SHERLOCK HOLMES
& *the* FABULOUS FACES

SHERLOCK HOLMES
& the FABULOUS FACES
THE UNIVERSAL PICTURES
REPERTORY COMPANY

by MICHAEL A. HOEY

BearManor Media

2011

Sherlock Holmes & the Fabulous Faces:
The Universal Pictures Repertory Company

© 2011 Michael A. Hoey

A version of the Roy William Neill chapter originally
appeared in *Monsters From The Vault* #28, 2011

For information, address:

BearManor Media
P. O. Box 71426
Albany, GA 31708

bearmanormedia.com

Typesetting and layout by John Teehan

Published in the USA by BearManor Media

ISBN—1-59393-660-5
978-1-59393-660-0

In Memory of my late wife, Katherine,
whose inspiration and love filled my life.

You will be missed forever

TABLE OF CONTENTS

INTRODUCTION

FROM MY EARLIEST MEMORIES I have loved the movies and they have been a part of my life. My father Dennis Hoey, who was what is known in the motion picture business as a character actor, made over seventy films in London and Hollywood between 1930 and 1952. He made his mark in Hollywood films with his portrayal of the slightly inept, but affable Scotland Yard Inspector Lestrade in six of the twelve Universal Studios Sherlock Holmes films. He was paid a $1,000 a week and would work roughly two out of the three weeks of each film's shooting schedule. The one exception was *Terror by Night* (1946) for which he was on salary for the entire three-plus weeks of filming. He also appeared in two of Universal's classic horror films, *Frankenstein Meets the Wolf Man* (1943) and *She-Wolf of London* (1946), curiously enough playing police inspectors in both films, but with somewhat more panache than poor old Lestrade.

Why Lestrade was portrayed in these films as such a dunderhead has been a matter of debate and some disapproval by true Sherlockians for many years. He certainly wasn't written that way by his creator, Sir Arthur Conan Doyle, who described him as "a well-known detective, a little sallow, rat-faced, dark-eyed fellow." Conan Doyle introduced Lestrade as a colleague and rival of fellow Scotland Yard Inspector Tobias Gregson in *A Study in Scarlet* and does imply that neither man, but particularly Inspector Lestrade, had the intelligence or temperament to match his master detective and hero, Sherlock Holmes. Conan Doyle even has Holmes describe Lestrade as "the best of the professionals" and "the pick of a bad lot," while still giving Lestrade a patronizing attitude toward Holmes's methods. They would work together on numerous cases, including *The Hound of the Baskervilles, The Sign of the Four* and 18 other stories, yet to the best of my knowledge, Conan Doyle never granted Lestrade a first name, merely assigning him the initial G. in "The Adventure of the Cardboard Box."

1

Dennis Hoey (c) as Lestrade, amuses Nigel Bruce and Basil Rathbone in
a publicity still for *The Spider Woman*.

Film historian Leonard Maltin's definition of character actors is
"Hollywood's Real Stars" and I agree. I have always held a great respect for
those unacknowledged stalwarts of the movies, particularly those men
and women who graced the films of the 1930s, '40s and early '50s. There
were so many marvelous supporting character players in the films of that
period that their names and photographs have filled such books as Warren B. Meyers' *Who Is That?*, Twomey & McClure's *The Versatiles*, and
David Quinlan's *Illustrated Directory of Character Actors*.

Roy William Neill directed nearly all of the Sherlock Holmes mys-
tery-adventures of the 1940s and, as was the case with directors John
Ford and Preston Sturges, he had a repertory company of character actors and actresses whom he liked to use. One might play a retired sea
captain in one film and a sinister shopkeeper in another, as was the case
with Harry Cording, or with Leslie Denison, who played a police sergeant in one and a barman in another, or Holmes Herbert as a courteous
auctioneer or a government official, or Sally Shepherd as a tobacconist
and a sinister housekeeper–the list goes on and on, ultimately including
more than 65 names, some familiar and others relatively unknown ex-

cept for their memorable faces. Today all of these old-timers are gone and forgotten, and character actors, as such, are virtually non-existent, with older leading men such as Dustin Hoffman, Jack Nicholson, Robert De Niro and Al Pacino frequently filling the bill. My intention in this book is to honor some of those wonderful performers of the past, who, like my father, appeared in supporting roles in hundreds of motion pictures, including many of Universal's horror films, but more importantly in the twelve Sherlock Holmes films produced by Universal Pictures between 1942 and 1946.

SHERLOCK HOLMES AND
THE VOICE OF TERROR

THE UNIVERSAL SHERLOCK HOLMES-Dr. Watson series sprang from the success of two Twentieth Century-Fox features starring Basil Rathbone and Nigel Bruce, *The Hound of the Baskervilles* and *The Adventures of Sherlock Holmes* (both 1939), followed by Rathbone and Bruce's growing popularity with their Holmes radio series over the next three years. In a *Hollywood Citizen News* article dated May 20, 1942, United Press Hollywood correspondent Frederick C. Othman discussed the chain of events that led to Universal taking on the Holmes stories. Claiming, inaccurately, that the two Fox films weren't successful, Othman went on to relate that Universal paid $300,000 to the Conan Doyle estate for the picture rights to 22 of the stories for a period of seven years. According to Othman, Universal was far more interested in securing the rights to the characters of Sherlock Holmes and Doctor Watson than to the actual stories. This agreement specifically excluded the four Holmes novels and did not include radio and stage rights to the short stories. Othman's article also mentioned that the studio had hired "one of the world's leading authorities on Holmes, Thomas McKnight, as technical director." McKnight, whose correct title was technical advisor, would receive a salary starting at $600 and increasing to $1,000 per picture during the run of the series. He would also direct Rathbone and Bruce in their radio series, *The New Adventures of Sherlock Holmes* on the Mutual Broadcasting System for several seasons during the mid-1940s.

It's interesting to note that Paul Harrison's *Harrison in Hollywood* syndicated column on April 26, 1939 quoted Basil Rathbone as saying he had agreed to do a second Sherlock Holmes film for 20th Century-Fox, but he was refusing a contract for a series because he feared he "might never be able to get away from the character of the famed sleuth." Apparently Rathbone already had concerns that the Holmes character might

Thomas McKnight (c) with Nigel Bruce and Basil Rathbone.

take over his life, which in his estimation it ultimately did. The article ended with an amusing quote from the actress Mrs. Patrick Campbell, who when appearing with Rathbone on the stage in London quipped, "Basil looks like two profiles pasted together."

The original adaptation entitled *Sherlock Holmes vs. Lord Haw-Haw* by Robert Hardy Andrews, writing under the name of Robert D. Andrews, was based loosely on " His Last Bow," Conan Doyle's eighth and final chapter in the fourth collection of Holmes's cases also entitled *His Last Bow* and published in 1917 during England's involvement in World War I. The decision had been made by Universal to bring the stories up into the mid-twentieth century and give them a wartime setting, hence the decidedly exploitative title. Lord Haw-Haw was the airwave name of several announcers on the Nazi's English- language propaganda radio program *Germany Calling*, broadcast to audiences in Great Britain and the United States during the war. In Conan Doyle's original story, Holmes entraps a German espionage agent named Von Bork by impersonating the American traitor Altamont; the yarn had nothing to do with mysterious radio broadcasts foretelling of acts of Nazi terrorism in wartime Britain. Those elements were added by Andrews and (in further drafts, now called *Sherlock Holmes Saves London*) by Lynn Riggs, the author of the play *Green Grow the Lilacs* upon which the Rodgers and Hammerstein musical *Oklahoma!* was based, and John Bright, whose greatest claim to fame must be that he was one of the contributing writers on the James Cagney classic, *The Public Enemy* (1931) and Mae West's first starring film, *She Done Him Wrong* (1933). Universal's Holmes project was given to Howard Benedict to produce and John Rawlins to direct. Benedict had only recently arrived at Universal from RKO Studios where he had supervised both the *Saint* and *Falcon* series. Rawlins was a former Columbia Pictures film editor who started directing "B" movies at Warner Bros. in the late 1930s and then moved to Universal to direct serials and programmers. His success with *Voice of Terror* would eventually lead him to higher budgeted films within the Universal catalog, such as the Jon Hall-Maria Montez starrers, *Arabian Nights* (1942) and *Sudan* (1945), but this would be his only film in the Sherlock Holmes series. Eventually the film's title was changed to *Sherlock Holmes and the Voice of Terror*, certainly no less exploitative, but more to the point.

In his unpublished autobiography, *Games, Gossip and Greasepaint*, Nigel Bruce wrote that in 1942 he received an offer from Universal Studios to sign a long-term contract at a salary of $850 a week with a 40-week guarantee and $100 raises every year. Bruce signed the contract and reported to Universal to begin work on *Eagle Squadron*, a story of the American volunteers flying with the British Royal Air Force before Pearl Harbor. Because Basil Rathbone was at that time under contract to M-G-M and had been since his agents, the Music Corporation of America, had negotiated a six-year contract in 1940, arrangements were made to borrow him from M-G-M for the Holmes series and allocate in the budget for each film the sum of $20,000 for his services. Most likely this money went to M-G-M to offset whatever they were paying Rathbone at that time. Universal began by paying Nigel Bruce $5,000 per film and gradually increased this amount to $15,000 for the final few films, so one can assume that Rathbone was being compensated accordingly.

Sherlock Holmes and the Voice of Terror, arguably the weakest of all of the series, opens with what would become the distinctive visual for all of the future Holmes films: an image of swirling fog dissolving into a close up of two pairs of feet. The camera then tilts up to hold a two shot of Basil Rathbone and Nigel Bruce as their names appear superimposed over their faces. The rest of the credits appear over a tracking shot of the feet moving through the fog. These visuals and the music written by Frank Skinner that accompanied them would in due course open all twelve of the Holmes film in the series. In order to prepare the audience for the fact that the story had been brought up to date, this title appeared following John Rawlins's directorial credit:

> *Sherlock Holmes, the immortal*
> *character of fiction created by*
> *Sir Arthur Conan Doyle, is ageless,*
> *invincible and unchanging.*
>
> *In solving significant problems of the*
> *present day he remains—as ever—the*
> *supreme master of deductive reasoning.*

A montage of an assortment of sabotage disasters is accompanied by the smarmy tones of the "Voice of Terror" (supplied by Edgar Barrier, who would later appear in 1943's *Phantom of the Opera* and 1944's *Cobra Woman).* At a contentious meeting of the Intelligence Inner Council, Sherlock Holmes joins the case. Somebody came up with an amusing inside joke that occurs just as Holmes and Watson are about to leave their flat to pursue the case: When Holmes picks up his deerstalker hat from the rack, Watson admonishes him with a shake of the head, "No, no, no, Holmes. You promised"—a subtle reference to the fact that we are no longer in the time of Queen Victoria and Edward VII, but rather the war-torn London of 1942.

The members of the Inner Council in *Sherlock Holmes and the Voice of Terror.*

The plot of *Voice of Terror*, filled with patriotic platitudes and wartime propaganda, is surprisingly lacking in suspense. Most of the action, except for a somewhat far-fetched excursion into the fog-bound London streets and a Limehouse pub, takes place either in the offices of the Inner Council or in Holmes's flat. Sherlock Holmes is unrealistically clever in his deducing of infinitesimal clues, such as the age of a scar on the villain's face and the anxiety of an official by the indentation of his footprints on a carpet, but nonetheless in the end he outsmarts the Nazi spies and thwarts an airborne invasion. The two bright spots, apart from Rathbone and Bruce, were the performances of Thomas Gomez as the enemy agent Meade and Evelyn Ankers as the tragic Kitty.

Director Rawlins' incessant and gratuitous overuse of full head close-ups throughout the film reduces their dramatic effect, but all in all the photography by Elwood (Woody) Bredell is excellent, capturing the same low-key atmospheric style of the earlier Universal horror films. This is not surprising, as Bredell, a fellow Englishman who began his career as a still photographer, had previously photographed six of these films, including *The Mummy's Hand* (1940) and *The Ghost of Frankenstein* (1942).

Evelyn Ankers and Thomas Gomez in *Sherlock Holmes and the Voice of Terror.*

The only true reference to *His Last Bow,* apart from the fleeting moment when Reginald Denny's Sir Evan Barham is revealed to be a Nazi spy named Von Bork, is the final quotation taken with only one small change from Conan Doyle's writing:

WATSON	It's a lovely morning, Holmes.
HOLMES	There's an east wind coming, Watson.
WATSON	No, I don't think so. Looks like another warm day.
HOLMES	Good old Watson! The one fixed point in a changing age. There's an east wind coming all the same. Such a wind as never blew on England yet. It will be cold and bitter, Watson, and a good many of us may wither before its blast. But it's God's own wind none the less, and a greener, better, stronger land will be in the sunshine when the storm is cleared.

Although Conan Doyle was of course referring to the earlier war of 1917, his words are remarkably timely and poignant given the circumstances in the England of 1942. And it is gratifying that John Rawlins chose to film this moment in a nicely framed two-shot over the two actors' shoulders, rather than resorting once again to full head close-ups.

The cast of *The Voice of Terror* contained many fine actors from the British contingent in Hollywood. Let us begin with EVELYN ANKERS who appeared in two Sherlock Holmes adventures, as well as appearing (between 1941 and 1945) in a Wolf Man, a Dracula, a Frankenstein and an Invisible Man film plus six more horror films, earning her the title of "Queen of the Horror Movies." Ankers was born in Valparaiso, Chile of British parents, and grew up in England. While still a teenager she made her first screen appearance in several important British films including *Rembrandt* (1936) and *Fire Over England* (1937) and soon won starring roles in several "quota quickies." During the period after The Great War, American films began to push British films out of theatres, and eventually British distributors had the Cinematograph Films Act of 1927 (also known as the Quota Act) passed. This ruled that a certain percentage of British films would be guaranteed play dates before any American films could be shown. Consequently, the American companies simply formed British subsidiaries and during the 1930s produced their own low-budget films ("quota quickies") in England. Ankers appeared in four of these films for Twentieth Century-Fox, several of them photographed by future film director Ronald Neame, before decamping to Hollywood and eventually being placed under contract to Universal Pictures in 1941. Her first so-called horror film was the Abbott and Costello comedy *Hold That Ghost* (1941) in which she and Richard Carlson supplied the love interest.

For her fifth film in 1941 she was assigned the romantic lead opposite Lon Chaney, Jr. in *The Wolf Man*, Universal's introduction of its first new creature into the horror genre following a long run of sequels from 1936 to 1940. Ankers would next appear in *The Ghost of Frankenstein* (1942), the fourth in the Frankenstein series, as Ludwig Frankenstein's (Sir Cedric Hardwicke) daughter Elsa. As was the case with most female roles in these films, the part of Elsa demanded little of Ankers aside from the prerequisite screaming when the Monster (Chaney, Jr. again) lumbered toward her. Her co-star, Ralph Belamy, had previously appeared with her in *The Wolf Man*. After appearing in a supporting role in 1942's *Eagle*

Evelyn Ankers as Kitty in *Sherlock Holmes and the Voice of Terror.*

Squadron and being loaned out to M-G-M for the forgettable *Pierre of the Plains* (1942), Ankers was cast in *Sherlock Holmes and the Voice of Terror*, in which she does a more than credible job of portraying a Cockney prostitute who agrees to help Holmes uncover the Nazi plot, giving a rousing, patriotic speech to a group of Limehouse dock rats and later being shot down for her patriotism by her Nazi paramour (Thomas Gomez). In 1944 she would return to the Holmes series as Giles Conover's (Miles Mander) nefarious girlfriend Naomi Drake in *The Pearl of Death*, giving her a chance to impersonate a Cockney dishwasher, a shabby old match woman and a bespectacled clerk. Between 1942 and 1944 Evelyn Ankers would appear in 15 films for Universal, including *Son of Dracula* (1943) and *The Invisible Man's Revenge* (1944) as well as *The Pearl of Death*, which shall be discussed in detail in a later chapter.

During this period, Ankers met and married actor Richard Denning, who during the five years he was under contract to Paramount Pictures appeared in over 45 pictures before temporarily leaving the business in 1942 to serve his country for three years in the U.S. Navy Submarine Service. Ankers left Universal in 1944 after appearing in a twelve-day quickie called *The Frozen Ghost* (1945) with her frequent co-star, Chaney, Jr. She was pregnant at the time and managed to conceal the fact from the camera with the help of designer Vera West's costumes and some propitiously placed pieces of furniture. By the time the film was finally released in June of 1945, Ankers was living the role of the dutiful war bride with her eight-month-old daughter Diana in a rented home in Malibu, California. Richard Denning soon returned from the Navy and he and Ankers would co-star in *Black Beauty* (1946) for Twentieth Century-Fox. Anker's career began to wind down as Denning's picked up momentum. He would co-star opposite Lucille Ball in the radio series *My Favorite Husband*, the precursor of the classic television series, *I Love Lucy,* as well as his own television series, *Mr. and Mrs. North* and *Michael Shayne.* In 1965 Denning joined his wife in retirement and they moved to Maui, Hawaii. A short time later the series *Hawaii Five-O* starring Jack Lord began filming in Honolulu and Denning was offered the part of Governor Philip Grey. He agreed, provided the role didn't require his full-time attention. Ankers was offered the role of the governor's wife but she refused, saying that she wouldn't be able to remember her lines. In truth, according to her husband, she just didn't want to have anything more to do with acting. The role of the governor would turn into a semi-regular job for Denning that would last throughout the entire twelve-year run of the series. Evelyn Ankers and Richard Denning would continue living on Maui and eventually build a small home in the mountains of Hakiau, Maui. According to their daughter Diana (Dee) Dwyer, who later lived with her own family on the Big Island, her mother loved gardening and the cooler climate of the mountain property on Maui. The Dennings would commemorate 43 years of marriage before Evelyn's death from ovarian cancer in August of 1985. She is buried in the Maui Veterans Cemetery on the island of Maui. Denning would die in 1998 in Escondido, California. Theirs was a true love story.

THOMAS GOMEZ, who played the villain who murders Evelyn Ankers, made his film debut in *Sherlock Holmes and the Voice of Terror*. Born Sabino Tomas Gomez, Jr. on July 10, 1905 in New York City, Gomez had two sisters and lived with his parents, Sabino, Sr. and Ida on 125th Street in Queens. In the 1920 Census, Gomez's occupation was listed as "Office Clerk," and the census also shows that the family had moved to 204th Street. In 1923, when he was just 17-years-old, Gomez received a scholarship to a prominent New York drama school headed by the Shakespearean actor Walter Hampden. Hampden later cast Gomez as a cadet in his production of *Cyrano de Bergerac,* and in 1925 Gomez played the role of Reynaldo opposite Hampden's Hamlet and Ethel Barrymore's Ophelia. Using the name S. Thomas Gomez, he continued with Hampden's com-

Thomas Gomez as Meade in *Sherlock Holmes and the Voice of Terror.*

pany until 1936 when he joined Alfred Lunt and his wife Lynn Fontanne in Robert E. Sherwood's *Idiot's Delight.* He remained with the Lunts for the next six years, appearing alongside company members Sidney Green-street and future directors Richard Whorf and Ralph Nelson. His performance with the Lunts in Sherwood's 1941 Pulitzer Prize drama *There Shall Be No Night* brought him to Hollywood's attention, and in 1942, at the age of 37 he was put under contract to Universal Pictures. His only appearance in any of Universal's Sherlock Holmes series was in *Voice of Terror,* but from 1942 to 1946 he appeared in 20 films for Universal including everything from a sex and sand opus, *Arabian Nights* (1942) for which he received "special praise" in the Sheboygan Wisconsin Press review, to a war film, *Corvette K-225* (1943), to a horror-mystery film, *Dead Man's Eyes* (1944), to a western, *The Daltons Ride Again* (1945). In 1947 Thomas Gomez (he had dropped the S. when he joined Universal), was nominated for an Oscar for his performance as Pancho the merry-go-round operator in director-star Robert Montgomery's *Ride the Pink Horse.* Other noteworthy performances followed, such as Father Bartolome in *Captain from Castile* (1947), Curly in *Key Largo* (1948), John Garfield's brother Leo in *Force of Evil* (1948) and Luigi Rossi in *Come to the Stable* (1949).

For the next few years he did his best to prop up some less than great films, even managing to get excellent reviews, such as this full paragraph in the U.S. Army's official newspaper the *Stars and Stripes* review of a better than average thriller, *The Sellout* (1952): "Thomas Gomez, one of the better character actors extant, plays the part of the corrupt sheriff admirably, getting the audience to hate and despise him almost from the start." In 1953 Gomez rejoined Basil Rathbone as Moriarty in an ill-fated Broadway staging of *Sherlock Holmes,* written by Rathbone's wife, Ouida Bergere. The play opened at the New Century Theatre on October 30th and closed the following night. Thereafter, Gomez divided his career between films and television, appearing only once more on Broadway when he temporarily replaced Leo McKern as Thomas Cromwell in *A Man for All Seasons* in December of 1961. I had the pleasure of working with Thomas Gomez in 1967 when he was signed for the role of Elvis Presley's cantankerous Grandpa in *Stay Away, Joe,* a screenplay I had written for M-G-M, based on a humorous novel by Dan Cushman. It was the story of a free-spirited young Navajo named Joe Lightcloud (played by Elvis), who returns to the reservation to carry out some wild schemes to raise money. Also in the cast were Burgess Meredith as Elvis's father and Katy Jurado as his mother, which meant that we didn't have a Native American in the whole bunch and we got clobbered later for this. Because I was also the Associate Producer I was with the production company in Sedona, Arizona where we filmed the location scenes. Tommy was 62-years-old when he made *Stay Away, Joe*. His gait had slowed down a bit, but his mind was still sharp as a tack and I enjoyed sitting with him outside his trailer between takes hearing him reminisce about his experiences in the Hollywood of the 1940s. He remembered working with my father on various radio programs in New York before either of them came out to California.

I had written Tommy's character of Grandpa as a sort of comic Greek chorus, always adding caustic comments to top off the scene. The director chose to throw out much of the written dialogue and have his cast improvise many of the scenes. In most cases it was disastrous, Tommy's character was the only one he couldn't screw around with; his one-liners remained as written and were beautifully delivered by this marvelous actor. This would be the penultimate film in Tommy's career and sadly in his final film, *Beneath the Planet of the Apes* (1970), his face would be hidden by a rubber ape mask in his one brief scene as the orangutan Minister blessing the ape soldiers before they invade the "Forbidden Zone." According to the film's director Ted Post, Gomez hated the makeup and found it claustrophobic. Thomas Gomez died on Friday, June 18, 1971 in Santa Monica, California from injuries sustained in an automobile accident. According to his obituary in the *Nevada State Journal*, he was in a coma for three weeks before his death. Thomas Gomez never married, and his only survivor was one of his sisters, who was still living at the time in New York City.

Barham Boulevard in Burbank, California was named after Doctor Frank Barham, publisher of *The Los Angeles Evening Herald*, one of Los Angeles' early newspapers from 1911 to 1931. Because Barham Boulevard runs past the back gate of Universal Studios, one has to wonder if that might not have been the inspiration for the screenwriters to name the head of the Intelligence Inner Council, Sir Evan Barham. As played by REGINALD DENNY, he is supposedly Doctor Watson's old school chum, but is, in fact, a German spy who killed the original Sir Evan and took his place many years before the war broke out. As the one who brings Sherlock Holmes into the case, he appears to be above suspicion—that is, until Holmes deduces that the scar on his cheek is too new to have been inflicted in a childhood accident.

Reginald Denny, born Reginald Leigh Dugmore in Richmond, Surrey, England in November 1891, was born into a theatrical family. His father was the actor-singer W.H. Denny, a member of the D'Oyly Carte Opera Company. When Reginald joined his father in the acting profession he also took on the name Denny and became quite well known in silent films. Denny also appeared on the Broadway stage, most notably in John Barrymore's much-admired 1920 production of *Richard III*, in which Denny played King Edward the Fourth. In 1921 Denny played the third lead in a silent adventure film called *The Iron Trail* that was directed by a young Roy William Neill, and in 1922 rejoined John Barrymore for a silent version of *Sherlock Holmes* for Samuel Goldwyn's film company. Later that year he began a series of shorts for the Universal Film Manufacturing Company (later Universal Pictures), that led to a featured contract that lasted for eight years and starred him in nineteen silent short films, twenty four silent feature films and two sound features. Denny's military demeanor came naturally to a man who had served in the Royal Flying Corps as an observer-gunner in World War I. During his service, he also became the brigade's heavyweight boxing champion. This would come in handy throughout his career in such films as *The Lost Patrol* (1934), *Join the Marines* (1937), *Captains of the Clouds* (1942) and of course *Sherlock Holmes and the Voice of Terror* (1942).

Including his silent short films, Denny appeared in over 175 films, but he also had another vocation that began as a hobby. His interest in the early 1930s in model plane building and eventually radio-controlled models led him to form Reginald Denny Industries, becoming one of the largest model plane kit concerns in America. In 1934 he opened the Reginald Denny Hobby Shop on Hollywood Boulevard. Although Denny sold his interest in 1937 to Walter H. Righter, the shop retained his name and

Reginald Denny as Sir Evan Barham in *Sherlock Holmes and the Voice of Terror.*

stayed open for many years, probably into the 1960s. I remember visiting it in the late 40s. It was a fascinating place, with dozens of model planes hanging from the ceiling and all types of model kits on sale. Denny's interest in radio-controlled model planes led to the development for the Army of a radio-controlled target drone for anti-aircraft gunners and the forming with several partners of the Radioplane Company with Denny as vice-president. Throughout World War II Denny's company manufactured thousands of these drones for both the Army and the Navy with wingspans of more than 12 feet and engines that grew from 5 ½ horsepower and speeds of 70 miles per hour to 60 horsepower and 250 miles per hour. A young woman by the name of Norma Jeane Baker, who worked for Denny's company at that time, would one-day star in films as Marilyn Monroe.

My one indirect contact with Reginald Denny was in 1965 when I was working at Paramount Studios as a sound editor and was assigned to *Assault on the Queen* (1966) starring Frank Sinatra. The plot, as described on the IMDb website, was lean and to the point: "A group of adventurers refloat a WWII German submarine and prepare to use it to pull a very large heist; they plan to rob the Queen Mary on the high seas." Rod Serling had written the screenplay and Jack Donohue, a former choreographer, was the director. We'd heard rumors during the filming that Donohue, who had directed Sinatra earlier that year in *Marriage on the Rocks* (1965), was having trouble with his star. Sinatra refused to do more than one take, even when his cameraman, the brilliant William Daniels, requested another due to a camera malfunction. Denny's role as the Queen Mary's Master at Arms took place in the final reels as the gang boards the ship. His role was brief, but I remember thinking at the time that his military demeanor brought a mark of realism to his scenes. Denny's final film was the *Batman* movie (1966) inspired by the success of the television series starring Adam West and Burt Ward, in which he played a character named Commodore Schmidlapp.

Denny was married twice, first to Irene Haisman and later to Betsy Lee, and had four children. According to Denny's son, Reginald Jr., Denny died as a result of a long series of illnesses while visiting relatives in England. His interest in model planes never left him and while he was in the hospital he purchased a model as a gift for a health care worker. Reginald Denny died on June 16, 1967, at the age of 76.

HENRY DANIELL, who played Sir Anthony Lloyd, one of the members of the Intelligence Inner Council, had already established himself with film audiences playing the villainous characters in classics such as *Marie Antoinette* (1938), *The Private Lives of Elizabeth and Essex* (1939) and *The Sea Hawk*, (1940) and he was used to good advantage as a red herring in *Voice of Terror* to help conceal the identity of the real heavy. Charles Henry Pynell Daniell was born in London, England on March 5, 1894, and by the time he was 17 was working as an insurance clerk to help support his widowed mother Elinor and his older sister Elinor Mary. He began as an apprentice actor by touring the provinces at the age of 18 and his first speaking role was on the London stage in Belgian Nobel laureate Maurice Maeterlinck's play, *Monna Vanna*. Unfortunately for him, the play opened on August 4, 1914, the day World War I was declared. "The first night, we played to a totally empty theatre," he said, "Except for

Henry Daniell as Sir Anthony Lloyd in *Sherlock Holmes and the Voice of Terror.*

my mother and sister." Daniell quickly found himself enlisted in the 28th Battalion, London Regiment (Artists' Rifles), a military unit formed in 1860 and originally comprised of painters, sculptors and actors. He was invalided home in 1915 and, after recovering from his severe shrapnel wounds, he returned the stage.

In an interview in 1920, Daniell complained that he found himself playing nothing but callow juveniles: "I'm so tired of being a juvenile and looking pretty I could go and jump in the Thames." He continued, "Someday I'm going to be the meanest, vilest, cold-blooded villain on any stage. You mark my words." That rather outlandish boast actually came true some years later in 1935, when he appeared on Broadway opposite Grace George in *Kind Lady.* In April of 1921 Daniell immigrated to New York to join Ethel Barrymore and her brother John in John's then wife Michael Strange's production of *Clair de Lune,* Daniell's first appearance on the Broadway stage. From there he went on to gain notice in seven additional Broadway productions between 1923 and 1935, including a successful revival of *The Second Mrs. Tanqueray* and the aforementioned *Kind Lady.* Daniell appeared in two early Hollywood sound films in 1929 and firmly established his credentials as a villain by playing the callous Baron de Varville opposite Greta Garbo in 1936's *Camille*. By this time he had married the English authoress Ann Knox and they and their daughter Allison were living comfortably in a modest canyon home in Southern California. According to humorist P.G. Wodehouse, Daniell and Ann were involved in a sex scandal in the 1930s. Wodehouse wrote about this in a letter to his daughter, "Apparently they go down to Los Angeles and either (a) indulge in or (b) witness orgies–probably both ... there's something pleasantly domestic about a husband and wife sitting side by side with their eyes glued to peepholes, watching the baser elements whoop it up. And what I want to know is–where are these orgies? I feel I've been missing something." When World War II broke out, Daniell made the easy transition from costume melodramas to uniformed Nazi officers in films, sometimes with subtle humor as Garbitsch in *The Great Dictator* (1940) and sometimes with evil intent as Von Stetten in *Hotel Berlin* (1945). His appearance in *Sherlock Holmes and the Voice of Terror* presaged a more important role to come as the arch-villain Moriarty in 1945's *The Woman in Green*. Henry Daniell was indirectly responsible for a major incident in my career, but that's a story for later.

OLAF HYTTEN made his first of five appearances in the Sherlock Holmes series in *Voice of Terror* as Admiral Sir John Fabian Prentiss, giving a very touching performance as the father of a soldier killed by Nazi saboteurs. Born on March 3, 1888, Alfred Olaf Hytten was the second of five children of Christian Olaf Hytten and Edith Emmeline Hytten. His sister Edith Maude was five years his senior and his brother Edwin was born in 1891, followed by two more sisters, Alice and Amy. His father was formerly a shipbroker from Tousberg, Norway, and the family resided at 24 Kenmure Street in Glasgow, Lanarkshire County, Scotland. Little is known of Hytten's early life except that he was firmly established in the acting profession and traveling with a repertory company in England by the time he was 26. The following year he joined the 8th Hampshire Regiment and fought in the Gallipoli Campaign, rising to the rank of 2nd Lieutenant. He debuted in his first silent film, *Money* in 1921, and between 1921 and 1929 acted in 29 silent films, all produced in England. In 1923 he appeared in Clive Brook's *The White Shadow* for which the 24-year-old Alfred Hitchcock not only wrote the screenplay, but was also the art director, editor and assistant director. Hytten traveled to America in 1924 to make his debut on Broadway in *Whitewashed* with the well-known British actor John Goldsworthy. Sometime around this period he married Edith Dudley who, according to a 1929 ship's manifest, followed him to the United States two

Olaf Hytten as Admiral
Sir John Fabian Prentiss in
*Sherlock Holmes and the Voice
of Terror.*

weeks after he did and settled with him in a small bungalow on Saturn Street in Los Angeles, California.

Hytten's career in sound films began with an uncredited role in *The Return of Dr. Fu Manchu;* Paramount's 1930 sequel to the previous year's successful production of *The Mysterious Dr. Fu Manchu* starring Warner Oland as the infamous master criminal. Hytten then began a run of nine consecutive films at Paramount, and the following year marked his first appearance in a Universal film, *The Impatient Maiden* (1932) starring Lew Ayres and Mae Clarke. Over the years Hytten appeared in over 280 films, frequently without receiving screen credit, with the list including such major productions as *Anna Karenina* (1935) , *Camille* (1936) and *The Good Earth* (1937), and such lesser titles as *A Feather in Her Cap* (1935), *Perils of the Jungle* (1953) and a Three Stooges short, *All the World's a Stooge* (1941). Hytten's first appearance in a horror film wasn't until 1941, when he played a small role in M-G-M's remake of *Dr. Jekyll and Mr. Hyde* starring Spencer Tracy, but he followed that by appearing in *The Wolf Man* (1941), *The Ghost of Frankenstein* (1942), *The Return of the Vampire* (1944), *House of Frankenstein* (1944), *The Brighton Strangler* (1945), *She-Wolf of London* (1946) and *The Son of Dr. Jekyll* (1951). Toward the end of his career, Hytten briefly segued into television, appearing in series such as *The Life of Riley* and *Adventures of Superman.*

In 1955 Hytten was signed for a small role in 20th Century-Fox's *The Virgin Queen* starring Bette Davis; it would be his 289th film role. He reported for work on March 11, eight days after his 67th birthday. A reporter for the U.S. Army's *Pacific Stars and Stripes* newspaper was on the set that day and interviewed Hytten, who likened his career to gambling: "It was all a matter of luck. Sometimes you do very little work and you get five or six weeks pay. I have only three days work on this one. It just happens that way, but money is money." Hytten seemed surprised that anyone would want to interview him, and when asked how long he intended to continue working he replied, "I suppose I will go on the rest of my life." Olaf Hytten fulfilled his prophesy when less than an hour later he suffered a heart attack on the set and died on his way to the studio hospital. He had just completed a short scene with Bette Davis, which unfortunately does not appear in the final version of the film. There is no mention of his wife in any of the brief obituaries marking his death, so one has to presume that Edith predeceased him. Olaf Hytten is buried in Santa Monica's Woodlawn Cemetery.

LEYLAND HODGSON is a perfect example of the fate of character actors; seldom receiving screen credit, he appeared in over 170 films during his career and yet only the most avid film buff, while recognizing his face in photographs, could come up with his name. In *Sherlock Holmes and the Voice of Terror*, the first of six Holmes films in which he appeared, he had one of his more important roles as Captain Roland Shore, one of the members of the Intelligence Inner Council. Born John Leyland Hodgson in London, England in October 1892, Leyland apparently began his acting career in Melbourne, Australia, as his occupation is listed as actor on the S.S. *Sierra*'s manifest when he arrived in San Francisco from Sydney, Australia in November 1929. While in Melbourne, Hodgson was married to Katherine Eda, who later followed him to California.

Hodgson's first film was *The Case of Sergeant Grischa* (1930) starring a young Chester Morris, later the star of a series of *Boston Blackie* films in the 1940s. The newspaper advertisements for *Sergeant Grischa* inexplicably announced to potential audiences: "You won't like this Picture! You'll hate it!!" And indeed that was the case as reviews for the film called it "vastly overlong and a boring talk-fest." Hodgson played Lt. Winifried and received good notices for his performance. "Leyland Hodgson, young English actor, makes his debut in the film as [Alec B.] Francis' aide de camp," reported *The Galveston Daily News* on Sunday, September 7, 1930 adding, "He brings an excellent voice to the screen."

Over the next few years Hodgson averaged four to five films a year, including a small uncredited role in *The Mummy* (1932), but in 1937 his career took an upturn

Publicity photo of Leyland Hodgson, who appeared as Captain Roland Shore in *Sherlock Holmes and the Voice of Terror.*

and he appeared in thirteen films and received screen credit in one, *The Adventurous Blonde* (1937) an entry in the Torchy Blaine series starring Glenda Farrell at Warner Bros. From then on, throughout World War II, he worked in dozens of films each year, many times as a British officer, in spite of which when he applied for United States citizenship, he put down as his occupation "actor unemployed." After *Sherlock Holmes and the Voice of Terror*, Hodgson appeared in five more films in the series, but would only receive screen credit again in the final film, *Dressed to Kill* (1946).

Leyland Hodgson's celebrity was so limited that a detailed search of obituary records has failed to turn up anything other than his death certificate. It would seem that he died without notice on March 16, 1949, and his place of burial is unrecorded. He was 57-years-old and had spent 19 years working in Hollywood.

MONTAGU LOVE rounds out the cast of excellent character actors portraying the members of the Intelligence Inner Council in *Voice of Terror*. Although he appears in every scene, along with the other members of the council, he has a limited number of lines and in fact is hardly seen in the first three minutes of the introductory sequence except as a shadowy figure and speaks only two clipped three-word comments. In his second scene the pattern repeats itself; although his comments increase by five-fold they are still short exclamations such as, "You must be joking" and "I can hardly believe it." Only in the final sequence that takes place in the ruins of the deserted church does Love as General Jerome Lawford have a few moments of authority with the British troops assigned to round up the Nazis, but ultimately his involvement is minimal.

Love's acting career goes all the way back to the early days of silent films and before that the theatre. Born Harry Montagu Love in Portsmouth, England, in March of 1881, Love dabbled briefly in careers in newspaper reporting and as an illustrator during the Boer War, but moved onto the British stage as a Vaudeville performer shortly thereafter. He developed his craft in touring companies, and in November 1913 arrived on Broadway, appearing in repertory at the Wallack's Theatre with British actor Cyril Maude. After performing briefly in three plays, the company opened in the comedy *Grumpy* on November 19 and had a successful run of 181 performances, closing in April of 1914. Shortly thereafter Love appeared in his first silent film, starring for Maurice Elvey in an adaptation of Robert Louis Stevenson's *The Suicide Club* (1914). While still managing to return periodically to Broadway, Love appeared in 98 silent films between 1914 and 1929, first as a leading man, and eventually as one of the highest regarded heavies in films. Love first worked for Roy William Neill when he co-starred with Constance Bennett in *What's Wrong with the Women?* (1922). He was the villain in Rudolph Valentino's final film *The Son of the Sheik* (1926) and fought a famous duel with John Barrymore in *Don Juan* (1926). His final performance on Broadway was in 1934. After that he moved to

Montagu Love (c) as General Jerome Lawford with Leyland Hodgson (l) and Reginald Denny (r) in *Sherlock Holmes and the Voice of Terror.*

his first home in Southern California, at 2109 North Fairfax Avenue in the hills above Hollywood, and concentrated exclusively on films. Some of his most notable roles were as Thomas Jefferson in *Alexander Hamilton* (1931), Henry VIII in *The Prince and the Pauper* (1937) and the Bishop of the Black Canons in *The Adventures of Robin Hood* (1938). His success would eventually allow him to buy a more palatial home on Rodeo Drive in Beverly Hills.

During early 1941, Love joined dozens of his British expatriates and contributed his services for a film being made to aid the British War Relief, *Forever and a Day*. The film told the story of a house and the family that lived in it from the time it was built in 1804 to 1940, when an American relative comes to England to sell it. The cast included stars such as Ray Milland, Claude Rains, Merle Oberon, Ida Lupino, Brian Aherne and Charles Laughton, as well as lesser-known actors such as Isobel Elsom, Patric Knowles, Cecil Kellaway and Eric Blore. Then there were the future members of the Sherlock Holmes repertory company, Billy Bevan, Aubrey Mather, Halliwell Hobbes, Mary Gordon, Dennis Hoey, Doris Lloyd, Alec Craig and Nigel Bruce. The film had seven directors and twenty-two writers, more than any other film in Hollywood's history. In order to accommodate its enormous cast (106 speaking roles) the film remained in production from May 1941 to January 1942 and opened at the Rivoli in New York City on May 12, 1943. Bosley Crowther's review the following day in *The New York Times* complimented the film on being "evenly constructed, well produced and nicely played. It should be a pleasant entertainment—especially for those who dote on the past."

Montagu Love married Marjorie Hollis in 1929; it was his second marriage. Although neither marriage produced any offspring, he did become stepfather to Marjorie's daughter Carol from a previous marriage. He and Marjorie remained married until his death of a heart attack on May 17, 1943 at the age of 62. He had listed "heart rheumatism" as a condition on his World War I Draft Registration Card and this may have contributed to his death. His final film appearance was as the Reverend Brontë, father of the Brontë sisters in *Devotion* in December of 1942. The film's release was delayed until 1946 as Warner Bros. and Olivia de Havilland, one of the film's stars, fought a court battle over her contract with the studio–a battle that she ultimately won.

HILLARY BROOKE makes a brief appearance in *Voice of Terror* as Sherlock Holmes' uniformed driver, but she would return far more prominently as the heroine in *Sherlock Holmes Faces Death* and as the villainess in *The Woman in Green*. Brooke, a fellow Virgo with whom I share a birth date of September 8, began working in films in 1937 when she appeared as a member of the chorus in RKO's *New Faces of 1937*. Born Beatrice Peterson in Astoria, New York, in 1914, she was attending Columbia University when on the subway one morning on her way to school she met John Robert Powers, head of the prominent modeling agency. Powers invited her to join the agency and she decided to give up school and take his offer. After a brief career as a model, Beatrice Peterson traveled to Hollywood and changed her name to Hillary Brooke because, as she put it, she thought her own name was "so long and so heavy." In her second film, *Stage Door* (1937), only her face was used in a photograph as Adolphe Menjou's wife. For the next five years Brooke worked frequently in small speaking roles in over twenty films, while never receiving screen credit. After appearing in a small bit in a minor M-G-M musical, *Two Girls on Broadway* (1940), she continued working off and on at M-G-M for the next two years. Her first leading roles came in 1941 in two low-budget westerns for PRC, one of the "Poverty Row" producing companies, *The Lone Rider Rides On* and *The Lone Rider in Frontier Fury*, which were most likely filmed back to back in twelve days in the San Fernando Valley. She was then seen briefly in the finale of *To the Shores of Tripoli* (1942) as a member of a crowd watching a parade; she catches John Payne's trousers when he tosses them while struggling to change clothes in a group of marching Marines. As acting roles began to improve, Brooke decided to give herself an edge over the other blonde actresses she was compet-

Hillary Brooke as Jill Grandis with Basil Rathbone and Nigel Bruce in
Sherlock Holmes and the Voice of Terror.

ing with by developing a cultured accent that she used when she went on
interviews. She was so successful that producers began to think of her and
cast her as the blonde with the British accent. Such was the case when she
was sent by the Universal Casting Department to audition for director
John Rawlins and producer Howard Benedict for the relatively brief role
of Jill Grandis, the British Women's Army driver who chauffeurs Holmes
and Watson about London in *Sherlock Holmes and the Voice of Terror.*
There will be more of Brookes' life and career when she returns in a later
chapter in *The Woman in Green* (1945).

And then there is the wonderful MARY GORDON. Although her
scenes were generally brief, she still managed to make an indelible impression as Sherlock Homes' kindly landlady, Mrs. Hudson. Born in Scotland in May of 1882 as Mary Clark Gilmour, she was the fifth youngest
of six children of Robert and Mary Gilmour of Glasgow. Gordon began
her stage career as a young girl singing with Harry Lauder and touring
throughout Scotland. The records are not clear on exactly when, but some
time around 1891 she married a man named Gordon and bore him a
daughter, also named Mary. By 1919 she was apparently divorced and

Mary Gordon as Mrs. Hudson, as she appeared with Basil Rathbone in
Sherlock Holmes Faces Death.

her father had died, as travel documents show that she arrived in Quebec, Canada, by steamship on the 13th of September, accompanied by her mother and teenage daughter. Gordon listed her occupation as "H'keeper" and their final destination as San Francisco. Taking the train to Vancouver, they crossed the border two days later at Seattle; from there they continued south to San Francisco to live with her uncle William Gilmour in the Bay City.

By the time of the 1920 Census, Gordon had made her way with her daughter to Los Angeles and set up housekeeping at 5012 Meridian Court, eventually graduating from making a living as a dressmaker to working in silent films as a day player. Altogether, Gordon appeared in 17 silent films and 265 sound films, with her first recorded appearance (for Universal Pictures as it turned out) as a non-credited character named Mrs. Hennessy in a Clive Brook drama titled *The Home Maker* (1925). This would be the first of many Irish characters this Scottish lady would portray; in fact, the following year she would appear as a Mrs. Murphy for her future Sherlock Holmes director, Roy William Neill in *Black Paradise* (1926). Over the years Gordon played so many cleaning ladies, scrub women and landladies that studio publicists would occasionally work up stories about her, always with the same theme: how she was discovered by some star or director working as a "scrub woman for $5 a week and meals at the old Robertson-Cole studios," or another one about "the 55 year old Irish widow, who jumped from restaurant cook to near stardom." One story that had a modicum of truth to it was an article that showed up in *The Reno Evening Gazette* about her receiving her first featured role while coaching Katharine Hepburn to perfect her Scottish dialect for *The Little Minister* (1934). Gordon did receive screen credit as Nanny Webster, and indeed also worked on the film as a dialogue coach, but she had in point of fact been receiving screen credit as an actress since she appeared opposite a young Jackie Cooper in an *Our Gang* comedy short for Hal Roach called *When the Wind Blows* (1930), playing Norman "Chubby" Chaney's mother, and the following year in the Charlie Chan film *The Black Camel* (1931) with Warner Oland, even traveling with the company to Honolulu to film some of her scenes on location. In *Pot O' Gold*, a relatively forgettable 1941 musical comedy starring James Stewart and Paulette Goddard, she had featured billing next to Charles Winninger and even managed to sing a few bars while briefly performing one of the songs. The film was produced by FDR's son James Roosevelt, who'd spent most of 1941 producing musical shorts called *Soundies* before making this film, his only feature. During the war, Gordon was a regular at The Hollywood Canteen entertaining the service men, who gave her the title of "Mother." She also spent her Sundays singing at nearby Army camps.

Mary Gordon was an extra in the original *Frankenstein* (1931) and ultimately appeared in eight more of Universal's horror films, including *The Invisible Man* (1933) and *Bride of Frankenstein* (1935). In 1939, Gordon was cast for the first time as Mrs. Hudson in 20th Century-Fox's *The Hound of the Baskervilles* and later that year repeated her role in *The Adventures of Sherlock Holmes*. All in all, she would portray Sherlock Holmes' doughty housekeeper in ten films (eight for Universal) as well as appearing on the radio series with Rathbone and Bruce. She would receive a salary from Universal of $100 a day and would generally work from one to three days in each film. Universal gave her a more prominent role in *The Mummy's Tomb* (1942), where she played Dick Foran's elderly sister Jane Banning who, after a few warm family scenes, was summarily dispatched by Lon Chaney, Jr.'s rather tacky looking Kharis, the Mummy. Gordon retired in 1950 at the age of 68 to live with her married daughter and ten-year-old grandson Douglas Dutton in Pasadena, California. She died there on August 23, 1963, after an extended illness. She is buried in Rose Hill Memorial Park in Whittier, California.

EDGAR BARRIER was the actor who supplied the radio voice for the *Voice of Terror;* his real name was Edgar Bromberg. He was born on March 4, 1907 in New York City, the only child of Anatoly Bromberg, a Russian Jew who immigrated to the United States in 1898 with his wife Rose (nee Gerstenzstang) and became a prosthetic dentist in New York. Barrier attended Colombia University and in 1928 appeared in his first Broadway play, an original comedy drama called *Pleasure Man* that opened and closed in two performances. Undeterred, Barrier was back on Broadway the following spring in a more successful production, *The Broken Chain*, and continued throughout the 1930s appearing in ten more plays, while alternating with work in various radio productions. It was there that he met and worked with Orson Welles in his *Mercury Theatre of the Air* and later in Welles' Broadway production of *Danton's Death*. Barrier was also featured in Welles' RKO film *Journey into Fear* (1943) and later in Welles' *Macbeth* (1948), for which he would receive praise for his performance as Banquo.

From 1942 to 1944 Barrier was under contract to Universal Pictures and appeared in eight films, portraying everything from a Japanese spy in *We've Never Been Licked* (1943) to South Sea islanders *Danger in the Pacific* (1942) and *Cobra Woman* (1944) and even another disembodied voice in *Bombay Clipper* (1942). Perhaps his most memorable performance during this period was as Raoul, the portentous police inspector and romantic rival of Nelson Eddy for Susanna Foster in *Phantom of the Opera* (1943), also starring Claude Rains. The Technicolor remake of the 1925 silent classic with Lon Chaney was finally put into production after many false starts on January 17, 1943. Universal art directors Alexander Golitzen and John B. Goodman won Oscars for their impressive sets of the catacombs beneath the Paris Opera House and their revamping of the original Opera House auditorium set from the earlier Chaney film. In addition, $100,000 was spent soundproofing the sound stage that housed the latter set .According to Clive Hirschhorn's *The Universal Story* the original set was an exact replica of the Paris Opera, containing five tiers of balconies and seating 3000 extras. For the 1943 Technicolor remake, they allocated $1,500,000 for opulent sets and costumes including the refurbishing of the Paris Opera set. Universal has maintained the opera house set on Stage 28 to this day; in 1986 I directed a sequence for an episode of *Blacke's Magic* in front of several tiers of balconies and box seats that still filled one wall of the stage and looked just as they did in the 1943 film. I don't want to say that the stage's history inspired me, but it certainly was an appropriate setting as the sequence I was filming involved an enormous crane shot of the star of the series, Hal Linden, rushing down a winding stone staircase in a castle set pursuing a terrified young woman, while lightning flashes through the barred windows. The show's producers were quite happy with my work and I was immediately signed to direct another episode, so I consider Universal's Stage 28 to be a lucky spot for me.

After starring in *Secrets of Scotland Yard* (1944), a grade "B" potboiler on loan-out to Republic Pictures, Barrier asked for and was granted his release from Universal. He went on to appear in over 80 films and television productions, including a co-starring role as the demented big game hunter Erich Kreiger in RKO's *A Game of Death* (1945), a remake of their 1932 produc-

Edgar Barrier as he appeared as Raoul D'Aubert in *Phantom of the Opera*.

tion *The Most Dangerous Game*. (In "Take Dead Aim," a 1961 episode of the television series *The Rebel* starring Nick Adams, Barrier played another mad hunter of humans, this one named Bianco.) In 1945 Barrier also starred briefly on NBC radio as Simon Templar, alias *The Saint*, and in 1946 returned to Broadway to co-star in *The Magnificent Yankee* opposite Louis Calhern. Sometime in the late 1940s Barrier married Ernestine Spratt, who began acting in television in the early 1950s under the name Ernestine Barrier. In 1953 she played Madame President in *Project Moon Base*, co-written by noted science-fiction author Robert A. Heinlein. They appeared together in an episode of the religious TV series *Crossroads* in 1957. Barrier's final screen appearance was in Billy Wilder's *Irma la Douce* (1963). He died in Los Angeles on June 20, 1964, and is buried at Westwood Memorial Park. Ernestine Barrier died in Los Angeles on February 13, 1989 at the age of 89.

HARRY STUBBS appeared in only two films for Roy William Neill, one of them a Sherlock Holmes film; the other was Neill's highly popular *Frankenstein Meets the Wolf Man* (1943). Stubbs would appear in many of Universal's other horror films of that period. His real name was Hildebrand Oakes Stubbs and he was born in Shifnal, a small market town

Harry Stubbs as the taxi driver with Basil Rathbone and Nigel Bruce in
Sherlock Holmes and the Voice of Terror.

in Shropshire, England, on September 1, 1874. His parents were Edward
William Stubbs, the curate of St. Milburga's Church in the nearby village
of Beckbury, and the former Ellen Jones. According to genealogical records compiled and printed in 1875 under the title, *A Royal Descent*, Harry Stubbs was a direct descendent of King Edward I (1239-1307), known
for his brutal conduct in attempting to subjugate the Scots and for issuing
1290's "Edict of Expulsion," which expelled the Jews from England.

By the time he was 16-years-old, Stubbs was on his way to the United
States to make his fortune as an actor. He toured with various stock companies in both Canada and the United States, perfecting his talents as a comedian, and on September 12, 1905, he made his Broadway debut in *The
Bad Samaritan*, a comedy that lived up to its name and wasn't good enough
to last more than 15 performances. The following year Stubbs was appearing with the W.S. Harkins stock company at the Gem Playhouse on Peaks
Island in Portland, Maine; Susan Titus Van Duser was performing at the
same playhouse. They were married in September of 1906 in the cottage on
Peaks Island that Susan and her mother were occupying at the time. Septem-
ber seemed to be a lucky month for Harry Stubbs: On September 29, 1908,
Stubbs luck changed again and he returned to Broadway to play opposite
Douglas Fairbanks in an original play called *A Gentleman from Mississippi*

which ran for over a year at the Bijou Theatre. From that point on, Harry and Susan Stubbs would tour the country with various stock companies, with Harry eventually becoming a theatrical manager of his own stock company.

Again in September, this time in 1922, Stubbs returned to Broadway and began appearing in a number of plays, some successful and some not, but his billing was improving. In 1925 he co-starred with James Gleason and wife Lucile Webster in George S. Kaufman's *The Butter and Egg Man* that ran until April of 1926 (243 performances). The following year he co-starred with Thomas Mitchell in a melodrama called *Nightstick* that was responsible for bringing him to Hollywood, where he recreated his role in the movie version now called *Alibi* (1929). His first role for Universal was in *Night Ride* (1930) in which he co-starred with Edward G. Robinson and Joseph Schildkraut. Over the next 13 years Stubbs appeared in over 70 films, including such Universal horrors as *The Invisible Man* (1933), *Werewolf of London* (1935), *The Mummy's Hand* (1940) and *The Wolf Man* (1941). Stubbs worked in his final film, Episode 2 of *Flesh and Fantasy* (1943) from July to Mid-August of 1942. When his beloved wife of 36 years, Susan Stubbs died on November 8, 1942, he retired from acting and never appeared in another film or play. He died in Woodland Hills, California, at the Motion Picture Country Home on March 9, 1950 at the age of 75 and was cremated with his ashes interred at the Chapel of the Pines in Los Angeles, California.

A number of other character actors make brief appearances in *Voice of Terror*, such as Harry Cording (Camberwell), Rudolph Anders (Schieler), Leslie Denison (London Bobby), Alec Harford (Grimes), Guy Kingsford (Foot Patrolman), Arthur Stenning (British Officer), and Ted Billings (Basement Dive Bartender). All of them appeared in future episodes of the series and will be discussed in detail as they make their appearances in these later films.

Sherlock Holmes and the Voice of Terror opened in theatres on September 18, 1942. The following day *The New York Times* published Bosley Crowther's review in which he described the film as having no "distinction or surprise." Crowther seemed particularly upset with Rathbone's "wind-blown hair-do" and the insertion of Nazi agents into the plot. He summed up his review this way: "The late Conan Doyle, who obviously never wrote this story, as Universal claims, must be speculating sadly in his spirit world on this betrayal of trust." Even so, the film was wholeheartedly received by the Hollywood trade press with comments such as "Picture is a neat concoction of suspenseful melodrama" (*Variety*) and "John Rawlins maintains the air of excitement in his direction, a first-class job" (*Hollywood Reporter*). The general public enthusiastically embraced the film and Universal quickly put a second film it had been preparing into production. Its working title, *Sherlock Holmes Strikes Back*, was quickly changed to *Sherlock Holmes and the Secret Weapon* and two new essentials were added to the mix: Roy William Neill took over as the director and would remain so for the remaining eleven films, becoming the producer as well on his third film, *Sherlock Holmes Faces Death*. The other addition to *Secret Weapon* was the inclusion of the Lestrade character as played by my father, Dennis Hoey.

ROY WILLIAM NEILL

I MET DIRECTOR ROY WILLIAM NEILL in 1944 when my father took a friend and me to Universal Studios in the San Fernando Valley to visit the set of the Sherlock Holmes film *The Pearl of Death*. It was Saturday, April 15, 1944 and I was nine-years-old and terribly excited, as I had never been inside a motion picture studio before. You might ask how I could remember the exact date. I couldn't, but I found it by reviewing the Universal Pictures production logs for the Sherlock Holmes films that are kept in the archives of the University of Southern California's Cinematic Arts Library.

Roy William Neill (r) with from left Dennis Hoey, Nigel Bruce and Alan Mowbray on the set of *Terror by Night*.

33

In 1944 Universal Studios was about half the size that it is today, but it still covered 230 hilly acres, most of it open land and back lot sets on the site of the original Taylor Chicken Ranch purchased by Carl Laemmle in 1915. The main building was a single-story Spanish-style structure next to the auto gate with the legend *Universal Pictures Company, Inc.* overhead. Next to it stood a second building that housed the Universal City Post Office. Carl Laemmle had incorporated his property and managed to convince the U.S. Postal Service to build a post office next to the studio. The main auto gate opened onto a street that ran down the center of the lot between the sound stages, office bungalows and dressing rooms, and on past the editorial department, makeup department and wardrobe department. On that particular Saturday, the Neill Company was working on Stage 14; *The Pearl of Death* had been in production for four days and today they were beginning several days' work on the Royal Regent Museum and Curator's office sets. According to the production logs, the set was a revamp of a standing set and the budget estimated the cost of the needed work to be $2,285, with a note from art director John B. Goodman to "endeavor to hold down to $2,000."

A panoramic view of the Royal Regent Museum set in *The Pearl of Death*.

Roy Neill greeted my father warmly and offered me his hand when my father introduced me to him. I have since read that Neill was missing several fingers on his right hand, but I must confess that I wasn't aware of it at that moment as I was too busy taking in the bustling activity on the set. I wouldn't truly learn to appreciate Roy Neill's talent until years later when I began working in the film business myself and revisited the Sherlock Holmes films and his remarkable visual contribution to *Frankenstein Meets the Wolf Man* (1943). Neill had the amazing ability to create atmospheric moments with lights, a few set pieces and an occasional fog machine and his scenes were always captivatingly composed and staged.

Neill had a prop man bring over director's chairs for my friend and me, and then he and my father went to work on a scene involving the theft of the Borgia Pearl by the film's heavy Giles Conover, played by Miles Mander. Conover, dressed in the coveralls of a janitor, takes the pearl from its case, rushes across the room, throws a small bench through a large, leaded glass window, breaking it into a thousand pieces, and escapes into the London streets beyond. Of course it was a stunt man who doubled for Miles Mander and he was paid the munificent sum of $35 for his efforts. Roy Neill gave my friend and me pieces of the broken glass as souvenirs and they turned out to be made of candied sugar. It was a momentous day for me; seeing Roy Neill at work instilled in me the ambition to become a director myself when I grew up. An ambition I one day achieved.

Appropriately enough, there is a great deal of mystery surrounding the life of Roy William Neill, beginning with his name and birthplace. All published biographies assert that his place of birth is Ireland. A biographic file in the Margaret Herrick Library at the Motion Picture Academy of Arts and Sciences says that his real name was Roland de Gostrie and that he was born in Dublin, Ireland, or possibly on a ship in Queenstown Harbor, County Cork. From extensive genealogical research developed for me by Scott Gallinghouse, it would appear that neither claim is correct. A comprehensive search of records reveals that his name was in fact Roy William Neill, that he most likely was born in San Francisco on September 4, 1887, and that his father's name was Robert Neill. Neill's father was in fact born in Ireland and immigrated to the United States in 1850, taking up residence in San Francisco. Gallinghouse refutes the authenticity of the de Gostrie name, stating, "From a genealogical viewpoint, there simply does not appear to be such a surname in any known records." Some stories imply that Robert Neill was a ship's captain and the name of his ship (upon which Neill was rumored to have been born) was the *Roland de Gostrie*.

In 1920 Neill, while directing films for Norma Talmadge's company, applied for a renewal of his U.S. passport, swearing under oath that his name was Roy William Neill. In that passport he declared that he was born in San Francisco in 1887. It's interesting to note that the application was witnessed by future Warner Bros. character actor Edward S. Brophy, who was at that time working as an assistant director for the Famous Players-Lasky Company and would later work as an actor for director Neill in *I'll Fix It* (1934). There is evidence of Neill living in San Francisco in 1909 and 1910, as his name appears in the San Francisco city directory for both years. The information for the 1909 volume would have been based on the results of a canvass of the residents in 1908, which would have been the year that Neill turned 21. A book published in 1920 discusses his acting career at the Alcazar Theatre in San Francisco. The book, *The First One Hundred Noted Men and Women of the Screen* by Carolyn Lowrey, includes Neill's name along with such film luminaries as Douglas Fairbanks, Wallace Reid and Mary Pickford and noted directors D.W. Griffith, Cecil B. DeMille, Marshall Neilan and Erich von Stroheim. Although Lowrey writes that R. William Neill, the name he was using to direct the fifty-three silent films he guided between 1917 and 1929, was born in Ireland, she adds that he attended St. Mary's College in San Francisco and was a member of Frederic Belasco's Alcazar Stock Company in San Francisco. (Frederic was the brother of writer-director David Belasco.) The 1910 listing for Neill in the San Francisco city directory lists Neill as "Assistant Manager-Alcazar Theatre."

In 1911 Neill embarked on a world tour with the Anglo-American Players, leaving the company in Manila and joining a friend on a tour through the Orient, including Egypt, Africa and India. A ship's manifest shows Neill arriving in London from Calcutta, India, on November 30, 1913, and declaring his profession as actor. He apparently quickly found work in *The Glad Eye*, creating the role of Flauge and enjoying a successful run in several London Theatres including the Globe and the old Strand. After several other engagements, his acting career suffered a setback and Neill returned to New York, attempting to find work on the Broadway stage, but with equally poor results. He then returned to California and secured an introduction to filmmaker Thomas Ince, known as the "Father of the Western." After serving as Ince's assistant for a few years, Neill began directing films for Ince's company, following him to Paramount. On his own he moved over to First National Pictures where he directed Norma Talmadge and her sister Constance in several films. By 1920 Neill's reputation was firmly established and he was working regularly, directing everything from a Buck Jones western, *The Cowboy and the Countess* (1926), to one of the first silent Technicolor films, *The Viking* (1928). A review for

The Viking in the *Key West Citizen* states that the film "...is something different, new, and far removed from the conventional photoplay, bringing to the screen a vastly different form of entertainment."

Sometime around 1916 Neill met and married Mary Elizabeth "Betty" MacLagan, a 21-year-old from Martin's Ferry, Ohio, and set up house at 3133 Sunset Boulevard in Hollywood. They eventually had two daughters, Barbara (born in 1919) and Patricia (born in 1923). In 1917 Neill, as a United States citizen, dutifully registered for the draft, once again stating on his registration card that he was born in San Francisco, while backdating his date of birth to 1884. That would have made him 30-years-old, and because he was now a married man, he was apparently exempted from service in The Great War. Notwithstanding the above, in the 1920 census Neill declared his place of birth to be Ireland, but then in September of that same year when he returned to the United States aboard the *S.S. Mexico* from a trip to Cuba, he affirmed in the ship's records that his birthplace was San Francisco, but now his birth date was listed as 1889. Apparently Neill had difficulty in remembering vital statistics.

As films grew in popularity, the public's interest in the stars and even some of the people behind the camera grew exponentially and publicity departments swung into action, delivering made- up stories to newspapers and fan magazines. Even Roy William Neill had his history embellished as newspaper stories began appearing about his having been a war correspondent during the 1911 Chinese Civil War (not entirely impossible as he was in the Orient at that time), a pilot during World War I (not likely as he was then busy directing films), and the first person to photograph the eruption of Mt. Etna in Italy. (Possible, but it's rather unlikely that he would have been the very first to photograph an eruption, as Mt Etna was an active volcano with hundreds of eruptions during the 1900s. However, Mt. Etna did have several eruptions in early 1923 and Neill, who directed only two films that year, was a passenger on the *S.S. Canada* that arrived in New York from Naples, Italy, on April 24, 1923).

The British Colony in Hollywood was quite extensive, even in the 1920s, and by 1940 it was filled with expatriate actors under the leadership of the stereotypical Englishmen Sir C. Aubrey Smith, who was the undisputed captain of the Hollywood Cricket Club. During the late 1930s it was required that every British-born actor in Hollywood show up in Griffith Park on Sundays to play cricket. Although there is no record of Neill ever playing in any of Smith's prerequisite matches, it would appear that Neill may have fostered the story of his Irish birth in order to embellish his image in Hollywood circles. Apparently Neill even developed a slight British-Irish accent, according to an interview that writer-director

Edward Bernds (*Return of the Fly* [1959], *The Three Stooges Meet Hercules* [1962]) gave to Tom Weaver and Michael & John Brunas for their book *Universal Horrors*. Bernds, who was a sound technician at Columbia Pictures in the 1930s and worked on a number of Roy Neill films, including *Black Moon* (1934) and *The Black Room* (1935), told the authors that Neill's speech "was that of an educated Irishman, somewhat British sounding, but with just a hint of the Irish lilt or brogue." Because Neill had spent some time in England as an actor, one can presume that he may have picked up the "brogue" from constant exposure to his surroundings. I do know that when I met Roy Neill I immediately assumed that he was British by both his speech and his appearance. Bernds also told Weaver and his partners that Neill liked to use a rocking director's chair on the set and this seems to be corroborated by a blurb in a syndicated Hollywood column called *Chatter of the Make-Believers* that appeared in the February 13, 1934 edition of the *Oakland Tribune*, which referred to Neill as "the only rocking chair director in captivity."

On October 25, 1929, Neill's wife Betty was involved in an automobile accident near their home in Beverly Hills; her car struck a car driven by Ellen De Kruis. Mrs. De Kruis, who was a nurse, later sued for damages, claiming that she had received injuries that resulted in the loss of the use of her left hand. An article in the *Los Angeles Times* on May 19, 1931, reported that after a three-day jury trial, Mrs. De Kruis, who had asked for damages of $56,213, was awarded a judgment of $17,019.

When sound arrived in 1929, Neill transitioned smoothly into the new medium, first directing two musicals, *The Melody Man*, based on an unproduced play by Herbert Fields, and *Cock o' the Walk*, starring Myrna Loy, for which he is also credited as the cinematographer. He then signed a contract with Columbia Pictures and directed the atmospheric mysteries, *The Menace* (1932), starring a young Bette Davis, *The Ninth Guest* (1934) and *The Lone Wolf Returns* (1935) with Melvyn Douglas. According to Edward Bernds, Neill attempted to give extra effort to Bette Davis' scenes in *The Menace*. Bernds recalled that Neill sensed Davis' potential "and tried to be an artist, a painstaking director, with her—which is a pretty tough job on a Columbia quickie budget. Besides, *The Menace* as I recall was a not-very-well-written, routine horror story, and Bette's chief dramatic contribution was a lot of terrified screaming." In 1934 Neill directed his first true horror film, *Black Moon*, a story about a voodoo curse and a young woman, starring Fay Wray and Jack Holt. The *New York Times* review published in June of 1934 declared, "*Black Moon*, although it is strictly studio-made, is admirably equipped to throw a double-barreled scare into the innocent entertainment-hunter."

Roy William Neill (seated with dog) on the set of *The Black Room*.
Thurston Hall (l), Boris Karloff and Marian Marsh stand facing him.

The following year Neill directed Boris Karloff in a dual role as twins, one of whom kills the other and assumes his identity, in another horror film with "black" in the title, *The Black Room* (1935). Neill's lush visual style is evident throughout this film, particularly in the darkly lit, gothic setting of the castle, and the early scenes in the Black Cat Inn (another "black" to add to the list) with its dulcimer player in the foreground serving as a precursor to similarly staged scenes in *Sherlock Holmes and the Secret Weapon*. Neill is ill served in *The Black Room* by a dreadful, bombastic musical score that frequently overpowers the dialogue, and the occasional reminders of Columbia's poverty row budgets, such as gravestones with names painted rather than chiseled on them. However, he manages to overcome these handicaps and elicits a bravura performance from Boris Karloff in all three of his incarnations and shows the same directorial technique that would come to grace the Universal films. It seems that films with "black" in the title would follow Neill throughout his career, starting with *Black Paradise* in 1926 and ending with his final film *Black Angel* in 1946.

In 1936 Neill completed his Columbia contract and sailed for England with his family, having signed a new contract with Warner Bros.' British subsidiary, First National Productions. For the next four years, with one notable exception, he directed mostly comedies (three of which he also wrote) at the company's Teddington Studios near London; the exception was the costume drama *Doctor Syn* (1937) starring George Arliss and Margaret Lockwood that was well received by both critics and audiences. According to some sources, Neill was producer Edward Black's first choice to direct his film *The Lost Lady* in 1937 and Neill took a company to Yugoslavia to film background shots. The project was abandoned when the company ran into trouble with the Yugoslavian police, who didn't like the way they were to be portrayed in the film. The following year Black hired Alfred Hitchcock to direct the film and changed the title to *The Lady Vanishes*. Hitchcock's suspenseful spy thriller on a speeding train became the most successful British film to that date, and some might say the partial inspiration for Roy Neill's later Holmes film *Terror by Night*.

Neill was still in England during the Nazi blitz of 1940, but when the United States entered the War in 1941 he returned to this country and eventually signed his contract with Universal Pictures, directing his first Universal films, *Eyes of the Underworld* and the Constance Bennett espionage melodrama, *Madame Spy* in 1942. Later that same year he took over the reins on *Sherlock Holmes and the Secret Weapon* and began his five-year association with the master detective with a beginning salary of $5,700 per picture that eventually graduated to $10,000. Basil Rathbone in his autobiography *In and Out of Character* expressed his admiration for his director: "He was endearingly known to his company as 'Mousie'. There was a nominal producer and some writers also, but Roy Neill was the master and final hand in all departments." In Nigel Bruce's unpublished memoir he too was under the impression that Neill was "an Englishman by birth who had become an American citizen." Bruce went on to describe his fondness for Neill: "He was a little man, very fussy about his clothes and like myself, he always smoked a pipe. He was an extremely kind and friendly person and all his assistants and the crews who worked for him were devoted to him. Roy was an extremely able director, having a great knowledge of film technique and of the use of his camera. During the many pictures we made under his direction we found him a joy to work for. Basil and I nicknamed him 'mousey' [note the difference in spelling to Rathbone's reference] during our first picture and the name stuck to him from then on. We both became extremely attached to Roy Neill." Rathbone's and Bruce's admiration for Neill was obviously shared by his studio, which promoted him in 1943 to producer-director on his third Holmes film, *Sherlock Holmes Faces Death,* and put out a press release stating that his work on the first two films was so "outstanding" that he was "being rewarded by being upped to producer status." He repaid Universal's faith in him by also directing that same year the highly atmospheric money-maker *Frankenstein Meets the Wolf Man* and then going on to produce and direct eight more Sherlock Holmes films as well as a Maria Montez starrer, *Gypsy Wildcat* (1944).

My father reprised his Lestrade character, including the same raincoat and bowler hat, in *Frankenstein Meets the Wolf Man* with perhaps a slightly more intelligent scowl and a different character name. This film has remained one of my favorite of the Universal horror films, particu-

Patric Knowles as Doctor Manning and Dennis Hoey as Inspector Owen in a scene that was dropped from *Frankenstein Meets the Wolf Man.*

larly the way Neill staged the opening sequence in the graveyard with its stunning introductory crane shot.

Neill also involved himself in writing, although despite his shared screen credit with Edmund L. Hartmann for the screenplay of *The Scarlet Claw* (1944) it would appear, according to the production budget, that Neill failed to receive any additional compensation from the studio for his work beyond his director's salary of $5,700. He also wrote the original story for a film called *Two Tickets to London* that he was originally penciled in to direct; the script eventually was completed by screenwriter Tom Reed and given to Edwin L. Marin to direct while Neill was in production on *Sherlock Holmes Faces Death (1943)*. Interestingly the cast of *Two Tickets* included most of his Universal repertory company, including Mary Gordon, Holmes Herbert, Mathew Boulton, Harry Cording, David Clyde, Leyland Hodgson, Mary Forbes, Colin Kenny, Arthur Stenning, John Burton, Harold De Becker and Doris Lloyd.

From April 9 to mid May of 1946 Roy William Neill directed what unhappily turned out to be his final film, *Black Angel*. The cast included Dan Duryea, Peter Lorre, and Universal contractee June Vincent, who

Dan Duryea, June Vincent and Peter Lorre. The stars of Roy William Neill's final film, *Black Angel*.

was replacing what would have been a far better choice for the role of the sultry nightclub singer, Ava Gardner. The film was Neill's only acknowledged attempt at film noir and he managed to pull it off with some success, particularly the final flashback staging of the murder. Reviews were unenthusiastic, with *Daily Variety* appraising Neill's direction as "Lacking that extra speed needed to give this type of film the desired sock." Over the years *Black Angel* has become a favorite of film noir aficionados and is considered an unjustly forgotten example of the genre. In fact Neill's signature expressionistic style in his staging of the Sherlock Holmes films; the below eye-level camera, evocative shadows, etc., was indeed true film noir. According to my father, who always spoke of Neill with affection, after the film was completed, Universal Pictures finally acknowledged Neill's well-proven talent by awarding him a high-budget film to direct in England. This would have made sense, as it was now after the war and Universal had frozen funds in England that could only be used on British co-productions. Film critic Edwin Schallert wrote in his *Los Angeles Times* column on October 19, 1946 that Neil was on his way to England to discuss an offer for a $3,000,000 film that would be produced in Ireland in Technicolor. In Nigel Bruce's memoirs he describes hearing from Neill a few days before he died and that he "told me that he was trying to arrange for Basil and myself to come over to England and make some Sherlock Holmes pictures there with him." According to another *Los Angeles Times* article, a company called Celebrity Films of Britain was pursuing Rathbone, Bruce and Neill to work in Britain on a Technicolor version of Sir Arthur Conan Doyle's *The Sign of the Four*. A ship's manifest shows that Neill sailed by himself for England aboard the *Queen Elizabeth* on October 31, 1946, and according to my father, Neill died onboard. However an Associated Press obituary stated that Neill died in London on December 14 at the home of his nephew Sidney Bracy. Neill's wife and two daughters were at their home at 540 North Croft Avenue in Hollywood at the time. This further increases the mystery surrounding Neill, because a Sidney Bracey (real name: Sidney Alfred Dunn) was a Hollywood supporting player until his death in 1942, four years before Neill's passing. Bracey, or Bracy as he was sometimes listed, appeared in several Neill films over the years. It is possible that the "nephew" is in fact the son of Sidney Bracy, who was married to an Evelyn Martin and had two daughters, Barbara and Iris and a son, Sidney Norton Bracy, Jr., who was born in 1908 and later attained the rank of captain in the Royal British Engineering Corps, which could explain his living in London in 1946. If Evelyn Martin's maiden name had been MacLagan, this would help established her as Betty Neill's sister since there is no record of Roy Neill having any siblings. However, since this is not the case, it is hard to find the connection making Sidney Bracy, Jr., Roy Neill's "nephew" as mentioned in the AP obituary. So the mystery surrounding Neill's life continues; however, given his apparent penchant for embellishing the facts, I think he would have rather enjoyed the more ironic and colorful myth that he was both born and died aboard ships off the coast of England. The real tragedy is that Roy William Neill died much too young (at the age of 59) before he could fully reap the rewards for his remarkable talent.

SHERLOCK HOLMES AND
THE SECRET WEAPON

THE SCREENWRITER FIRST ASSIGNED to develop the second in Universal's Sherlock Holmes series was Edward T. Lowe, who had begun his writing career during the silent era and in the 1930s had created the screenplays for a number of Charlie Chan and Bulldog Drummond films at Paramount and Fox. He was followed by W. Scott Darling, a prolific writer from Canada, who had written the screenplay earlier in 1942 for *The Ghost of Frankenstein* and would contribute to 1944's *Weird Woman* and *Cobra Woman*. The final screenplay was completed by Edmund L. Hartmann, who would later collaborate with Roy William Neill on the script of *The Scarlet Claw* (1944). The first revised draft, still titled *Sher-*

lock Holmes Fights Back, was submitted by Universal's C.R. Metzger to the Production Code Administration's offices on May 5, 1942. The Production Code, which is now known as the Motion Picture Association of America, was authorized to rate all motion pictures before their release. The organization's Joseph I. Breen of the Production Code responded the following day, warning Mr. Metzger that the story contained "a specific Code violation, in that reference is made in a three-page scene to opium smoking and there are scenes of opium dens." Over the next few weeks Hartmann revised the script, now referred to by its final title, changing the opium den setting to a Limehouse pub. This revamped script received the blessing of the "Breen Office," as the Production Code was frequently called, and Neill began filming on June 8, 1942.

The opening sequence of *Sherlock Holmes and the Secret Weapon,* while ostensibly taking place in Switzerland, was in fact some excellently photographed scenes by cinematographer Les White on Universal's back lot European Street. White and Roy William Neill made their auspicious debut into the series with impressive style, as the night scenes with their glistening streets and deep shadows are similar to the look of Carol Reed's *The Third Man* (1949). White, who had previously filmed *Invisible Agent* (1942) for the studio and was also the permanent cameraman for all of the *Andy Hardy* series at M-G-M, would return to Universal in 1943 to film *Sherlock Holmes in Washington.*

Based loosely on Conan Doyle's short story "The Adventure of the Dancing Men," which first appeared in the United States in a 1903 issue of Collier's magazine, *Secret Weapon* introduces Holmes' use of disguises with a well-done makeup of an elderly bookseller posing as an accomplice of two Nazi spies (Rudolf Anders and Paul Fix). Two more masquerades, first of a rough-looking native seafarer and later one of Doctor Tobel's scientist accomplices are equally effective. Fast-paced action then carries us through Holmes and Tobel's escape to London and the introduction of the secret bombsight. William Post, Jr.'s Swiss accent is most credible for a man born in Montclair, New Jersey, and holds up quite well opposite the authentic accent of Berlin-born Kaaren Verne who plays his love interest. (Verne would wed Peter Lorre in May of 1945, but the marriage would last only five years.) Tobel's use of the Dancing Men code came from the previously mentioned short story "The Adventure of the Dancing Men," which was included as one of the chapters in Conan Doyle's *The Return of Sherlock Holmes.*

The plot thickens as Tobel is kidnapped by Holmes' arch-enemy Moriarty, played by veteran character actor Lionel Atwill. Atwill's performance has been criticized by many movie buffs as being too lacka-

Lionel Atwill as Moriarty and Basil Rathbone as Sherlock Holmes in
Sherlock Holmes and the Secret Weapon.

daisical, but I believe that his reputation as a prime villain in so many films, including the Universal chillers *Man Made Monster* (1941) and *The Mad Doctor of Market Street* (1942), enhanced his admittedly laid-back performance. However, as compared to Henry Daniell's "delectably dangerous" interpretation of Moriarty in *The Woman in Green,* as expressed by Basil Rathbone in his autobiography, Atwill's performance does suffer by comparison. And the finale, with Holmes and Moriarty debating the proper way to eliminate each other, with Moriarty settling on slowly draining Holmes' blood supply, while Watson, Lestrade and the police follow a trail of luminous paint to his hideout, seems oddly anticlimactic. Moriarty's death, presumably by falling through an open trap door off stage, leaves open the possibility of his return, which as it turns out is the case a few films later. The final moment, with Rathbone as Holmes answering Doctor Watson's comment: "Things are looking up, Holmes. This little island is still on the map," with a much abridged version of the Duke of Lancaster's speech from Shakespeare's *Richard II*: "Yes. This fortress, built by nature for herself. This blessed plot. This earth, this realm... this England," is quite moving when viewed from the perspective of 1943 and World War II.

Dennis Hoey as Lestrade (fifth from left) in his first screen appearance in
Sherlock Holmes and the Secret Weapon.

When Lestrade was first introduced in *Sherlock Holmes and the Secret Weapon,* there is no description of the character in the script. Although most of the other characters are depicted in detail, there is absolutely nothing to characterize Lestrade—not his clothes, nor manner of speech, or physical appearance. Lestrade is more reserved and perhaps even more resourceful as written; it is he who deduces that the sea chest carrying the bound-up Holmes might have a false bottom, thereby rescuing Holmes from two of Moriarty's henchmen. My father's physical appearance certainly didn't match Conan Doyle's description, as he stood six foot three and weighed over two hundred pounds, and was anything but "a little sallow, rat-faced, dark-eyed fellow." Ironically, Lestrade doesn't even appear in the original "Dancing Men" story and the decision to give him a Cockney dialect was a choice made between director Roy William Neill and my father and did not come from Conan Doyle's design. As time and the films continued, the dialect and the ineptitude seemed to increase as both the films and my father's character grew in popularity. However there were still moments of sincerity, as when Holmes has apparently perished in a fall in *The Spider Woman* (1944) and Lestrade and Watson grieve his passing. Lestrade admires Holmes's old chair, saying, "Funny duck, he was. Said to me ol' woman only this morning, if it hadn't been for him I'd still be a sergeant." When Watson replies, "Pity you didn't mention it when he was alive," Lestrade answers with a sad nod and adds, "Perhaps we understood each other better than you think, Doctor." Affectionately touching Holmes's pipe rack, he mutters, "One of his old pipes." Then, with a burst of pain and accusation, he shouts, "What you let him fall in that blasted river? Why didn't you jump in after him, you big blunder head!!" When Watson offers one of Holmes's pipes to him, Lestrade mutters, "I wouldn't mind," and, picking up an old Calabash, adds, "This is the one I want, it's the one I remember best." When Holmes suddenly reappears and Lestrade surreptitiously tries to return the pipe to its place in the rack, Holmes tells him that he may keep the pipe and he accepts it with a grateful smile. I think that I can safely say that this was one of my father's favorite scenes, as it most certainly was mine, and that Lestrade was most likely his favorite role. My father ultimately appeared as Lestrade in six of the films, and would most likely have appeared in a seventh, *Dressed to Kill* (1946) except for a scheduling conflict with a 20th Century-Fox film he was appearing in at that time, *Anna and the King of Siam* starring Rex Harrison and Irene Dunne.

I have discussed my father's life in great detail in one of my previous books, but I will briefly outline his career once again for those of you who haven't read *Elvis, Sherlock and Me: How I Survived Growing Up in Hollywood.*

DENNIS HOEY was born Samuel David Hyams on March 30, 1893, the eldest son of Ellis Hyams, a tailor journeyman from Poland, and his wife Leah, who managed a boarding house at 13 Landsdowne Place in the town of Hove, England, a short distance from the seaside resort of Brighton. There were two brothers, Harry and Morris, and two sisters, Rita and Miriam. I met only Rita and that was a brief afternoon tea in her suite at New York's Waldorf Astoria Hotel, when she was visiting the United States in 1946; my one impression was that she looked like my father in drag and terrified me.

My father originally intended to become a teacher after graduating from Brighton College, but worked briefly as a stockbroker before joining the Army on December 23, 1916 and serving for two years in the Devonshire Regiment, 13th Works Battalion. Shortly before enlisting, he married his first wife, Sara Pearl Lyons, but according to what my father told me years later, the marriage was quickly annulled. It was in the Army that my father developed his singing talents while entertaining the troops. As Dennis Hoey, a name he later claimed was borrowed from a

Dennis Hoey as Lestrade.

well-known actress of the early 20th century name Iris Hoey, he made his first stage appearance at London's Drury Lane Theatre in *Shanghai* (1919) and quickly followed that up by portraying Arif Bey in the musical *Katinka* at the Shaftsbury. He initiated the role of Ali Ben Ali in the London production of *The Desert Song*, which ran for 432 performances at the Drury Lane in the late 20s, and traveled to America to costar on Broadway in two more musical operettas: *Hassan*, in which he had the dubious distinction of appearing in blackface, and, during the fall season of 1926, in *Katja*, in which he had a more prominent role and enjoyed a very respectful run of 112 performances at the 44th Street Theatre. He also toured in England, playing Long John Silver in *Treasure Island*; the *Evening Express* reported that he was "…as delightful a pirate as ever shivered his timbers." He appeared in his only silent film, *Tip Toes* in 1927 for British filmmaker Herbert Wilcox, appearing opposite Dorothy Gish and Will Rogers.

He married my mother, Josephine Marta Ricca, who everyone called Jo, in 1933 and I was born the following year. By 1934 my father had appeared in fourteen British films alongside such stars as Anna May Wong, in *Chu Chin Chow* (1934), and John Gielgud, Jessie Matthews, Jack Hawkins and Edmund Gwenn in *The Good Companions* (1933). The latter was a Victor Saville film musical taken from J.B. Priestley's hugely successful novel about a theatrical group touring the provinces. In 1935 he appeared with two of the cinema's top horror icons, Tod Slaughter in *The Murder in the Red Barn* and Bela Lugosi in *The Mystery of the Marie Celeste*. Like most actors on the British stage, my father had learned his craft by appearing in many of the Bard's plays. For several seasons he was a member of Sydney W. Carroll's Shakespearean troupe and in 1931 he toured the provinces in Sir Godfrey Tearle's production of *Hamlet*, before being signed to play the lead in a new film called *McCluscky the Sea Rover* and leaving for Tripoli to begin filming. At that time the Italians controlled Tripoli and a disagreement with the Italian authorities regarding the use of firearms by the Bedouin tribesmen, who were to appear in the film as extras, forced the film's cancellation. Ronald Neame, who was working on the film as an assistant cameraman, later became a noted director and wrote about this incident in his autobiography *Straight from The Horse's Mouth*.

In 1936 Dennis Hoey starred in his only film as a leading man, an Australian epic called *Uncivilised* that was produced and directed by Charles Chauvel, the man who had discovered Errol Flynn. By today's standards the film is an embarrassment, although at the time it did fairly brisk business, particularly in Australia; Paul Hogan insists that it was the inspiration for his film *Crocodile Dundee* (1986). Later that same year, having been signed by a theatrical agent, who promised he could get him plenty of work on radio, my father decided to move to New York and see what this new agent could do for him. Almost immediately, he was rushing from studio to studio, doing a soap opera in the morning (*Pretty Kitty Kelly*) and dramatic shows such as the *U.S. Steel Hour* in the evenings. His success prompted him to arrange to have my mother and me join him the following year. In December of 1936, the Theatre Guild signed my father to the role of Edward Rochester opposite Katharine Hepburn's Jane Eyre.

Hepburn, who was considered box-office poison by the film exhibiters at that time, supposedly planned to tour with *Jane Eyre* until she had built up her confidence enough to open the play on Broadway. As it turned out, Hepburn never truly intended to bring *Jane Eyre* to New York. She was merely buying time while family friend Philip Barry finished writing his play, *The Philadelphia Story* as a vehicle for her.

When the war started in Europe my father (who was touring with Ruth Chatterton, portraying Colonel Pickering in Shaw's *Pygmalion*) had a hunch that Hollywood would soon have need of character actors with British accents who could also be called upon to do a convincing German dialect. So we left New York and traveled by train to join him in Los Angeles. He was right; before too many months had passed he had portrayed an RAF Intelligence officer in *A Yank in the R.A.F.* (1941) and two really nasty Gestapo officers in *They Came to Blow Up America* (1943) and *Bomber's Moon* (1943), all for Twentieth Century-Fox Studios. Over the next ten years my father appeared in over forty five films, including *Kitty* (1945) with Paulette Goddard and Ray Milland, *Golden Earrings* (1947), with Milland and Marlene Dietrich, *Wake of the Red Witch* (1948) with John Wayne, and of course the Sherlock Holmes-series plus the two horror films for Universal, *Frankenstein Meets the Wolf Man* (1943) and *She-Wolf of London* (1946). He even played a butler on a couple of occasions in *This Above All* (1942), *Christmas Eve* (1947) and *The Secret Garden* (1949).

My father had several talents besides acting; since he started as a singer, he still practiced his vocalizing every day and would on occasion sing for guests at our home. He was also an amateur artist and a pretty good one at that. One Sunday he borrowed a water color set that someone had given me and proceeded to make an excellent copy of a photograph that had appeared in the morning paper of some sailboats moored in a harbor at sunset. He also tried his hand at writing and in 1945 he returned to New York to appear in *The Haven,* a play that he had written based on a book by Anthony Gilbert. With a setting similar to an Agatha Christie mystery and a cast, besides my father, that included such well-known performers as Dennis King, Valerie Cossart and Melville Cooper, it should have been a success, but unfortunately for my father it opened and closed in three nights. It also caused a rift in my parents' marriage, as my father soon divorced my mother and married a young woman he had met while in New York. Barbara Collingwood was the sister of newsman Charles Collingwood and she seemed to be a very nice person when I met her during a summer I spent with her and my father; however the marriage lasted only a year or so and then ended in divorce. My father remained single until 1951 when he married Henrietta Russell, a wealthy widow who divided her time between a Park Avenue cooperative and a house on the bay in Tampa, Florida. She wrote poetry under the name of Bayka Russell and published it herself. She and my father would remain married until his death in 1960.

From 1946 to 1951 my father appeared in nineteen films, including *Terror by Night* (1946) and *She-Wolf of London* (1946) at Universal and played such diversified characters as a British ambassador in *Anna and the King of Siam* (1946), Hedy Lamarr's drunken brute of a father in *The Strange Woman* (1946), a Nazi Gestapo officer in *Golden Earrings* (1946), and a western land baron in *The Kid from Texas* (1950), starring Audie Murphy as Billy the Kid.

In May of 1951, my father, who was now living part time in New York, appeared in a revival of George Bernard Shaw's *Getting Married* at the ANTA Playhouse. Appearing with him was writer-actress Edith Meiser, who had been instrumental in getting the Sherlock Holmes radio series on the air and had written a great many of the radio scripts for Rathbone and Bruce. My father tried his hand at playwriting again with a comedy called *Stag at Eve*, which he also starred in at the summer playhouse in Bridgeport, Connecticut. Dennis Hoey's final screen appearances were in *Plymouth Adventure* (1952) for M-G-M and *Caribbean* (1952) for Paramount. After that he returned to New York and continued appearing in theatre and live television programs, such as a 1956 episode of the television series *Omnibus,* hosted by Alistair Cooke, in which he portrayed Sir Arthur Conan Doyle while dressed in a deerstalker hat and carrying a Calabash pipe—props which obviously were more associated with Conan Doyle's creation than with the author himself.

My father suffered from emphysema in his later years. Although they maintained an apartment in Manhattan, his wife preferred spending much of her time at her mansion in Tampa, so he was regularly subjected to the humid Florida climate, which aggravated his condition. He died of complications from the emphysema on July 25, 1960 in a Tampa hospital at the age of 67. My father and I had a difficult relationship for a very long time and in fact were estranged for five years until the 1959 birth of my son, who I named after him, brought us together again and we had a brief period of reconciliation while he was visiting my family the year before he died. For some reason, when he became ill his wife failed to let me know until after he had died, so I was only able to attend his funeral. I'm grateful that we had spent some wonderful time together the previous year when he came to California to meet his grandson and his granddaughter, Karin. In 2008 my wife Katie and I visited the Myrtle Hill Memorial Park in Tampa where he is buried and I placed a small stone in remembrance on his headstone. I've always appreciated David Stuart Davies' comments about my father in his study of the Holmes' films, *Starring Sherlock Holmes* and when we met a few years ago at a Sherlockian film convention put on by publishers Steven Doyle and Mark Gagen in Indianapolis, I thanked him for writing: "Hoey's Lestrade added a strange kind of endearing charm to the series. If he had not been there, we would have missed him."

The actor most suited to play Professor Moriarty, LIONEL ATWILL (Full name Lionel Alfred William Atwill) was born in the London suburb of Croydon on March 1, 1885, the eldest of four children. His father Alfred Atwill was a civil servant and insurance agent and his mother was the former Ada Emily Dace. Because the family was prosperous (his grandfather was a successful architect), Atwill was educated by private tutors and later attended Mercer School in London with the idea that he too would become an architect. However, Atwill quickly abandoned his original vocation and took up a study of Shakespeare, appearing in several Shakespearean recitals in the London suburbs. He made his professional debut in 1904 at the Garrick Theatre as a supernumerary in *The Walls of Jericho* and soon was touring England in a repertory company performing such plays as *The Flag Lieutenant* and *The Prisoner of the Bastille*. Atwill gained prominence in *Milestones*, which played for over 600 performances at the Royalty Theatre, and by 1915 he had appeared in five more London productions including a less than successful appearance in *Mrs. Thompson* with the legendary Lily Langtry that opened and closed in short order. On April 19, 1913, Atwill married his first wife Phyllis Mary Relph, a fellow actor, and in 1915 their son John Arthur Atwill was born. The Atwills crossed the Atlantic together to make their joint debut on the Broadway stage in 1917 in *The Lodger* based on Marie Belloc-Lowndes' novel about Jack the Ripper. From this choice of play, one might presume that Atwill was already turning to the dark

Lionel Atwill as Professor Moriarty in *Sherlock Holmes and the Secret Weapon*.

side of his character, but that was not the case. This production of *The Lodger* bore no resemblance to Alfred Hitchcock's (1927) or Laird Cregar's (1944) interpretations, but was in fact a comedy that Atwill also directed while playing the title character as a lovesick free spirit. *The New York Times* did not care for the play and was not very kind in its comments on Ms. Relph's performance, but saved its most vitriolic remarks for Atwill: "Mr. Atwill drives in his every point as if he were bound that no defective in the last row of the gallery should miss one of them. It is acting of the hammer-and-tongs school." Atwill would quickly recover from this drubbing, receiving excellent notices later that year for his next performance as the disreputable Courtenay Urquhart opposite Grace George in *Eve's Daughter*. He would then reprise his role in the silent film version of the play, now opposite Billie Burke, and begin his long association with motion pictures. The Atwill's marriage ended in divorce in 1919 and the following year Atwill married another actress, Elsie Mackay. This union would be dissolved when Atwill, who in 1925 was directing his wife in a new play entitled *Deep in the Woods,* became suspicious that she was having an affair with her leading man, Englishman Max Montesole, and had detectives raid an East side apartment to discover Mackay with the actor.

From 1918 to 1932, Atwill appeared in a half-dozen silent films while continuing to direct and perform in twenty-five Broadway productions, achieving star status with his acclaimed performance as the French mime Jean-Gaspard Deburau in Sacha Guitry's eponymous play *Deburau,* which ran at producer David Belasco's theatre from December 1920 to June 1921. Also in the cast was the future Charlie Chan, Sidney Toler and Atwill's soon to be wife Elsie Mackay, plus a young actor named Frederick Bickle, who would later change his name to Fredric March. This would be the beginning of a very successful relationship between Atwill and David Belasco that lasted for several years and included such hits as *The Grand Duke* and *The Comedian.* At the same time, Atwill was beginning to appear in films and in 1927 he purchased a house in Pacific Palisades, California, at 13515 D'Este Drive and ceremoniously placed his hand in wet cement on the porch to commemorate the date, October 9, 1927. Atwill soon returned to Broadway to co-star opposite Katharine Cornell in *The Outsider,* playing a role not dissimilar to those he would soon be portraying in his many horror films, a bogus doctor who heals a crippled girl whom experts had said was incurable.

The divorce from Elsie Mackay was finalized in 1928 and two years later Atwill married for the third time—this time gaining not only a beautiful wife, but a wealthy one as well. Henrietta Louise Cromwell Brooks MacArthur was the stepdaughter of Philadelphia millionaire Edward T.

Stotesbury and had previously been married to Brigadier General Douglas MacArthur from 1922 to 1929. Several biographers have stated that MacArthur, who was Superintendent at West Point Military Academy when he married Louise, earned the ire of his superior General John J. Pershing, who transferred the couple to a post in the Philippines. Lionel and Louise were married at the bride's Eccleston, Maryland estate Rainbow Hill on June 8, 1930 and, according to the wedding announcement in *The New York Times*, left for their honeymoon on their new yacht that was waiting for them at the pier of the Maryland Yacht Club.

In 1931 producer Lee Schubert signed Atwill to play the role of Sir Austin Howard in *The Silent Witness*. The play had a successful run at the Morosco Theatre from March to June of that year and then went on tour, ending its run in Los Angeles. As it happened, Fox Studios purchased the rights to the play as a vehicle for Greta Nissen and asked Atwill to recreate his role in the screen version. Having already decided that he liked the idea of appearing in films, Atwill agreed to make his sound film debut in *The Silent Witness*. Mr. and Mrs. Atwill moved into his home in Pacific Palisades and Louise became one of the reigning Hollywood hostesses. The February, 1932 *New York Times* review of *The Silent Witness* exclaimed: "Mr. Atwill appears in the role he acted on the stage last Spring. His portrayal is easy and convincing, particularly in a court room sequence in which he, as Sir Austin Howard, is on trial for his life." Gregory William Mank, who has written extensively about Lionel Atwill in several books and magazine articles, had this to say about his performance: "It was an impressive, but remarkably ironic Hollywood bow. After committing perjury, Lionel, in the happy ending, says to Bramwell Fletcher, 'Tony, old boy, why, self-sacrifice is one of the great luxuries in life. And when you do it for someone whom you love—very deeply—why, my boy, it becomes a positive orgy!' Both the perjury and the orgy would follow in Lionel Atwill's real life about a decade later."

Atwill's career took a major turn with his next film when Warner Bros. assigned him the title role in their two-color Technicolor chiller *Doctor X* (1932) costarring Fay Wray, of *King Kong* fame. The film was a great success and after appearing in the low-budget *The Vampire Bat* (1933) for Majestic Studios and *The Secret of Madame Blanche* (1933) for M-G-M, Warner Bros. called Atwill and Fay Wray back to star in another Technicolor thriller, *The Mystery of the Wax Museum* (1933), which many would consider to be his most famous screen performance. All in all, Atwill appeared in eight films during 1933 most of which were in the horror genre, with Paramount's *Murders in the Zoo* calling for Atwill to pay for his evil deeds by dying wrapped in the coils of a giant snake. Atwill liked the snake so much that he bought it from the studio and added it to his own zoo on his estate at D'Este Drive. Atwill attempted to explain his departure from Broadway for Hollywood horror films after his success in *Wax Museum* in this later interview: "The first thing I knew, my agents had offers for far more horror films than I could possibly appear in, with misshapen limbs, distorted features, secretive backgrounds, and graveyard atmosphere. The high spot of that series, perhaps, was *Murders in the Zoo*, when I threw my wife to the crocodiles."

1939 was a banner year for Lionel Atwill. It was the year that he appeared in both *Son of Frankenstein*, which premiered on January 13 and marked his return to the horror genre after a four-year hiatus, and *The Hound of the Baskervilles*, his introduction to Sherlock Holmes. Josephine Hutchinson, who appeared with him in *Son of Frankenstein*, once gave an interview in which she explained the origin of Atwill's nickname of "Pinky": "I think it was because he had red hair when he was young." 1939 was also the year that Louise Atwill moved out of their home on D'Este Drive and returned to Washington, D.C. The following year a widely reported party, or orgy as the gossip mongers dubbed it, which Atwill admitted hosting at his home, became the basis of a scandalous trial in which he categorically denied under oath owning or showing any pornographic films. Following the trial, where Atwill was deemed an "innocent party," he returned to Universal for a series of films, including *The Mad Doctor of Market Street* and *The Ghost of Frankenstein*, finishing the year with his portrayal of Professor Moriarty in *Sherlock Homes and the Secret Weapon*. The day following completion of filming Atwill was indicted for perjuring his testimony during the earlier trial and was eventually convicted. It was at this time that Atwill received even more devastating news. His son John, who had returned to England with his mother Phyllis Relph to study to become a doctor and had later become a pilot officer in the R.A.F. when the war broke out, was killed in action on April 26, 1941. The young pilot (26) was buried at St. Michael Church in his mother's village of Blewbury.

The ensuing scandal made Atwill an object of scorn and unwelcome at most of the Hollywood studios except for his old stamping grounds at Universal, where director Roy William Neill and producer George Waggner hired him the following year to play the Burgomaster of Vasaria in *Frankenstein Meets the Wolf Man*. Shortly after, when the Hays Office issued a mandate to the studios not to hire the convicted felon, Atwill found that he was unemployable. After reappearing before the judge and changing his plea to guilty of exhibiting pornographic movies, Atwill was exonerated of all charges. But the situation still remained bleak and Atwill decided to return to the stage, appearing across the country in several summer stock productions. Finally in 1943, Republic hired him to play the super villain "The Scarab" in their serial *Captain America*. Next he made two low-budget thrillers for PRC and then returned to Republic for another quickie *Secrets of Scotland Yard* (1944), joining a large contingent of fellow Roy William Neill repertory players including, Martin Kosleck, Frederick Worlock, Matthew Boulton, John Abbott, Mary Gordon and Arthur Stenning.

In Las Vegas on Friday, July 7, 1944, with Louise Atwill having finally divorced him earlier that year, Atwill married wife number four, 27-year-old singer and radio producer Mary Paula Pruter. Atwill, who was 59 at the time, tried to ameliorate the 32-year difference by announcing his age as 50 and hers as 35. The following year, while he was appearing at Universal in a cameo role in *House of Dracula*, his son Lionel Anthony Guille Atwill was born at Cedars of Lebanon hospital on October 14, 1945. Shortly thereafter, Atwill was diagnosed with bronchial cancer, but continued working as best he could in another production for Universal, the 13-episode serial *Lost City of the Jungle* (1946). Unfortunately Atwill's health continued to deteriorate and he was unable to finish his work in the serial, succumbing to the cancer on April 22, 1946. The studio was forced to use a double to complete his sequences in the serial. Ironically, the final scene that Atwill completed before having to leave the production due to his failing health was in fact his death scene in the final chapter. Lionel Atwill was cremated and his ashes were interred at the Chapel of the Pines in Los Angeles, where they remained for 57 years until his son, Lionel Anthony reclaimed them in 2003 and had them interred near his home in Vermont.

RUDOLPH ANDERS, who was born in Waldkirch, Germany on December 17, 1895 and whose real name was Rudolph F. Amendt, appeared in *Sherlock Holmes and the Secret Weapon* as the Nazi spy, Braun. At that time he was using the screen name Robert O. Davis, which he acquired while appearing on the Broadway stage and later used while playing numerous Nazi villains in World War II films. Later he would take on Rudolph Anders as his professional name, occasionally changing the spelling of the first name from Rudolph to Rudolf.

Anders came to the United States for the first time to appear as a young man in an original Broadway play called *Yosemite*. The 1914 play had a short run of 24 performances and Anders went back to Germany to join the Max Reinhardt School. He returned to Broadway in 1926 and appeared in a number of plays between 1926 and 1933, returning periodically to his homeland to work in German films. On September 18, 1930 in Berlin he married Julia Lindemann from Milwaukee, Wisconsin and they would remain married for 47 years until her death in 1977. Anders continued working in films, including several Spanish-language productions and in 1933 he traveled to Mexicali, Mexico and formerly applied for Naturalization, walking across the border into Calexico on the California side. He was granted citizenship in December of 1933 and returned to New York to appear briefly as the Blind Beggar in the play *Yoshe Kalb*. After that he came back to California and took up residence with Julia at 167

Rudolph Anders as Braun in *Sherlock Holmes and the Secret Weapon.*

Westgate Avenue in West Hollywood and began working in his first Hollywood film at Columbia Pictures, *When Strangers Marry* (1933) starring Jack Holt. Over the next 35 years Anders would appear in over 100 films, beginning his long run of portraying Nazis in *Confessions of a Nazi Spy* (1939) and including *Sherlock Holmes and the Voice of Terror* and *Sherlock Holmes and the Secret Weapon* (both 1942.) Anders complained in an interview, given on the set of *The Strange Death of Adolf Hitler* (1943) where he had a featured role as a Gestapo officer, that he was "...weary of being a hated man. Such roles make me unhappy, I've been a screen Nazi," he continued, "Because I felt that I was needed to help arouse the emotions of movie-goers by portraying these European warlords as they actually are." When the war ended, Anders was somewhat freed of his unpleasant burden and went on to play a variety of characters, including doctors, scientists and café hosts in both films and television, including an amusing cameo as a studio makeup specialist examining Judy Garland's face in *A Star is Born* (1954).

I met Rudolph Anders in 1951 when I appeared in my first play as a professional actor. The play was entitled *The Burning Bush* and was written by two former screenwriters, Heinz Herald and Geza Herczeg; refugees from Hitler's Europe, they had collaborated on the screenplay for Warner Bros.' *The Life of Emile Zola* (1937), for which they had received an Academy Award. The play dealt with the Jewish pogroms in Russia during the 19th century, specifically a trumped-up murder trial. Rudy played the Counsel for the Defense and I (judging from a photo taken during a performance) played a rather rigid police officer. The director was another German émigré named Walter Wiclair who didn't seem to have much time to devote to a novice actor like me; however Rudy took pity on me and went out of his way to help me with my characterization and my makeup. His wife Julia accompanied him to every performance and waited patiently in his dressing room each night for him. They invited me to their home, but unfortunately I was never able to accept their invitation.

A few years later, Anders had a successful run playing Anne Frank's father in a 1959 touring company of the play *The Diary of Anne Frank* and still later did a series of readings of the poetry of Hugo von Hofmannsthal while still continuing to perform in films and television until 1968 when he and Julia retired to their home in Woodland Hills, California, after playing one more of his hated Nazi heavies in an episode of the ABC-TV series *Garrison's Gorillas*. Julia Anders died in May of 1977 and Rudolph Anders on March 27, 1987. Their death notices identified both of them as Julia L. and Rudolph Amendt.

PAUL FIX, the gentleman playing Rudolph Anders' fellow Nazi, Mueller in *Secret Weapon,* would go on to play grizzled characters in dozens of westerns—many with his good friend John Wayne—not to mention convicts, soldiers, pirates, doctors, sheriffs and judges. Peter Paul Fix was born March 13, 1901, in Dobbs Ferry, a village in Westchester County, New York. His parents had immigrated to the United States from Germany in the 1870s; his father was the brewmaster for Manilla Anchor Brewery. Fix grew up in a home on the brewery property with his two sisters and three brothers, all of whom were older than him. His father died when he was 15 (his mother had died two years earlier) and Fix was sent to live with his married sisters until he joined the Navy at 17 in 1918, serving on the troopship U.S.S. *Mount Vernon* which was torpedoed off

Paul Fix as Mueller with a disguised Basil Rathbone in
Sherlock Holmes and the Secret Weapon.

the coast of France. (This was the second time Fix's life had been placed in jeopardy. In a 1953 newspaper interview with Hollywood columnist Jimmy Fidler, he told how he had accidentally shot himself in the head with a .22 rifle when he was 10-years-old.) Fix had tried his hand at acting in local productions and upon his discharge from the Navy in 1919 decided to pursue an acting career in the burgeoning film industry in California. He married Frances (Taddy) Harvey in 1922 and they moved to Hollywood.

Fix's first acting assignments in Hollywood were once again in local stage productions. He met a young Clark Gable and Stu Erwin when the three of them were hired by stage actress Pauline Frederick for her touring company, which traveled up and down the West Coast performing such plays as *Lucky Sam Macarber* and *Madame X*. All in all, Fix and Gable appeared in twenty plays together. Fix next appeared with Nancy Carroll in *Chicago* and with Mae West in *Sex*. In 1925, Fix and Taddy's daughter Marilyn was born while the family was living at 7151 Sunset Boulevard. Fix had formally changed his name to Paul Peter Fix and had appeared in his first silent film, a western starring William S. Hart. After several more uncredited roles in silent films, Fix got his first screen credit in *The First Kiss* (1928), starring Gary Cooper and Fay Wray. Fix first met John Wayne in 1931 when they both appeared in the film *Three Girls Lost* co-starring Loretta Young. Legend has it that Fix was the one who taught Wayne his distinctive walk, and at Young's suggestion, coached Wayne and gave him acting lessons on the set. This was shortly after Wayne had made a name for himself in his first starring role in Raoul Walsh's *The Big Trail* (1930). The two remained close friends and appeared together in twenty-six films. According to Fix's daughter, he had written a number of plays over the years and at Wayne's request he worked as a script doctor on two of Wayne's films that he also appeared in, *Back to Bataan* (1945) and *Wake of the Red Witch* (1948). Also for Wayne's production company, he shared a screenplay credit with Michael Hogan for *Tall in the Saddle* (1944) and with James Edward Grant and Philip MacDonald for *Ring of Fear* (1954), a rather off-beat circus-set mystery starring animal trainer Clyde Beatty and crime author Mickey Spillane. He was the author of the original story for the movie *The Notorious Mr. Monks* (1958) in which he also played the title role.

In 1958, Fix signed on as Sheriff Micah Torrance in the television series *The Rifleman* with Chuck Connors and stayed with the highly popular series until its completion in 1963. In an interview in the syndicated column *TV Keynotes* (May 1960), Fix spoke about his well-earned fear of guns, stemming from his childhood accident where he accidentally shot himself just below his eyes. Over the years Fix had managed to overcome his phobia, which was probably a good thing as he ultimately appeared in close to ninety western films and television shows. Other non-western roles included the dying industrialist in *The High and the Mighty* (1954), Elizabeth Taylor's father in *Giant* (1956) and the judge in *To Kill a Mockingbird* (1962). His last film with John Wayne was *Cahill U.S. Marshal* (1973), where he celebrated his 50th year as an actor. However, he was far from finished, continuing on for another eight years in two more features and twenty- eight television episodes. His final appearance as an actor was in 1981 in an episode of *Quincy M.E.* aptly title "For Want of a Horse."

Paul and "Taddy" Fix's daughter Marilyn married actor Harry Carey, Jr. on August 12, 1944, while Carey was on leave as a Navy Corpsman. In his book *Company of Heroes*, Carey described his father-in-law: "Paul Fix was one of those guys that my friend Wendell Corey called a blue shirt actor. To him, that signified an old pro who could do it all on a moment's notice. That was Paul in a nutshell—an old Hollywood pro." Paul and "Taddy" divorced in 1945 and four years later Paul married Beverly Pratt, who remained his wife until her death in 1979. Paul Fix died on October 14, 1983 in Sherman Oaks, California of renal failure; he was 82-years-old. He was survived by his daughter and son-in-law Marilyn and Harry Carey, Jr., three grandchildren and several great-grandchildren. He is buried next to Beverly at the Woodlawn Cemetery in Santa Monica, California.

HOLMES HERBERT, who played Sir Reginald Bailey, the grandfatherly representative of the British Government in *Sherlock Holmes and the Secret Weapon*, began working in films during the silent era as a leading man, ultimately appearing in 229 films between 1915 and 1952 including five of the Sherlock Holmes series. Herbert, whose real name was Horace Edward Jenner, was born in Mansfield, England on July 30, 1882, the first son of British actor-comedian Ned Herbert (real name Edward Henry Jenner) and Agnes Clay Jenner. According to an Olean, New York *Evening Herald* article (December 10, 1921), Holmes Herbert was educated at Rugby School (where the game of Rugby football was invented) and trained at the same dramatic school as British stage and screen actor Percy Marmont, best remembered for his portrayal of the title character in the 1925 silent film version of Joseph Conrad's *Lord Jim*.

On June 1, 1909, Horace Edward Jenner and Beryl Sabine Pasley Mercer were married at St. Mary Parish in the London borough of Hammersmith and Fulham. Both husband and wife were 26-years-old and Horace was about to change his name to Holmes Edward Herbert, taking the stage name of H.E. Herbert. On August 28, 1912, the couple sailed from Liver-

Holmes Herbert as Sir Reginald Bailey in *Sherlock Homes and the Secret Weapon.*

pool on the S.S. *Adriatic* for New York, where H.E. Herbert, having appeared in the London production of *The "Mind-the Paint" Girl* with Billie Burke, would make his Broadway debut with Ms. Burke in the same play. After a winning run of 136 performances, Herbert was soon enjoying another success, performing with Grace George in *Half an Hour,* the top half of a two-part evening of plays at the Lyceum Theatre.

Immediately upon closing in *Half an Hour,* Herbert appeared in his first two silent films for Mutual Film, *His Wife* and *The Fisherwoman* and in 1917 he starred as Lt. Philip Nolan in Edward Everett Hale's moving story *The Man Without a Country.* After one final appearance on Broadway in *The Case of Lady Camber,* Herbert devoted his career exclusively to working in films, with leads opposite such diversified actresses as Pearl White (*Any Wife,* 1922) and Alice Joyce (*The Inner Chamber,* 1921). He starred in his first film for Roy William Neill, who both produced and directed *Toilers of the Sea,* in 1923. By 1930 Herbert had apparently divorced Beryl Mercer, with whom he had a daughter, and moved permanently to Los Angeles. Mercer would later play Lionel Atwill's wife in *The Hound of the Baskervilles* (1939). Now 48-years-old, Herbert found his career as a leading man had ended as he received fourth billing to Conrad Nagel, Kay Johnson and Carmel Myers in his first sound film *The Ship from Shanghai* (1930). Thereafter he would move permanently into supporting roles as a character actor in such memorable films as *The Count of Monte Cristo* (1934), *Captain Blood* (1935), *The Adventures of Robin Hood* (1938) and even a few horror films such as *Dr. Jekyll and Mr. Hyde* (1931), *Mystery of the Wax Museum* (1933) and *Tower of London* (1939). In a 1937 two-reel version of *The Man Without a Country* he played Aaron Burr and in 1939 he joined the cast of *The Adventures of Sherlock Holmes* as the Justice of the Court in the opening sequence of the trial of Professor Moriarty.

In 1930 Herbert married former actress Elinor Kershaw, the widow of famous producer Thomas H. Ince who had died under mysterious circumstances aboard newspaper publisher William Randolph Hearst's yacht in 1924. Ince was one of the early pioneers in silent films, directing, producing and eventually building his own studio in Culver City that would one day become David O. Selznick's home base and even later part of the Desilu complex of Desi Arnaz and Lucille Ball. Ince was aboard Hearst's yacht that night attending a party and there was a great deal of conflicting testimony as to what actually happened, but the most frequently repeated story told of Hearst discovering his mistress Marion Davies in bed with Charles Chaplin. When Chaplin ran out of the cabin, Hearst pulled a gun and followed him onto the deck, firing several shots at him. The shots missed Chaplin, but struck Ince who was standing on the deck. The first reports carried the headline "Movie producer shot on Hearst yacht!" Later reports, prompted by Hearst spokeswomen Louella Parsons who was also aboard that night, changed the cause of Ince's death to acute indigestion and no charges were ever filed. Other versions included a sordid account of rape involving Ince and Marion Davies' secretary, who also died under mysterious circumstances a few months later. According to newspaper accounts at the time of Holmes Herbert and Elinor Ince's marriage, Thomas Ince's will, which left his estate of $1,600,000 to his widow and their three sons, stipulated that Mrs. Ince remain unmarried for a period of seven years. When Herbert and Ince married in April of 1930 there was still one year to go to fulfill the provision. I could find no record of how the matter was ultimately resolved, but her marriage to Herbert was dissolved in January of 1934 and Elinor Herbert petitioned the courts to restore her first married name.

Holmes Herbert continued acting in films for the next eighteen years, supplying a raft of wonderful performances (many of them without credit) in films such as *Intermezzo: A Love Story* (1939), *Johnny Belinda* (1948) and *The Stratton Story* (1949); his final film appearance was in 1952 in *The Brigand*, a costume melodrama starring Anthony Dexter, the actor who had the previous year portrayed Latin lover Rudolph Valentino in the biopic *Valentino*. Herbert married for a third time, to Scottish actress Agnes Bartholomew, who passed away in September of 1955, just over a year before Herbert's death on the day after Christmas (known as Boxing Day in his native England) in 1956. He is buried at Forest Lawn Memorial Park in Glendale, California.

HARRY CORDING became something of a good luck charm for Roy William Neill, appearing in seven of the Holmes films, more than any other actor with the exception of Mary Gordon's eight films. His role in *Sherlock Holmes and the Secret Weapon* as one of Moriarty's henchmen was his second appearance in the Sherlock Holmes series. Like his mentor Neill, Cording's origin is difficult to pin down, as various sources have him born in Somerset, England, Cardiff, Wales, New York City and even Australia, where one newspaper article indentified him as "Australia's greatest actor." After digging though numerous records, it appears that Hector William Cording was actually born in India on April 26, 1894 and was christened on June 10, 1894. His father was Edmund Cording and his mother was the former Rose Helen Pierce. The family was living in Murree, Bengal, India at the time of Cording's birth while his father, a soldier in the 1st Rifle Brigade (Prince Consort's Own), was on duty in Africa. About the time that

Harry Cording as Jack Brady in *Sherlock Holmes and the Secret Weapon.*

Cording was celebrating his sixth birthday, the family returned to England, settling into the District Royal Artillery, Clarence Barracks in Portsmouth. Cording had four siblings: an older sister Lillian, who died in 1903 at the age of 15; an older brother, Lewis, who later joined the British diplomatic service; another older sister, Elsie and a younger brother, Victor. There's little known of Cording's education, but in 1910 at the age of 16, he apparently followed his father into the military, serving from June 20, 1910 until his discharge on January 28, 1919. According to his cousin, Cording served as an artillery gunner during The Great War. In September of 1918, two months before the end of the war, Hector William Cording married a Marjorie S. W. Wheaton in Epsom, Surrey. How long this marriage lasted is not known, but Cording would marry again in 1938.

What we do know is that a Hector Cording, sometimes calling himself Harry Cording, worked as an assistant steward on several transatlantic passenger ships from early 1920 until mid-1922. Arriving in New York City on July 20 of that year, Hector William Cording filed for his naturalization papers and then showed up a few years later in Hollywood, working as an actor in silent films. Cording's first film, in which he received screen credit as Harry Cording, was *The Knockout* (1925), a boxing film directed by Lambert Hillyer who would go on to direct over seventy "B" westerns, but would make two memorable horror films in 1936, *Dracula's Daughter* and *The Invisible Ray* starring both Karloff and Lugosi. It's interesting to speculate on how Harry Cording might have broken into films, with one possibility being that he may have begun as a stunt man. Cording, having spent nine years in the British army and several years working on ships, would certainly have been in excellent physical condition. This might explain the gap of three years between his arrival in New York and his first appearance in *The Knockout*, in which he presumably played a boxer. However he accomplished it, he obviously made enough of an impression on Hillyer to convince him to hire him for a featured role in his very first film.

After appearing in supporting roles in a dozen more silent films Cording made his talkie debut in 1930 in Universal's *Captain of the Guard,* an absurdly inaccurate dramatization of the life of Rouget de Lisle, the composer of France's national anthem "La Marseillaise." In 1934 Cording had his one brief moment of stardom in an exploitation film called *Narcotic* in which he played a disreputable doctor who sells a drug-laced patent medicine called "Tiger Fat" and eventually becomes a victim himself to the lure of opium. Presumably based on the life of the author Hildegard Stadie's uncle, the film wasn't well received and reviews, such as the *Oakland Tribune*'s (January 20, 1934) described the story as "melodrama that is so lurid that it loses ground steadily as it progresses." Later that year Cording appeared in Edgar Ulmer's *The Black Cat* (1934) as Thamal, Bela Lugosi's mute servant and soon after in *The Man Who Reclaimed His Head* (1934). During the next five years, Cording acted in over sixty films, seldom receiving screen credit, but wearing the costumes of everything from a pirate in *Treasure Island* (1934) and a trapper in *The Last of the Mohicans* (1936), to an executioner in *Marie Antoinette* (1938).

In 1939 Cording was signed by 20th Century-Fox to play the role of the escaped convict hiding on the moors in *The Hound of the Baskervilles*. On February 15, 1939, a syndicated cartoon series called "Seein' Stars" by Feg Murray appeared in newspapers in which Harry Cording's caricature turned up wearing the convict's beard and thick hair. It's not known how much of his role Cording completed, but one story has it that upon completion of filming, the studio decided that he didn't look convincingly half-starved and recast and reshot his sequences with another actor, Nigel de Brulier, playing the role. Presumably the only portion of Cording's performance that was retained in the film was the moment when Holmes and Doctor Watson discover his body. The actual film is edited so that there is no master shot that ties Holmes and Watson with the convict lying on the ground, but there are stills from the film that illustrate that moment and it does appear to be Harry Cording lying at the feet of Rathbone and Bruce wearing the same beard and thick hair as in the Feg Murray cartoon and

Harry
Cording as
the escaped
convict in *The
Hound of the
Baskervilles.*

looking much heavier than Nigel de Brulier's skinny physique. Also, when Holmes and Watson pick up the convict's body, it shows a thickness about the waist that belies a lack of food.

In 1938 Cording married Margaret Fiero, the daughter of a wealthy Detroit drug store chain owner, and this time the marriage took, lasting until Cording's death in 1954. According to a certificate of citizenship, Harry Cording, formerly Hector William Cording, appeared before the U.S. District Court in Los Angeles, California on May 9, 1941 and took the oath to become a citizen of the United States of America. Margaret and Harry Cording lived for many years in the San Fernando Valley, first at 4104 Farmdale Avenue, North Hollywood, and later in 1946 at 10115 La Tuna Canyon Drive in Sun Valley, where Harry Cording became heavily involved in civic affairs, joining the Kiwanis Club and the Loyal Order of Moose as well as running for honorary mayor. In 1951 Cording became a block warden of the Civil Defense Team and in 1954, vice president, Metropolitan District, Loyal Order of Moose, all the while continuing to act in over 164 films. His total of 279 films sets some sort of a record in the business.

In my father's final screen appearance as the Head Constable in the opening sequence of M-G-M's color extravaganza, *Plymouth Adventure* (1952), who should turn up at his side as he interrogates the Pilgrims waiting to board the *Mayflower* on the Southampton dock, but Harry Cording playing his aide. Cording would continue acting in films with only one foray into television, a *Schlitz Playhouse* episode titled "How the Brigadier Won His Medals," in which he appeared in 1954 shortly before his death. His final film *East of Eden* was released in 1955. It's interesting to note that all of the H Cordings of record, including a Harry Cording born in Somerset, England and a Harold Cording born in Cardiff, Wales show the identical date and place of death as Hector Cording: September 1, 1954 in Los Angeles California. However the certificate of citizenship, noted earlier, seems to confirm the true identity of actor Harry Cording, who is buried at the Glen Haven Memorial Park in Sylmar, California. Cording's wife Margaret apparently lived for many years in Laguna Beach, California, as public records show her still living there as late as 1993.

LESLIE DENISON, who appeared in six of the Holmes films in such various small roles as an air raid warden, a transport pilot and various police sergeants, appears briefly in *Sherlock Holmes and the Secret Weapon* as a London Bobby. He was born in 1901 in Northamptonshire, England; his father was a farm laborer named John William Denison and his mother was the former Margaret Harriet Humphries. Leslie was the

Leslie Denison as he appeared as Sergeant Bleeker in *The House of Fear*.

youngest of their six surviving children (three had died in childhood, and another son would be born when Leslie was nine-years-old). The family lived on Cowley's Lane in the village of Crick, and Leslie and his siblings were educated at the village school. By the time his brother Harry was born in 1910 the family had moved to the village of Ullesthorpe in the district of Lutterworth.

Denison, like so many of the Roy William Neill repertory company members, never rose above the ranks of journeyman actor and consequently very little was written about his early life. All that is known for certain is that he began appearing on the Broadway stage in 1930 at the age of 29 in *Made in France* a farce that opened and closed in a few days. His next appearance was far more successful; Denison played one of Elizabeth Barrett's brothers in the original 1931 Broadway production of *The Barretts of Wimpole Street* opposite Katharine Cornell and Brian Aherne. Vernon Downing, another future member of the Neill repertory company, played another brother and Ian Wolfe portrayed Henry Bevan—but unlike the other two, Denison was not brought out by M-G-M to recreate his role in the film version. Like most actors working on the stage in New York in the 1930s, my father included, Denison undoubtedly tried to find work in radio to help pay the bills. The numerous radio soap operas popular during this period and the dramatic programs such as *The Shadow* and *Jack Armstrong, the All-American Boy* offered many actors the opportunity for employment. Years later Denison would augment his bank account by doing voiceover work for Disney studios. Denison continued to turn up in featured roles on Broadway until the end of 1938, when he moved to California to begin his career in films.

After his third film, *International Squadron* (1941), Denison found himself playing scores of military officers, secret service agents, and Scotland Yard detectives, often in films with my father such as *A Yank in the*

R.A.F. (1941), *Bomber's Moon* (1943), *Kitty* (1945), and *Golden Earrings* (1947), not to mention the six Sherlock Holmes films in which he appeared. This continued until well after the end of the war, with Denison still playing an R.A.F. officer in the 1949 film *Twelve O'Clock High* starring Gregory Peck. All in all, Denison appeared in forty-nine films between 1941 and 1945.

According to a *Los Angeles Times* article on September 18, 1943, Denison was involved in a real life mystery surrounding the death of fellow actor David Bacon. Bacon, the son of the then lieutenant governor of Massachusetts, had been stabbed to death by a mysterious assailant and died in a Venice bean field after collapsing at the wheel of his car while apparently trying to drive for aid. Although he didn't know the murder victim, Denison lived in the upstairs half of a Laurel Canyon duplex, the ground floor of which Bacon had recently rented. Denison told police that the apartment had never been occupied except for the Sunday when Bacon was killed. "I do believe someone was there," Denison reported, "because I have the water heater for both places, which is slow acting, and on Monday morning it was cool like most of the hot water had been run out." Apparently Bacon, who lived with his wife at another home about a mile away from the Laurel Canyon apartment, had rented the place a short time before and had told his wife it was for a man who was to be employed at their home. The only clue was a sweater of the crew-necked type knitted for Navy and Merchant Marine seamen that was found in Bacon's car and which the police determined was much too small for Bacon to have worn. A few strands of blond hair were found on the sweater and the police announced that they were looking for a man of about 140 pounds, 5 feet 8 inches tall and having blond hair as a suspect. David Bacon's murder was never solved.

In 1946 Denison worked as a voice actor for the Walt Disney Studios, supplying the voice of Donald Duck's lookalike in the cartoon *Donald's Double Trouble* and again in 1948 as the suave Donald in *Donald's Dream Voice.* He then shared the soundtrack in 1949 with narrator Basil Rathbone when he voiced the character of the Weasel to whom Mr. Toad sells Toad Hall in order to buy his motor car in Walt Disney's *Adventures of Ichabod and Mr. Toad.* Denison played a prominent role in a 1954 black & white science fiction movie called *The Snow Creature* that was produced and directed by Billy Wilder's older brother W. Lee Wilder and written by Billy Wilder's nephew Miles Wilder.

For some reason, starting around the early 1950s when he began appearing on television, Denison's screen credits appeared with a double "n" in his last name. Leslie Denison's final appearance was in the M-G-M film

Signpost to Murder (1964) starring Joanne Woodward and Stuart Whitman in which he once again played a police inspector. He was 63-years-old at that time, having appeared in 120 films and television series, and apparently never worked again in films, television, or Theatre. There is a confusion regarding his acknowledged date of death; the date that is reported, September 25, 1992, which would have made him 91-years-old, could very well have belonged to another Leslie Denison who reportedly died in Austin, Texas. Another Leslie Denison was a teenage girl, a Bridgeport High School senior in Ft. Worth, Texas who was killed as the result of an awning collapsing on her in August of 2009. Unfortunately, the date of actor Leslie Denison's death remains obscure.

Sherlock Holmes and the Secret Weapon premiered in New York on January 4, 1943 and once more Bosley Crowther grumbled about Universal's updating of the Conan Doyle stories and Basil Rathbone's "wind-blown hair." He concluded however, by grudgingly admitting that, "the aura is still mysterious, the action is fast and tense. And the plot sufficiently fantastic that no one is likely to swallow it." Even Hollywood's trade papers were divided in their opinions, with *Variety* claiming that the picture, " strictly a programmer, will hold up mild interest only in its normal billings." *The Hollywood Reporter* countered, "The picture is a tightly-woven excitement from beginning to end." Going on to praise the cast, it continued, "Lionel Atwill makes a fine thing of Moriarty, William Post, Jr. impresses as the Swiss inventor, and Kaaren Verne is excellent as his wife. Others of those credited in supports who count are Dennis Hoey's Scotland Yard Inspector, Holmes Herbert's Sir Reginald and Mary Gordon's loveable landlady."

SHERLOCK HOLMES
IN WASHINGTON

IN THE LATE SUMMER OF 1942, Universal put into development its third film in the series. Having successfully brought Sherlock Holmes into the mid 20th century, Universal now took him from London all the way to America's capital in *Sherlock Holmes in Washington*. The picture was budgeted for 15 shooting days at $150,000, with all exteriors (except for the airport sequences) to be filmed on Universal's back lot and with extensive use of process photography utilizing second unit footage filmed in Washington D.C. by Universal's New York-based Newsreel Department. Roy William Neill managed to bring the film in under budget ($138,365.47)

despite going two days over schedule. The usual $12,500 was allocated for Story Rights, which was Universal's way of amortizing its arrangement with the Conan Doyle estate, but for some reason the allocation for Basil Rathbone's salary was reduced to $16,666 for this one picture only, while Nigel Bruce's remained at $5,000. Bruce was suffering from phlebitis of the right leg due to severe wounds he had suffered in World War I and he had been examined by a physician, Doctor Howard O. Dennis of Beverly Hills. On July 24, 1942 Doctor Dennis wrote a letter addressed

Nigel Bruce relaxing on his lawn chair and chatting with Dennis Hoey.

"To Whom It May Concern," stating that he "had repeatedly warned Mr. Bruce that he should not use this leg more than eight hours daily," for fear of causing a return of a severe acute reaction. Bruce's war wound had been serious enough that he had been confined to a wheelchair at one time. In 1945 he needed a further operation to remove varicose veins from both legs. Behind the scenes photographs of Bruce show that he always used a canvas and wood lawn chair, rather than the standard director's chair, to elevate his legs.

As opposed to the previous two films, *Sherlock Holmes in Washington* had no direct connection to the Conan Doyle stories; the original story *Sherlock Holmes in U.S.A.* was written by Bertram Millhauser, who was paid $3,666.65 for his services to write a screenplay. Millhauser, who would go on to write four more films in the series, had previously adapted the William Gillette play *Sherlock Holmes* and written the screenplay for the 1932 Fox Films production starring Clive Brook, which the actor later claimed was "a terrible film." After Millhauser completed his work on the screenplay, Lynn Riggs, who had contributed previously to *Sherlock Holmes and the Voice of Terror*, was brought in to do a polish. The script was then submitted to the Production Code Administration for approval. Joseph I. Breen of the Code office objected to the presence of drinking in the script, specifically the engagement party that Nancy Partridge's aunt Annie hosts for her. Breen's note specifically requested that the studio "Keep any actual drinking at this cocktail party to the absolute minimum necessary for characterization." As it turned out, there was a minimum of drinking and a great deal of smoking in the scene. On July 13, 1942, Roy William Neill began filming the opening sequences of the film, which took place at the London Airport and later on board a passenger plane en route to the United States and didn't require either Rathbone or Bruce.

Once again the film opened with the same written prologue that had appeared in *Sherlock Holmes and the Voice of Terror*. Apparently Universal was still trying to convince the Sherlockians that it was all right to meddle with the master's environment. The film itself was a rather standard espionage drama that begins on a plane and then on a train travelling toward Washington, D.C., where a British courier, John Grayson (Gerald Hamer), is kidnapped by a group of spies led by William Easter (Henry Daniell). Sherlock Holmes and Doctor Watson are brought into the case by Atkins of the British Foreign Office (Holmes Herbert), who tells them that Grayson was actually Alfred Pettibone, who was carrying a secret message of vital importance. When Holmes and Watson go to Pettibone's home to speak with his mother (Mary Forbes), they are almost killed by a loose stone dropped on them from the roof. The trail now leads to Washington,

Don Terry (l) and Marjorie Lord and John Archer (far right) with the V for Victory matchbook in *Sherlock Holmes in Washington*.

D.C., where they are met by British official Bart Lang (Gavin Muir) and Detective Lt. Grogan of the Washington police (Edmund MacDonald).

Neill and Millhauser pay homage to Alfred Hitchcock by including their version of a MacGuffin, a book of matches carrying hidden microfilm containing high-secret government documents. The microfilm (actually two frames of 35mm motion picture film) has been secured between the sides of the matchbook cover, which is easily identified by the well-known "V for victory" on its face. Neill uses the cocktail party for Nancy Partridge (Marjorie Lord) and her fiancé, Naval Lt. Peter Merriam (John Archer), to present a very skillfully staged sequence where the matchbook passes from hand to hand, falling briefly into the possession of the heavies (Don Terry and Bradley Page), who are unaware of their windfall, before it returns safely to Nancy Partridge's purse. The penultimate scene in the film was a rather ridiculous shoot-out in the confined office of the heavies, where Holmes has come to rescue Nancy. The chief heavy, Heinrich Hinkle (George Zucco), manages to escape only to come a cropper in the final moments of the film in the office of Senator Babcock (Thurston Hall) when he is surrounded by police and Holmes reveals the location of the microfilm, which has been in Hinkle's possession all along. Without Lestrade to help carry the burden, Nigel Bruce's Doctor Watson seems more of a buffoon than ever, slurping ice cream sodas, chewing gum, quoting slang phrases from a guide book and receiving a fair share of rebuffs from Rathbone's Sherlock Holmes. All in all, under Roy William Neill's able direction the cast of first-rate actors performed admirably.

A number of the members of the Neill repertory company made return appearances in *Sherlock Holmes in Washington,* including Henry Daniell, up to his usual nastiness as William Easter, the main henchman seeking the microfilm, Holmes Herbert as Mr. Ahrens from the Home Office, this time wearing a neat mustache, Leyland Hodgson as an airport official at the London Airport, John Burton as the army officer who accompanies Sir Henry Merchant to the plane, Leslie Denison as the pilot of the plane that brings Holmes and Watson to Washington, D.C., and of course Mary Gordon in a brief appearance as Mrs. Hudson. In an even briefer appearance, Colin Kenny played a hotel doorman who opened the door of a taxi for Holmes and Watson. He would return in a slightly larger role as a museum guard in *The Pearl of Death* and finally in *Terror by Night* an even larger role as a bogus constable.

GEORGE ZUCCO is the most important of the new arrivals as Richard Stanley, the owner of the antique store; Holmes reveals him to be Heinrich Hinckel, a former secret agent from the First World War who is now the head of an international spy ring. Although not technically a member of the Neill repertory company, as this would be his only appearance in a Holmes film, Zucco had portrayed Holmes' archenemy Professor Moriarty with great aplomb in *The Adventures of Sherlock Holmes* (1939) and would grace five of Universal's classic horror films during the mid-1940s.

George Desylli Zucco was born in Manchester, England on January 11, 1886. His father was a Greek importer named George Deayilla Zucco who died shortly after his birth, and his mother, the former Marian Rintoul, had once been a lady-in-waiting to Queen Victoria. After her husband's untimely death, Marian Zucco moved the family to London where she took on work as a dressmaker. Zucco attended several London schools and then completed his education at the Borden Grammar School in Sittingbourne, Kent, where he excelled in mathemat-

George Zucco as Richard Stanley in *Sherlock Holmes in Washington.*

ics and played on the soccer and cricket teams.

Sometime around 1903 or 1904, a teenage Zucco made his way to Winnipeg, Canada, where he first worked on a large wheat farm, later moving into the city and finding employment as a clerk at the grain exchange. It was in Winnipeg that Zucco first became interested in acting, joining a touring stock company that traveled up and down the West Coast, making his professional debut in Regina, Saskatchewan in 1908 in a play called *What Happened to Jones*. The acting company crossed into the United States several times, first in December of 1910 at Sumas, Washington and in 1911 visited Ketchikan, in the territory of Alaska. Zucco stayed with the troop for several years, eventually arriving in New York City in 1913, performing a Vaudeville sketch called *The Suffragette*. The assassination of Archduke Ferdinand of Austria-Hungary in 1914 and the outbreak of World War I put a hold on Zucco's acting career, as he immediately returned to England to join the West Yorkshire Regiment, 7th Battalion as a private. Sent to the front line trenches in France, Zucco was severely wounded in his right arm, nearly losing it. An operation on the arm was successful, but he lost the use of two fingers on his right hand, as they were permanently turned down. Although this affected his ability to shake hands, he still managed to conceal this hindrance from audiences by frequently holding a prop in his right hand.

When Zucco, having attained the rank of lieutenant, was discharged from the army on September 25, 1918 he returned to London, taking a flat at 44 Springfield Road, intent on resuming his acting career. Zucco enrolled for one term at the Royal Academy of Dramatic Arts, during which time he also began appearing on the London stage in such productions as *The Freedom of the Seas* (1918), and *The Crimson Alibi* (1919). In July of 1920 Zucco opened in *At the Villa Rose*, A. E. W. Mason's adaptation of his mystery novel starring noted Shakespearean actor Arthur Bourchier. Later that same year Zucco joined the New Shakespeare Company in Stratford Upon Avon and in 1921 went on a year-long tour of South Africa and the Far East. After spending almost twenty years as an actor, Zucco, who had appeared in more than a dozen plays in London's West End, was signed to appear in what would be his final stage appearance in England, albeit quite an extended one and for which he received a great deal of praise. R. C. Sherriff's *Journey's End* was originally presented as a two-performance tryout, under the direction of newcomer James Whale, in December of 1928 by the Incorporated Stage Society at the Apollo Theater. The two leads were played by Laurence Olivier as the tormented commanding officer Stanhope and Maurice Evans as Raleigh, Stanhope's brother-in-law, who dies in his arms. Zucco played the ex-schoolmaster Lt. Osborne, who quotes from "The Walrus and the Carpenter" from *Alice in Wonderland* before going to his death: "The time has come, the Walrus said, To talk of many things: Of shoes–and ships–and ceiling wax–Of cabbages–and kings." Zucco's performance was acclaimed by many; in an issue of *Theatre Arts Monthly* for example, drama critic and war veteran W. A. Darlington, who was overwhelmed by the power of the play, wrote, "George Zucco, as Osborne, was perfect. That I was not alone in thinking this was shown after the final curtain, when the deeply moved audience called for Mr. Zucco and gave him an ovation, while being no more than politely enthusiastic over Mr. Olivier and Mr. Evans." The play transferred to the Savoy Theatre where it ran for three weeks with the entire cast reprising their roles, with the exception of Olivier who had left the production and was replaced by Colin Clive. The cast and play then moved over to the Prince of Wales Theater where it continued its run for a total of 500 performances.

During the run of *Journey's End*, Zucco met stage actress Stella Francis who was introduced to him by Charles Bennett (whose later screenwriting credits included *The Man Who Knew Too Much* [1934] and *The 39 Step* [1935]). Francis, whose real name was Frances Dorothy Hawke and had already starred in a number of West End productions including *The Blue Lagoon* and Sir James Barrie's *Dear Brutus*, remembered her impression of Zucco's performance in an interview she gave in 1998 to Gregory William Mank for his book *Hollywood's Maddest Doctors*: "Oh, I thought he was tremendous," she recalled. "He was absolutely amazing in *Journey's End*, I think–a beautiful performance…" Francis and Zucco joined Bennett and his fiancée for a late supper and soon after they began dating. After six months, Zucco proposed and was turned down, primarily because of the difference in their ages (Zucco was 43 at the time and Francis was only 29). Zucco pursued his objective and after another six months Stella finally accepted. "George and I had a double wedding with Maggie and Charles Bennett," Francis told Mank, "at the Registrar's Office in London on June 6, 1930." It was the first marriage for both; Stella Francis gave up her acting career to become Mrs. George Zucco and the mother of their daughter Frances Marion who was born in Hampton Court, Surrey on May 30, 1931. The Zuccos remained a devoted couple for almost 30 years until his death in 1960.

Building on his success with *Journey's End*, George Zucco appeared in several more plays between 1931 and 1932, including *Machines* and *Autumn Crocus*, as well as a season of Shakespeare at the Old Vic. He made his debut in films in 1931 in *The Dreyfus Case* starring Cedric Hardwicke and in 1933 appeared in Victor Saville's musical drama based on J.B. Priestley's novel *The Good Companions* alongside Jessie Matthews, John Gielgud, Edmund Gwenn and my father, who played Joe Brundit, one of Matthews' musical group, The Dinky Doos. The following year Zucco reprised his role of the Reverend Edward Mayne in the film version of *Autumn Crocus* and then appeared in seven more "quota quickies" before making his final film in England, *The Man Who Could Work Miracles* with Roland Young and Ralph Richardson. The film was released in 1936, but by then Zucco, having been signed by Henry Miller to appear on Broadway as Benjamin Disraeli opposite Helen Hayes and Vincent Price in *Victoria Regina,* had already made his way with his family on the S.S. *Britannic* to New York, arriving on November 14, 1935. A smash hit, the play opened on December 26, 1935 and ran until June of 1936, when it temporarily closed to give the cast a month's vacation, then reopening and running for another ten months, a total of 969 performances. Zucco however was not with the cast when it returned from vacation, having been signed to a term contract by M-G-M studios in Hollywood. His reviews in the play had all been excellent with Percy Hammond's review in *The New York Herald Tribune* a typical example: "I think you will particularly enjoy Mr. George Zucco's vivid study of Disraeli –a triumph of florid reticence as at Balmoral he bends the pregnant hinges of a showy sycophant." Patricia Morison, who would play Sherlock Holmes' final nemesis in *Dressed to Kill,* was Helen Hayes' understudy in *Victoria Regina* and remembered George Zucco for interviewer Gregory William Mank in *Classic Images Magazine:* "I loved him! What an actor! Oh, he was wonderful onstage! A perfect Disraeli. He was another elegant villain, an elegant actor, a very gentle, nice man."

George and Stella Zucco sold their home in Hampton Court, England and moved into a ranch home at 3381 Mandeville Canyon in Brentwood, California. According to Stella Zucco, the property had "11 acres, with a fresh water stream that ran down the hill. We had horses, rabbits, chickens, turkeys, pigs–you name it we had it." George ultimately bought three German Shepherds and the family took up horseback riding, with their daughter Frances becoming an accomplished jumper at the age of eight or nine and winning many showmanship blue ribbons at the Riviera Country Club and at many other Southern California horse shows. She would later briefly become an actress, appearing in minor roles in five films between 1952 and 1953, and marry several times.

Shortly after the new year of 1937, George and Stella Zucco traveled to Ensenada, Mexico for a brief stay before George, accompanied by Stella, walked back across the U.S. Border at San Ysidro, California on January 25, 1937 and requested permanent residence, declaring his intention of becoming a naturalized United States citizen. He officially became a citizen on November 13, 1942.

Zucco's first film at M-G-M was a "B" mystery called *Sinner Take All* (1936), but he was soon supporting M-G-M's mega-stars such as William Powell and Myrna Loy in *After the Thin Man* (1936), Clark Gable in *Parnell* (1937), Gable and Jean Harlow in her final film, *Saratoga* (1937) and Greta Garbo in *Conquest* (1937). Zucco remained under contract to M-G-M until 1938, when he moved over to 20th Century-Fox to appear opposite Tyrone Power and Loretta Young in *Suez*. Zucco played the British Prime Minister while future Roy William Neill repertory company member Miles Mander took on the role of Benjamin Disraeli, and Nigel Bruce, who was also in the film, played Sir Malcolm Cameron. The following year, Zucco joined Nigel Bruce and Basil Rathbone in the second of Fox's Holmes' films, *The Adventures of Sherlock Holmes* (1939) as the memorable Professor Moriarty.

From this point on, Zucco's livelihood seemed to alternate between appearing in important films such as *The Hunchback of Notre Dame* (1939), *The Black Swan* (1942) and *Captain from Castile* (1947) and lower-case horror films such as *The Mad Monster* (1942), *Dead Men Walk* (1943) and *Voodoo Man* (1944). He would also appear in three of Universal's horror series, *The Mummy's Hand* (1940), *The Mummy's Tomb* (1942) and *The Mummy's Ghost* (1944), as well as *The Mad Ghoul* (1943) and *House of Frankenstein* (1944). In the late 1940s, after appearing in a prominent role in *The Pirate* (1948) with Judy Garland and Gene Kelly, Zucco's luck seemed to improve and from that point on, with only a couple of exceptions, he was cast in important films such as *The Barkleys of Broadway* (1949) and *Madame Bovary* (1949). His one foray into television was in 1951 in an episode of NBC's *Fireside Theatre* called "Drums in the Night."

A peculiar United Press release headlined "Sherlock Holmes Seeks Police Aid" that appeared in the *Berkshire Evening Eagle* of Pittsfield, Massachusetts on Saturday, December 4, 1943, revealed that "actor George Zucco, who portrays Sherlock Holmes on the screen," [sic] called the police upon finding the "remains of a human skeleton" in the backyard of his home (presumably the Mandeville Canyon ranch). The article went on to quote the police as saying that "the few bones indicated the victim was a man and that he had been dead for several months." One wonders if this might not have been the brainchild of an over-eager studio press agent, since nothing further was ever written about the incident. However it was not completely forgotten, for when George Zucco died the United Press obituary mentioned that he had once "played Sherlock Holmes before Basil Rathbone took the role." As far as can be ascertained, no record exists of Zucco ever having played Sherlock Holmes, either on the stage or on the screen. In the mid-1940s, the Zuccos moved into a new home at 928

Chautauqua Boulevard in Pacific Palisades, California and discovered that actor and fellow Professor Moriarty interpreter Lionel Atwill lived nearby. According to Stella Zucco, they saw Atwill as little as possible.

George Zucco and my father both appeared in a number of films, including *Where There's Life* (1947), *Joan of Arc* (1948), *The Secret Garden* (1949) and *David and Bathsheba* (1951). However, the only film where they shared scenes was *Where There's Life,* an amusing Bob Hope comedy in which both Zucco and my father played ministers of an Eastern European duchy who have come to America to force Hope, the heir apparent, to return to their country.

After Zucco completed *David and Bathsheba* for 20th Century-Fox, he was signed for a role in *The Desert Fox,* the biopic of German Field Marshal Erwin Rommel starring James Mason as the general. Zucco had been on the film for only a short time when he reportedly began behaving strangely. Stella Zucco described what happened in her interview with Mank: "He couldn't remember his lines and didn't know where he was." Director Henry Hathaway was willing to shoot around him until he was feeling better, but it was discovered that Zucco had suffered a severe stroke and his condition was too grave for him to continue and he was replaced in the film. Stella Zucco tried caring for him at home, but over the next couple of years his condition became worse. "I had to put him in a nursing home," she told Mank. "The Motion Picture Hospital wouldn't take George, because they were afraid he'd wander off–which he was apt to do." Zucco was placed in the Monterey Sanitarium in South San Gabriel and soon after Stella was forced to sell their home in Pacific Palisades and move into an apartment in Beverly Hills. Her financial situation became perilous, and Frances' small salaries as a bit player were of little help, so Stella went to work as a receptionist for a doctor.

Stella and Frances would visit Zucco at the sanitarium, "George would always know me, and our daughter Frances," Stella recalled. "But he didn't know other people, his friends." He did however retain the dream of acting once more and, according to an interview with producer Alex Gordon that appeared in Tom Weaver's book *Poverty Row HORRORS,* Gordon and Zucco's agent tried to give him that opportunity by offering him a role in Gordon's upcoming film *Voodoo Woman* (1957). Stella drove her husband to a meeting at Gordon's office, where the producer told the actor how much he admired his work and described the film to him. Zucco politely rejected the offer, thanking Gordon, but announcing that he had done so many low-budget horror films that he would prefer to do something "a little more in the classical vein." When the film was made, Tom Conway played the role that had been offered to Zucco.

Zucco remained at Monterey Sanitarium for another three years, until he finally succumbed to pneumonia on May 27, 1960. His funeral service was held at 11:00 A.M. on Tuesday, May 30 at the Church of the Hills, Forest Lawn Memorial Park. He was cremated and his ashes were interred at the Hollywood Hills Forest Lawn Cemetery. Less than two years later, Stella Zucco suffered another tragedy when her daughter Frances Zucco Maguire succumbed to throat cancer, leaving her husband James R. Maguire and her son George C. Canto from a previous marriage. Stella lived to be 99- years-old, dying on May 11, 1999 in Woodland Hills, California.

Whether he was playing Margaret O'Brien's compassionate doctor in *The Secret Garden* (1949) or the deranged scientist in *The Mad Ghoul* (1943), George Zucco's classical training always guaranteed an understated and totally believable performance and for that he deserves his vaunted position in the pantheon of Hollywood character actors.

GERALD HAMER's performance as John Grayson, alias Alfred Pettibone the Home Office clerk who is the courier of the hidden microfilm, is first-rate as he stumbles and stutters his way onto the plane, only to then study his fellow passengers with a cunning eye. Hamer, who would have an even greater opportunity to display his talent in *The Scarlet Claw*, was born in Northern Wales on November 16, 1886. His real name was Geoffrey Earl Watton and he was the eldest child of John and Evelyn Watton of the village of Llandudno, today one of Wales' most popular beach resorts, on the north shore of the Irish Sea. John Watton was a newspaper proprietor and the family was wealthy enough to have two servants. A second child, Winifred, was born two years later.

There is nothing recorded of Geoffrey Watton's education, but it is highly possible (as his father was a man of some means) that he would have been sent to the recently opened secondary school in Llandudno, Ysgal John Bright, named after the Victorian radical politician John Bright who came to the town for respite and whose young son was buried there. The first recorded entry for Geoffrey Watton was in 1911 when Watton, now calling himself Gerald Hamer and working as a professional actor, was living in a shared flat in Warwickshire, near Stratford Upon Avon. His roommate was a theatrical business manager named Crofton Jones and it appears that they might have been working together in a theatrical company. Hamer appeared in a number of Shakespearean plays during this period, including *Henry V* and *The Taming of the Shrew*. At some point he became associated with actor-producer Harley Granville Barker, sailing from Liverpool on the S.S. *St. Louis* in October of 1915

Gerald Hamer as Alfred Pettibone in *Sherlock Holmes in Washington.*

with a group of actors and Granville Barker and his wife, the actress Lillah McCarthy, to appear in a repertory season of plays at Wallack's Theater on Broadway, starting with the premier of George Bernard Shaw's *Androcles and the Lion.* A fellow passenger was the tour manager, a young man named Claude Rains, who was also the understudy for several of the roles. Rains' then wife Isabel Jeans was also a member of the company. Following *Androcles,* Hamer appeared in Barker's production of *The Man Who Married a Dumb Wife* and a revival of Shakespeare's *A Midsummer Night's Dream.* The company then went on a tour of American universities, presenting the Euripides plays *The Trojan Woman* and *Iphigenia in Taurus.* When Barker disbanded the company and returned to London, Hamer revisited Broadway in a revival of *The Merchant of Venice* starring Sir Herbert Beerbohm Tree. For the next fifteen years Gerald Hamer continued appearing on Broadway in both revivals and original plays with such actors as Bela Lugosi in *The Red Poppy,* Roland Young in *The Devil's Disciple,* and Fay Bainter, Walter Hampden and Estelle Winwood in *The Admirable Crichton.*

On December 19, 1924 a short article, datelined New York, appeared in the *New Castle News* in Westchester County. It told of the purchase of a house at 244 W. 70th Street in New York City where a Joseph Brown Elwell had been murdered five years earlier. The crime had never been solved and the house had since become a "high class lodging house" and appeared to be haunted by Elwell's ghost. In March of 1925, an illustrated article appeared in the Sunday supplements of newspapers across the country. The article declared that the property had been purchased by a Captain B. Daveney, a retired sea captain of the British maritime service and his partner the actor Gerald Hamer, who was currently appearing on Broadway in a revival of Shaw's *Candida.* The article went on to say, "There are persistent rumors that these purchasers, both Englishmen, are representing Sir A. Conan Doyle and other distinguished English spiritualists and that the latter will fill the house, as soon as leases now running have expired, with trained investigators who will bend their every intelligence to getting into communication with the ghost of Elwell." Of course nothing more seems to have been written about this mystery and it does seem interesting that the first article appeared one week after *Candida* had opened at the 48th Street Theater and the second article appeared just a month before it closed. Could it be that press agents in New York were just as creative as their brethren in Hollywood?

In 1926, Hamer returned for a brief visit to England on the S.S. *Aquitania* to marry. He then brought his bride Dorothy and his sister Winifred back to New York with him. The 1930 census shows them all living together in Queens, along with their daughter Gwinifrede, who was born in 1927, and a maid named Margaret Dawson. A son, Christopher Earl Watton, was born in 1931. Gerald Hamer has been widely listed as the father of British film director Robert Hamer (*Kind Hearts and Coronet* [1949]); however this is not the case. Robert Hamer was born in Kidderminster, Worcestershire in 1911, at which point, according to the 1911 census, Hamer was pursuing his acting career in Stratford Upon Avon as a single man living in the village of Leamington. Robert Hamer's father was in fact a bank clerk in Kidderminster, Owen Dyke Hamer, and his mother was Annie Grace Hamer. They had been married for just a year when Annie gave birth to twins, Robert and Barbara. Robert Hamer began in the film business as a second assistant cameraman, or clapper boy, then joined the editing department and worked his way up to film editor, then associate producer and finally director. His career was marked by successes and failures and he was never really able to achieve his true potential as a director before dying at the age of 52 of pneumonia in 1963.

Gerald Hamer's final appearance on Broadway was in 1933 as a police constable in the original production of Kurt Weill's *Threepenny Opera*, in which another future Roy William Neill repertory company member, Rex Evans, also appeared. Hamer's first film appearance was in 1936 in the Fred Astaire-Ginger Rogers musical *Swing Time* in which he plays a well-dressed drunk involved in a complicated game of strip poker with gambler Astaire. From that point on, Hamer's film career was for the most part unremarkable, marked by small uncredited roles in dozens of films and television series, until his retirement in 1966. His most outstanding accomplishments were in the five Sherlock Holmes' films that he made at Universal between 1943 and 1946. He died of a heart attack at the age of 85 on July 6, 1972.

GAVIN MUIR, one of the few members of the Roy William Neill repertory company who wasn't British born, still managed to affect a convincing accent in most of the films in which he appeared. Born in Chicago, Illinois on September 8, 1900 (he shares a birthday with actress Hillary Brooke and me), his parents were John and Jessie Muir who would later retire to Miami, Florida. Muir's sister Agatha had been born two years earlier and it would appear that the Muir family relocated themselves to

Gavin Muir as Bart Lang in *Sherlock Holmes in Washington.*

Great Britain a few years later. In 1905 Agatha and Gavin Muir sailed with their mother Jessie on board the S.S. *Sicilian*, arriving in Glasgow, Scotland in August of that year. Muir received his education in British schools and returned to the United States when he was 19 in April of 1920.

He would mark his debut on the American stage with his appearance in *Enter Madame* at the Garrick Theatre on August 16, 1920. Produced and directed by the founder of the Tony awards, Brock Pemberton, the play had a successful run of 350 performances. Muir was soon appearing on Broadway with some frequency, even trying his hand at producing a 1923 play called *The Love Set*, which closed after eight performances. In 1924, while appearing in Chicago in a pre-Broadway tryout of a play called *The Best People*, Muir married the former Frances Logan-Herz. After *The Best People* closed on Broadway in December of 1924, Muir took his bride to England for a brief visit, returning to New York in May 1925 and immediately going into rehearsals with Laura Hope Crews and Frieda Inescort for Noel Coward's *Hay Fever*. Over the next twelve years, with the exception of one brief appearance in a Vitaphone short with singer Ruth Etting in 1932, Muir concentrated on developing a name for himself as a successful Broadway juvenile in comedies. His youthful appearance helped to keep this illusion going well into his late thirties, when he appeared in his final play, a comedy called *Bachelor Born* that had another successful run of 400 performances. One of Muir's fellow actors in this 1938 play was Aubrey Mather, who would rejoin him some years later in *The House of Fear*.

In 1936 Muir signed a year's contract with Twentieth Century-Fox and began his 35- year career in films. He first appeared as a doctor in a Frances Dee and Brian Donlevy comedy at Fox called *Half Angel* (1936); the studio then loaned him out to RKO studios to take on the role of the Duke of Leicester in John Ford's *Mary of Scotland* (1936) and still managed to have him appear in two more films before the year was out. Muir kept equally busy for the next few years, including his return to Broadway for his appearance in *Bachelor Born*, and by 1941 was almost exclusively playing British military officers in films such as *A Yank in the R.A.F.* (1941), *Captains of the Clouds* (1942), and *Eagle Squadron* (1942). According to the Internet Movie Database (IMDb) he supposedly supplied the voice of a BBC radio announcer in *Sherlock Holmes and the Voice of Terror*, but in viewing the sequence, which takes place at the end of the film, it's difficult to confirm that the voice is really his and in fact could be Edgar Barrier using a more upbeat-sounding version of his Voice of Terror persona. Muir would appear in another Brian Donlevy film for Universal, *Nightmare* (1942), before his debut for Roy William Neill in *Sherlock Holmes in Washington* in 1943. He would work again for Neill in *Sherlock Holmes Faces Death* (1943) and again in *The House of Fear* (1945).

Muir's career continued to flourish and he and his wife Frances bought a home in Beverly Hills at 2020 Coldwater Canyon, where they lived until her death in August of 1960. Muir continued acting, dividing his time between television and an occasional film. In 1960 he appeared as Betty Hutton's stuffy butler in her eponymous television series and the following year made his final film, playing the drunken sea captain in Curtis Harrington's *Night Tide* (1961). Shortly thereafter, Gavin Muir moved to Fort Lauderdale, Florida where he passed away on May 24, 1972 at the age of 71. There were no survivors as his mother had died in Florida in 1954 and he and Frances had no children.

IAN WOLFE made his first of four appearances in the Holmes' series in *Sherlock Holmes in Washington* as the antique store clerk. Like Gavin Muir, Wolfe was not an Englishman, but rather a product of Canton, Illinois who managed to perfect a cultured accent when needed. Born on November 4, 1896, Wolfe moved with his family when he was three-years-old to Grand Island, Nebraska. His father was Marcus A. Wolfe and his mother was the former Mary Rose Wilson. Wolfe was raised a Baptist, the youngest of three children; his brother Otis was eleven years older and his sister Blanche nine years older. When Ian Wolfe was eight years of age the family moved again to Kansas City, Kansas where he remained until his 19th year when he joined the Army as a medical orderly, eventually attaining the rank of sergeant. In 1924, Wolfe married Elizabeth Schroder; they would have two daughters, Moya and Deirdre.

Ian Wolfe as the Antique Store Clerk in *Sherlock Holmes in Washington*.

Wolfe's first appearance on Broadway was in 1921 as a doorman in *The Claw* starring Lionel Barrymore. He would rejoin Barrymore many years later in 1942 in the radio series, *Mayor of the Town*, having already appeared with him in the films *You Can't Take It with You* (1938) and *On Borrowed Time* (1939). Wolfe had a successful run on Broadway for the next few years in plays such as Maxwell Anderson's *Gods of the Lightning* with Sylvia Sidney and Charles Bickford, but his greatest success was in 1931 when he replaced John Seymour as Henry Bevan in *The Barretts of Wimpole Street* starring Katharine Cornell. When Ms. Cornell took the play on tour, Wolfe remained with the company, eventually landing in Hollywood and being signed by M-G-M to recreate his role in the film version with Norma Shearer taking over Cornell's role as Elizabeth Barrett.

In an interview he gave to Alanson Edwards of United Press to publicize his film debut in *The Barretts of Wimpole Street*, Wolfe told of an interesting experience he had when appearing with Lillian Gish and an acting troupe in Central City, Colorado performing *Camille*. "Central City," Wolfe related, "is three tortuous hours by mountain road above Denver. The altitude is 7,000—odd feet. We found a ghost city awaiting us. Miner's shacks with gaping holes for windows leaned at grotesque angles. Saloon doors hung open on rusted hinges. The opera house stood tall and forbidding in the midst of this ruin." Wolfe went on to explain how the lure of Lillian Gish brought the crowds to Central City and "… soon the town became a beehive of activity. Opening Night, was like a carnival. Every seat in the house was sold far in advance and hundreds came just to see the place." The director, Robert Edmund Jones, was worried that the crowd's feelings were so high that the delicacy of *Camille* would be lost on them, but Wolfe described how "…the ethereal atmosphere always surrounding Miss Gish held the audience spellbound until the final curtain."

Ian Wolfe made six more films during the next twelve months, including his first for Universal, *The Raven* (1935), with one of his favorite films coming toward the end of 1935 when he played Maggs, Captain Bligh's stool pigeon in *Mutiny on the Bounty*. From that point on, he managed to average between six to seven films a year.

And so began a career that spanned 56 years and 288 films. It seemed to me that I noticed that weasel face and receding hairline in practically every film I saw and I used to joke that Ian Wolfe couldn't get out of bed in the morning unless he had a film job to go to. From October of 1943 to December of 1944 Ian Wolfe made 11 films in a row for Universal Pictures. I always thought that Wolfe should have held the award for the most performances by an actor, but Turner Classic Movies host Robert Osborne seems to have incorrectly given that honor to horror icon Christopher Lee, who with only 265 films doesn't even come close, albeit he is still working and may one day break Wolfe's record.

The 1952 Los Angeles Registered Voters Index shows Wolfe, his wife Elizabeth and daughter Deirdre, all registered Democrats, living at 4652 Noble Avenue in Sherman Oaks, California. In what spare time he managed to steal from his acting jobs, Wolfe also wrote and self-published two books of poetry, *Forty-Four Scribbles and a Prayer* and *Sixty Ballads and Lyrics in Search of Music*. Wolfe, who continued acting well into his 90s, appeared mostly in television series in the later years, including running roles on *WKRP in Cincinnati* and *Wizards and Warriors*, but he made his final appearance in a featured role in Warren Beatty's over-the-top musical adaptation of Chester Gould's comic book hero, *Dick Tracy* (1990). Ian Wolfe died of age-related ailments on January 23, 1992 at the age of 95.

JOHN BURTON is a perfect example of the legion of character actors whose face is familiar to audiences, but whose name they cannot place. In fact there are 24 John Burtons listed on IMDb–everyone from six separate actors, both British and American, to sound technicians, cameramen, art directors and animation producers, and in civilian life there are several politicians, fundraisers, a chef and even a county coroner. "Our" John S. Burton appeared in four of the Sherlock Holmes films starting with *Secret Weapon* and ending with *The Woman in Green*, and played the army officer at the London Airport at the beginning of *Sherlock Holmes in Washington*. Burton, who always played small, uncredited roles such as military officers, or radio announcers in the Holmes' films, was born on April 6, 1904 in Norwich, England. Research shows that he traveled to the United States in September of 1927 with fellow actor John Knox-Orde, with both men staying at the Times Square Hotel on Broadway in New York City. There is no record of either of them having appeared in any Broadway plays, but on December 30, 1927 Burton traveled from Southampton to Halifax, Nova Scotia on his way to Montreal, Canada to appear at the Monument-Nation Theatre, a well-known Vaudeville site at that time. He would continue to commute from England to the United States for several more years, even after he started appearing in films in Hollywood in 1936.

John Burton as the Army Officer in *Sherlock Holmes in Washington*.

Burton's first film was Twentieth Century-Fox's *Lloyds of London* (1936) in which he portrayed Lord Horatio Nelson, boyhood friend of the film's hero, Jonathan Blake played by Tyrone Power. A great many of Hollywood's British Colony and future Roy William Neill repertory company members also appeared in the film, including Gavin Muir, Miles Mander, Montagu Love, Arthur Hohl, Billy Bevan, Holmes Herbert and Olaf Hytten. Burton continued playing famous characters, such as Lafayette in *Marie Antoinette* (1938) and Nostradamus in several of the *John Nesbitt's Passing Parade* short subjects at M-G-M. When the War came along, he, like every other British actor of a certain age, began portraying officers in films such as *A Yank in the R.A.F.* (1941), *Eagle Squadron* (1942) and *Invisible Agent* (1942).

Burton apparently dabbled in writing as well, according to a newspaper article that appeared in the *San Antonio Light* in 1938. The article told of Burton having written a play, *As We Dream*, which was to have its initial production in London the following fall, as well as a book of poems called *Trackless Winds*. Burton continued acting in films until his final performance as a British radio announcer in *The Day the Earth Stood Still* in 1951; which would mark the fifth time he portrayed a radio announcer in films. In 1953 Burton made his one television appearance in the syndicated *Boston Blackie* series starring Kent Taylor. He would eventually return to England, where he would live until his death in London on September 29, 1987 at the age of 83.

Much of the cast was American and first-timers to the Holmes oeuvre, such as MARJORIE LORD and JOHN ARCHER, real-life husband and wife, who played the young lovers Nancy Partridge and Naval Lt. Peter Merriam. According to a *Hollywood Reporter* blurb on July 20, 1942,

one week after filming had begun, but before they were scheduled to appear, Lord replaced the original choice of Evelyn Ankers, and John Archer took over the role of Lt. Merriam from Robert Paige. Universal had previously signed Lord to a term contract and she had already appeared in three low budget films for the studio.

Lord, whose real name was Marjorie Wollenberg, later gained fame as Danny Thomas' wife in *The Danny Thomas Show* on television and John Archer, born Ralph Bowman, who starred as the rock-

Marjorie Lord as Nancy Partridge in *Sherlock Holmes in Washington*.

etship commander in George Pal's *Destination Moon* (1950), had two children. Their daughter, Anne Archer, grew up to become a highly successful, Oscar-nominated actress with whom I had the pleasure of working in her second film, *Cancel My Reservation* (1972), a mostly unfunny Bob Hope comedy that turned out to be his final feature film and I'm sure one that Anne Archer omits from her resume. Lord and Archer were divorced in July of 1953 and John Archer died on December 3, 1999 at the age of 84. Marjorie Lord is still living.

John Archer as Lt. Peter Merriam in *Sherlock Holmes in Washington.*

DON TERRY, a Universal contract player played Howe, one of Richard Stanley's (Zucco) henchmen. Terry, whose real name was Donald Prescott Loker, was born in Natick, Massachusetts on August 8, 1902. He was educated at the Huntington School in Boston and the Philips Academy and graduated from Harvard in 1925. A quick trip to Hollywood led to his costarring in his first film, *Me, Gangster* (1928), and to his name change. His first film for Universal was a small role in *Her First Mate* (1933), but he was then signed by Columbia Pictures and starred in a series of seven action films there, before moving back to Universal in 1939. He would star in eighteen films and is best remembered as Commander Don Winslow in the Universal serials, *Don Winslow of the Navy* (1942) and

Don Winslow of the Coast Guard (1943). In 1943, Terry enlisted in the Navy, becoming a lieutenant commander and was awarded a Purple Heart in 1944. After the war he left the film business and over the years became a noted philanthropist and founding member of the California Cancer Center and the California Museum of Science and Industry Foundation. He and his wife, Katherine B. Loker, donated $1.5 million to the USC School of Theatre in 1977. He died on October 6, 1988 in Oceanside, California survived by his wife and two daughters.

Don Terry as Howe in *Sherlock Holmes in Washington.*

Clarence Muse as the Club Car Porter in *Sherlock Holmes in Washington*.

CLARENCE MUSE, who had been appearing in films for twenty two years by the time he appeared as the club car porter in *Sherlock Holmes in Washington*, was truly a Renaissance man; a lawyer, actor, screenwriter, director, opera singer and composer, he co-wrote the song "When It's Sleepy Time Down South." Muse was born in Baltimore, Maryland on October 14, 1889 and would become the second African-American actor, after Paul Robeson in *The Emperor Jones* (1933), to star in a film, *Broken Earth* (1936). In 1939 Muse collaborated with acclaimed author, Langston Hughes on an original screenplay for producer Sol Lesser called *Way Down South* (1939). Muse, who played many roles in his 58-year career, including everything from bootblacks and a diaper delivery man to seventeen separate appearances as a Pullman porter, always managed to maintain a sense of dignity and purpose. He was a talented singer and sang in a number of films including *Porgy and Bess* (1959) in which he sang "Here Come de Honey Man." Clarence Muse died in Perris, California on October 13, 1979, one day before his 90th birthday and four days before the release of his final film, *The Black Stallion* (1979).

THURSTON HALL had been a successful actor on Broadway for eighteen years, dividing his time between the stage and silent films, before joining the list of character actors in Hollywood as Commodore Jason T. Thatcher in *Hooray for Love* (1935), starring Ann Sothern and Gene Raymond. Hall always seemed to be the stuffy judge, businessman or, as in this film, Senator Henry Babcock, using the booming voice and bombastic personality that added a comedy element to every performance he gave. Best remembered as the blustering boss to Leo G. Carroll's Topper in the television series of the same name, he would continue in films and television until his death in 1958.

Thurston Hall as Senator Henry Babcock in *Sherlock Holmes in Washington*.

EDMUND MACDONALD, who played Lt. Grogan, the lantern-jawed Washington detective helping Holmes and Watson unravel the mystery, began his movie career playing a cad who impregnates the heroine in an exploitation film called *Enlighten Thy Daughter* (1934). He had a relatively brief career playing supporting roles in 47 films, many of them at Universal, including director Roy William Neill's second film for the studio, *Madame Spy* (1942). He also starred in a Uni-

Edmund MacDonald as Detective Lt. Grogan in *Sherlock Holmes in Washington.*

versal serial called *The Mysterious Mr. M* (1946) and three other films for the studio *Destry Rides Again* (1939), *Black Friday* (1940) and *Corvette-225* (1943). In Edgar G. Ulmer's classic film noir *Detour* (1945), MacDonald had the pivotal role of the gambler who gives drifter Tom Neal a ride and then dies, giving Neal the opportunity to assume his identity. He made his final film, *Red Canyon* (1949) for Universal-International Pictures before his premature death of a cerebral hemorrhage at the age of 43 in 1951.

Sherlock Holmes in Washington opened in New York on April 30, 1943, but the Hollywood trade papers had published their reviews the previous month. On March 26 *The Hollywood Reporter* wrote, "Direction by Roy William Neill takes full advantage of the excellently contrived twists of the story. Basil Rathbone is just what he should be in the title role, and Nigel Bruce as Doctor Watson is supplied with much bright comedy of which he is quick to make the most." The reviewer seemed to be offended by the fact that Holmes smoked cigarettes in this film instead of the usual pipe. "It is difficult to believe," he complained, "that even an up-to-date Holmes would forego his famous pipe for cigarettes." *Daily Variety* echoed the previous review's praises, saying, "Resultant tale is a melodramatic and suspenseful tale that will provide plenty of entertainment for addicts of detective yarns, and slip neatly into the program houses." The reviewer also singled out Neill's staging of the "MacGuffin" sequence for praise, writing, "Idea of following the match packet provides good drama and suspense in film form."

SHERLOCK HOLMES FACES DEATH

UNIVERSAL RETURNED SHERLOCK HOLMES to his traditional surroundings in their next production, in fact creating a venue for him that properly reflected the Conan Doyle influence. Bertram Millhauser was brought back to the studio to develop a screenplay, which he called *Sherlock Holmes Faces Death*, based on the Conan Doyle short story "The Musgrave Ritual" that appeared in Britain's popular *Strand* magazine in May of 1893. Taking his cue from Conan Doyle, Millhauser created an original story filled with gothic horror elements such as an old dark house, a clock striking thirteen that foretells of a Musgrave's death, ghosts that walk in the west wing and, adapting some elements from Conan Doyle's story, an eavesdropping butler and the eponymous ritual that Holmes must eventually decipher.

Millhauser created a prologue that takes place in the village of Hurlstone, in a pub called the Rat and the Raven, where the pub's proprietor (Harold De Becker) sets the film's mood of dark foreboding by telling two curious British sailors (one of whom is a young Peter Lawford) the legend of Musgrave Manor; the "corpse lights and wailing" seen and heard by villagers in the Manor's greenhouse, and the family's sinister history. Millhauser took the setting of Hurlstone Manor in Sussex from the Conan Doyle story and changed it to Musgrave Manor in Northumberland, bringing it up to date as a locale for rehabilitating military officers from World War II. The locale change from Sussex to Northumberland was an appropriate revision given that the Nazis were relentlessly bombing the south of England at that time and the northern district would therefore be a more appropriate locale for a sanctuary for convalescent officers. It's interesting to note that the publican, played by Harold De Becker, refers to the Musgraves' home as Musgrave Manor, but when Doctor Watson returns the medical file to the cabinet in the study, the label on the drawer says "Case Histories of Officers Convalescent at Hurlstone Towers Northumberland." Later, Sherlock Holmes refers to the home as both Hurlstone Towers and Musgrave Manor at Hurlstone with no explanation ever given as to this discrepancy.

Millhauser completed his first draft screenplay on April 5, 1943 and it was submitted to the Production Code Administration for approval. The code's administrator Joseph L. Breen objected to the use of the expression "Good Lord," noting that it was on the "list of banned words and phrases and could not be approved." Millhauser quickly completed his changes and the film went into production on April 12. Roy William Neill, directing his third installment in the Sherlock Holmes' series and recently awarded the title of producer as well, skillfully utilizes Universal Studios' marvelously creepy European village set, illustrating his flair for the genre, including the atmospheric antique shop from *The Wolf Man* that art directors Russell A. Gausman and Edward R. Robinson turned into the exterior for the Rat and the Raven.

Following the prologue at the Rat and the Raven the film establishes Musgrave Manor in a stunningly atmospheric, windy exterior and then introduces the current Musgrave family: two brothers, Geoffrey and Phillip, played by Frederick Worlock and Gavin Muir, and their sister Sally, played by Hillary Brooke. This scene also established the brothers' objections to Sally's romance with U.S. Army Captain Pat Vickery, played by Milburn Stone, and the tendency of everyone to eavesdrop on everyone else, including the butler, Alfred Brunton, played by Halliwell Hobbs and Mrs. Brunton the housekeeper, played by Minna Phillips. Nigel Bruce's Doctor Watson is established as the physician in charge of the welfare of the military patients at the Manor in a scene that ends with his assistant Doctor Bob Sexton, as played by Arthur Margetson, stumbling into the study and collapsing with a knife wound to his neck. Watson brings this mysterious attack to the attention of Rathbone's Sherlock Holmes in the one scene that plays out in his Baker Street lodgings and gives Mary Gordon's Mrs. Hudson her brief moment on screen. When Holmes deduces that a killer is loose at Musgrave Manor, the team arrives to find Inspector Lestrade (Dennis Hoey) already at work interrogating Doctor Sexton. Geoffrey Musgrave's body is soon discovered in front of the greenhouse and the mystery is now a case of murder. Lestrade decides that Capt. Vickery is the culprit and arrests him, as a hysterical Sally pleads with Holmes for help. With the tower clock once again chiming thirteen, Phillip disappears, only to be later found dead in the boot of Sally Musgrave's car. Learning of the ritual, which must be recited upon the death of a Musgrave, Holmes now swings into full investigative form. In a scene adapted from the Conan Doyle story, Holmes imagines himself in Sally Musgrave's place and tries to discern where she would have hidden the piece of paper on which is written the words of the ritual. He quickly deduces that the paper is hidden in Sally's bedroom clock and then sets about to decipher the meaning of the questions and answers.

Millhauser has cleverly changed the ritual to resemble a chess match and Roy William Neill stages the sequence stylishly with the help of cinematographer Charles Van Enger. In fact, the entire film is filled with scene after scene of atmospheric lighting and gothic visuals with one of the most startling being the bolts of lightning that flash in the storm outside the windows during Sally's recitation of the ritual, ultimately crashing through one of the windows and striking a suit of armor that stands beside her. If this reminds one of the lab effects in *Frankenstein* (1931) and *Bride of Frankenstein* (1935), that is because these effects were created by the same man, Kenneth Strickfaden.

The film's finale plays out in the Musgraves' ancient burial crypt, which Holmes, having deciphered the meaning of the ritual, has located beneath the cellar, and where he finds the body of the murdered butler. Holmes makes it appear that he has left the Manor, then suddenly reappears in the crypt to confront Doctor Bob Sexton and after a brief struggle exposes him as the killer. In a wrap-up scene where Holmes reveals the motives for Sexton's crimes, complete with brief flashbacks to illustrate Holmes' explanation, one can readily see where the creators of the television series *Murder, She Wrote* found their inspiration. The old land grant that Sexton was seeking is destroyed by its rightful owner, Sally Musgrave, who doesn't wish to take the land away from the farmers who have toiled it for centuries. The film's final moment finds Holmes and Watson driving away from Hurlstone village and reviewing what has occurred. In an original piece of writing, rather than using quotes as had been done in the previous films, screenwriter Millhauser has Holmes reflect on Sally's unselfish act: "There's a new spirit abroad in the land. The old days of grab and greed are on the way out. We're beginning to think of what we owe the other fellow, not just what we're compelled to give him. The time is coming, Watson, when we cannot fill our bellies in comfort while the other fellow goes hungry, or sleep in warm beds while others shiver in the cold." Holmes finishes his speech with the plea, "And, God willing, we'll live to see that day, Watson." Isn't it a shame that we're still waiting to see that day arrive?

Several members of the Roy William Neill repertory company were making return appearances in *Sherlock Holmes Faces Death*, including Dennis Hoey (Lestrade), Hillary Brooke (Sally Musgrave), Mary Gordon (Mrs. Hudson), Gavin Muir (Phillip Musgrave), Gerald Hamer (Major Brunton) and Olaf Hytten (Captain MacIntosh). The new arrivals were Frederick Worlock (Geoffrey Musgrave), Vernon Downing (Lt. Clavering) and Harold De Becker (Pub Proprietor).The romantic leads in the film were played by Hillary Brooke (Sally Musgrave) and Milburn Stone (Capt. Pat Vickery). Hillary Brooke was making her second appearance and would return once more in *The Woman in Green* so I'll save further discussion on her until she joins us again in this later film.

MILBURN STONE, who will always be remembered as the crusty Doc Adams on the long-running television series *Gunsmoke,* was born in Burrton, Kansas on July 5, 1904. His uncle was the Vaudeville comedian and Broadway actor Fred Stone who created the role of the Scarecrow in the original 1903 production of *The Wizard of Oz* and played Grandpa Vanderhof in the Moss Hart-George S. Kaufman 1936 comedy hit *You Can't Take*

Milburn Stone as Capt. Pat Vickery with Hillary Brooke as Sally Musgrave in *Sherlock Holmes Faces Death.*

It With You, which ran for two years on Broadway. While still in his teens, Milburn Stone left home to join a Vaudeville troupe as part of a song and dance team and eventually joined his uncle on the Broadway stage in the 1934 production of *Jayhawker*. Stone came out to Hollywood the following year and spent the next eight years playing bit parts and second leads for the poverty row studios. In 1943 he was signed to a contract by Universal Pictures and spent the next six years alternating between supporting roles in features and leads in several serials. By the time he was signed to play Doc Adams in 1955 he had appeared in over 163 films and television episodes. He ultimately appeared in nearly 500 episodes of *Gunsmoke* and made the unfortunate mistake in 1961 of selling his residual rights to CBS for a mere $100,000. This undoubtedly seemed like a lot of money at the time and who would imagine that the series would still be playing in syndication 49 years later, but there is no doubt that Stone ultimately regretted his decision. Stone was married three times, although in fact he divorced then remarried his second wife Jane Garrison and remained married to her for 41 years until his death of a heart attack on June 12, 1980 at the age of 76. He is buried in the El Camino Memorial Park in San Diego, California.

FREDERICK WORLOCK makes his second of six Holmes appearances in *Sherlock Holmes Faces Death* as Geoffrey Musgrave—he had appeared briefly in *Sherlock Holmes in Washington* as a BBC radio announcer, superimposed over a stock shot of London, reporting on the disappearance of John Grayson, and would reappear in *The Woman in Green, Pursuit to Algiers, Terror by Night and Dressed to Kill*. Frederick George Worlock was born on December 14, 1886 in the Marylebone district of London, the first son of Thomas Worlock and the former Sophia Elizabeth Thornhill; another son, Gerald, was born the following year. Frederick received his education at the Royal College of St. Peter, more commonly known as Westminster School, on the grounds of Westminster Abbey in London. He first appeared on the stage in Francis Benson's Shakespearean repertory company around the same time as Halliwell Hobbes and most likely competed with him for leading roles. He also toured Australia, New Zealand and South Africa as a leading juvenile for the noted Australian Shakespearean actor Oscar Asche and his wife Lily Brayton. In February of 1911, while appearing at the Haymarket Theatre, Worlock married actress Olive Noble (five years his senior) and moved into her home at 36 Holbein House, Sloan Square. When war began, Worlock enlisted in the 14th London Regiment and went to France, serving continuously for three years and rising to the rank of major. Seriously wounded, he received a medical discharge in 1917 and was awarded the Military Cross.

Frederick Worlock as he appeared as Colonel Cavanaugh in *Dressed to Kill.*

In 1923 Worlock traveled to North America for the second time, having tried his luck with little success in Canada two years earlier, but this time he was signed to appear in Rafael Sabatini's *Scaramouche* at the Morosco Theatre. One of the play's leading actors was Sidney Blackmer and as soon as *Scaramouche* finished its run, Worlock joined Blackmer in another play, *The Moon-Flower*. It was here that he met leading lady Elsie Ferguson; he went on to tour as her leading man in both *The Moon-Flower* and *The Wheel of Life* and appeared with her again on Broadway in *The Grand Duchess and the Waiter*. In 1924 they would marry and continue their acting careers, but no longer as co-stars. In April of 1930 Elsie Ferguson, who had been starring in films since 1917, was signed by Warner Bros. to appear in the screen version of *Scarlet Pages,* a play she had performed on Broadway the previous year. The Worlocks traveled to Hollywood where they were the guests of Lionel Barrymore and his wife at their Beverly Hills home. Elsie reported to the Warner Bros.' studios on Hollywood Boulevard to recreate her role of Mary Bancroft for director Ray Enright.

Worlock returned to Broadway later that year to appear in a very successful comedy by Zoe Akins called *The Greeks Had a Word for It*, which ran for 253 performances. (He and Elsie would divorce at the end of the year and she would marry her fourth husband Captain Victor Egan four years later.) Also in the cast of *The Greeks Had a Word for It* was stage and screen actress Verree Teasdale who would eventually marry Adolphe Menjou and star in several films with him. In 1939, after sixteen years of performing on the stage, Worlock returned to Hollywood to make his first feature film appearance in director Tod Browning's final film, *Miracles for Sale*. The film starred Robert Young and a host of wonderful character actors, with Worlock playing the magician Sabbat, whose murder in an apparently locked room sets off the mystery. Among the supporting players were Henry Hull (*Werewolf of London*, 1935) and Gloria Holden (*Dracula's Daughter*, 1936).

Worlock had appeared in several short subjects at the beginning of his film career and he appeared in several more in the '40s, as well as a number of big-budget films such as *The Black Swan* (1942), *Madame Curie* (1943), *Jane Eyre* (1944) and *A Double Life* (1947). In the 1950s he continued in films, but also began appearing in various anthology television series. In 1961 he supplied the voice for Inspector Craven in Walt Disney's *One Hundred and One Dalmatians*. He also recorded an album of Robert Burns' poetry, complete with a very strong Scottish burr.

In 1966 I worked with Freddy Worlock at M-G-M in one of a series of Elvis Presley films I was associated with. It was called *Spinout* and Freddy played the butler to the family of one of the female leads in the film, Shelley Fabares. My first impression of Freddy was based on the scowling, rather disagreeable characters he had portrayed in the Sherlock Holmes films, but I found him to be a delightful person, very warm and personable. He was 80-years-old and slowing down a bit, but his mind was still sharp. He remembered my father with fondness and spoke of the many films they had both appeared in beside the Sherlock Holmes films, including *National Velvet* (1944), *She-Wolf of London* (1946), *Ruthless* (1948) and *Joan of Arc* (1948).

Frederick Worlock died on August 1, 1973 of a cerebral ischemia——a decreased supply of blood to the brain caused by a blockage of the supplying blood vessels–and was buried at the Valhalla Memorial Park in North Hollywood, California.

VERNON P. DOWNING was born in Suffolk, England on January 6, 1913. Little is know about his family and his early life, but some time around his seventeenth birthday he traveled to the United States and began making the rounds on Broadway. He apparently impressed Guthrie

Vernon P. Downing as Lt. Clavering with Basil Rathbone in
Sherlock Holmes Faces Death.

McClintic, who signed him to appear in his production of *The Barretts of Wimpole Street* and on February 9, 1931 he opened at the Empire Theatre in support of McClintic's wife Katharine Cornell, playing one of her brothers. The play was a terrific success, somewhat of a tour de force for Ms. Cornell, and it ran for 370 performances, until December of 1931. Cornell revived the play four years later with her co-star Brian Aherne, and again in 1945, also with Aherne. M-G-M bought the play as a vehicle for Norma Shearer and in 1934 began filming it under the direction of Sidney Franklin. Fredric March and Charles Laughton played Robert Browning and Edward Moulton-Barrett respectively and two members of the original Broadway cast, Downing and Ian Wolfe, were brought out from New York to recreate their original roles, except that director Franklin decided that he wanted Vernon Downing to play Octavius Barrett instead of his original role of brother George and to cultivate a nervous stutter. Downing used this affectation in several other roles, including that of Lt. Clavering in *Sherlock Holmes Faces Death.*

M-G-M liked Downing's performance in *The Barretts of Wimpole Street* and brought him back the following year to play the sadistic midshipman Hayward in *Mutiny on the Bounty* (1935). In the meantime Downing had appeared in four other films, including *Clive of India* (1935) and *Les Miserables* (1935). A press release at the time told of an incident that supposedly took place aboard the *Bounty* while the company was filming off the coast of Catalina Island. According to the article that appeared in *The Chicago Tribune* on September 1, 1935, Clark Gable was supposed to punch Dowling on the jaw, but didn't want to do it because he felt that it would make him look like a bully to his fans. Director Frank Lloyd finally talked him into doing it and, according to Rosalind Schaffer, the author of the article, "The boys made the scene several times, faking the punch, but it just looked fakey. Finally Lloyd and Gable went into a huddle to talk it over. 'Well, boys, let's try it again,' he announced, and this time with no warning to Downing, Gable delivered a real sock to the jaw, landing Downing in a neat bundle on deck, suffering as much from astonishment as from the blow." The article concluded with the tag, "Don't let anyone tell you making movies is a softie's game."

Some time around 1939 (once again the records are unclear), Downing apparently married and the following year, on March 8, 1940, his daughter Victoria Downing was born in Los Angeles. Over the next seven years, Downing appeared in fifteen films, frequently as a British military officer and always uncredited. It wasn't until his appearance in *Sherlock Holmes Faces Death* in 1943 that he would receive screen credit and his name included on the film's posters. Then, after two more films, *Corvette K-225* (1943) and *A Guy Named Joe* (1943), in which he again appeared as British officers and was again uncredited, he received screen credit in *The Spider Woman* (1944).

Immediately upon finishing the small role of another English officer in William A. Wellman's *This Man's Navy* at M-G-M in the summer of 1944, Downing joined the American Field Ambulance Service and was shipped overseas, returning in October of 1945. His first film upon returning from the war was the Abbott and Costello comedy *The Time of Their Lives* (1946) at Universal, which reunited him with "Spider Woman" Gale Sondergaard. On September 9, 1946, Downing once again performed the role of Octavius Barrett on the Lux Radio Theatre's production of *The Barretts of Wimple Street* on CBS starring Brian Aherne and Loretta Young.

With exception of his work in *The Macomber Affair* (1947), Downing never again received screen credit on any of the films he appeared in over the next seven years. He did better in the few television series he worked on, such as a 1952 episode of *Dangerous Assignment* with Brian Donlevy and fellow *Barretts of Wimpole Street* alumni Leslie Denison, and a 1954 episode of *Four Star Playhouse* titled "The Bomb" that was written and directed by Blake Edwards. Downing's final film was a "B" costume drama directed by future horror maven William Castle called *The Iron Glove* (1954). At some point after that, Downing returned to New York, where he died in December of 1973. Vernon Downing's soft, youthful features and supercilious manner made him the perfect choice to play autocratic bullies and overbearing officers.

HAROLD DE BECKER was a marvelous addition to the Roy William Neill repertory company, having come from a theatrical family and having spent 36 years performing on the Broadway stage before moving permanently to Hollywood in 1942. He would appear in four of the Holmes films, first as Peg Leg, one of Moriarty's gang of thugs in *Sherlock Holmes and the Secret Weapon*, then as the proprietor of the Rat and the Raven in *Sherlock Holmes Faces Death,* then as the Café Boss in *The Pearl of Death* and finally as a shoelace seller in *The Woman in Green.*

De Becker was born on June 8, 1889 in London England, the fourth child of Nicola and Kate De Becker. The rest of the clan included sisters Marie and Nestor and brother Nicola. Father Nicola, whose family was originally from the Netherlands, worked as a clerk in a London firm and when he died in 1901, Kate and her children immigrated to the United States.

All of the family, with the possible exception of brother Nicola, had aspirations to become actors and as it happened everyone except mother Kate and Nicola were working on Broadway shortly after they arrived in New York. The play, a drama that previously had a successful run in London's West End, was called *A Message from Mars* and opened at the Garrick Theatre on October 7, 1901. Making his Broadway debut along with Marie, Nestor and Master Harold De Becker was Henry Stephenson, who would many years later play Sir Ronald Ramsgate in *The Adventures of Sherlock Holmes* (1939). The play had an interesting premise for 1901; A Martian Messenger (Stephenson) is sent to Earth to cure a young man of selfishness. It had a very successful run of 184 performances and then returned to Broadway, with the original cast, in March of 1903 for another lengthy run. By the time *A Message From Mars* opened for a third run in October of 1904, both Nestor and Harold, who was now 15 and had dropped the "Master" from his billing, had moved over to the Lyceum Theatre to appear in *The Serio-Comic Governess*, a comedy-drama by the Jewish author Israel Zangwill, who first coined the phrase "The Melting Pot" as a definition of the United States. Once this play closed, the De Becker family went their separate ways professionally, with even mother Kate eventually making it to Broadway.

Harold De Becker as he appeared as Peg Leg in *Sherlock Holmes and the Secret Weapon* with a disguised Basil Rathbone.

Over the next seven years Harold De Becker appeared in five plays, including as a member of the chorus in a musical called *The Balkan Princess*. Then, in March of 1912, he played a Japanese student in *The Typhoon* and for the next few years he appeared to be type-cast, playing a Chinese in *Innocent* and another Japanese in *The Willow Tree*, which had a healthy three-month run and then went on tour. In 1918 De Becker registered for the draft, moving his birth date back to 1887 and thereby making his age 31 and escaping the draft. He also applied for citizenship that year. He continued to appear on Broadway with some regularity, even hiring a press agent to keep his name featured regularly in the gossip columns. The press agent turned out the usual drivel, such as "One of the reasons we like the old songs best, pessimistically comments Harold De Becker, is because they are sung less often than the others."

In 1928 De Becker appeared in his twenty-fifth Broadway play, *The Skull*, which had a decent run of 96 performances, but then came the Crash of 1929 and Broadway shut its doors. With typical British optimism, De Becker chose this moment to marry and move with his wife Dorothy Daniels from his mother's apartment to a new home, where their son, Karoldor was born the following year. By March of 1931 De Becker was back at work, appearing with Lionel Atwill in *The Silent Witness*, and from that point on he remained active right up to 1939, when he had the enviable dilemma of appearing in two plays at the same time. His ever-diligent press agent fed the story to Charles B. Driscoll's "New York Day by Day" column, who built it up with the following: "Fortunately, De Becker's part in one show was all in the first act. In the other show, performing in a playhouse across the street, his entrance didn't come until the last act. He managed the double job, but it took some fast makeup work." The truth was that De Becker did have a one-day overlap between *Foreigners* at the Belasco Theatre and *The Woman Brown* at the Biltmore Theatre, but neither play lasted longer than a week.

In 1942, De Becker moved to Hollywood to appear in his first film, the Tyrone Power- Joan Fontaine starrer *This Above All* with fellow Roy William Neill repertory company players, Holmes Herbert, Dennis Hoey, Miles Mander, John Abbott, Billy Bevan, Leyland Hodgson, Olaf Hytten, David Thursby, Doris Lloyd and Nigel Bruce. De Becker's wife Dorothy made her only appearance in this film as a WAAF, and De Becker's 12-year-old son, who changed his name to Harold De Becker, Jr. for professional reasons, appeared in two films, *National Velvet* (1944) and *Kitty* (1945). De Becker's sister Marie, who died on March 22, 1946, appeared in eight films, including *Mrs. Miniver* (1942) and *Random Harvest* (1942), and would have appeared in *The Spider Woman* as a charwoman, but her scenes were deleted.

Together with the four Sherlock Holmes films, De Becker appeared in a total of 29 films, including *The Return of the Vampire* (1944), *A Thousand and One Nights* (1945), *The Picture of Dorian Gray* (1945), *Cluny Brown* (1946) and *Golden Earrings* (1947). He died on July 24, 1947 in Los Angeles, having just celebrated his 58th birthday the previous month.

HALLIWELL HOBBES, another marvelous character actor, makes his only appearance in a Sherlock Holmes film as the butler Alfred Brunton, although he was certainly well-suited to play any number of roles given to other actors. Born Herbert Halliwell Hobbes on November 16, 1877 in Stratford Upon Avon, Hobbes' career encompassed 59 years of both stage and screen performances, but he is perhaps best remembered for the 20 films in which he played a butler, including *Sherlock Holmes Faces Death*. In fact Hobbes began his career as a Shakespearean actor who cut quite a handsome figure in his doublet and tights.

Hobbes made his stage debut in 1898 at the age of 21 in Francis Robert Benson's Shakespearean repertory company touring throughout England, and in the late summer of 1906 he traveled with the famous Shakespearean actor Johnston Forbes-Robertson and his wife Gertrude Elliott to New York to appear with them in George Bernard Shaw's *Caesar and Cleopatra* at the New Amsterdam Theatre. In March of 1908 Hobbes played Tybalt opposite Matheson Lang's Romeo in Lang's production of *Romeo and Juliet* at the Lyceum Theatre in London. When World War I began, 38 year-old Hobbes (who had just married a young actress by the name of Nancie Brenda Marsland) enlisted in the 7th Battalion of the Royal East Kent Regiment, known as the "Buffs," and went off to serve in France, eventually attaining the rank of Captain.

After the war Hobbes returned to his wife and his son Peter, who had been born in August of 1917, and resumed his acting career, sometimes appearing in the same company as his wife. In September of 1923 they sailed from Liverpool aboard the S.S. *Celtic* for New York to appear

Halliwell Hobbes as Alfred Brunton and Minna Phillips as Mrs. Brunton in *Sherlock Holmes Faces Death.*

together in *The Swan* with Basil Rathbone, Philip Merivale and Eva Le Gallienne. For the next few years Halliwell and Nancie Hobbes commuted between England and Broadway continuing to performing together, although Nancie would maintain her billing as Nancie B. Marsland. In 1929 the family moved to Hollywood and Halliwell Hobbes appeared in his first film, *Lucky in Love*, a musical starring radio singer and songwriter Morton Downey. In 1931 Hobbes portrayed his first butler in *The Bachelor Father* and before the year was out he had played butlers in four more films, managing to end the year with a break in this pattern by appearing as Brigadier General Sir Danvers Carew in the Fredric March version of *Dr. Jekyll and Mr. Hyde*. Hobbes was once interviewed about the curse of type-casting and reported that he had tried refusing to play butler's roles. "The only trouble with that decision," he said, "was that Hollywood knows me only for my work in two types of role: butlers and the Archbishop of Canterbury. Archbishop parts come once every 24 years, so I picked up my silver tray again and I've kept it ever since."

Throughout the 1930s and 1940s Halliwell Hobbes did in fact appear in many of the classic films of the period and not always as a butler, including Frank Capra's *Lady for a Day* (1933), *Captain Blood* (1935), *Mary of Scotland* (1936), *You Can't Take It with You* (1938), *That Hamilton Woman* (1941) and *Here Comes Mr. Jordan* (1941). He also appeared in several of the popular horror films: *Dracula's Daughter* (1936), *The Undying Monster* (1942) and *The Invisible Man's Revenge* (1944).

Halliwell Hobbes returned to New York in the late 1940s to appear in a number of Broadway productions and live television series and from that point on he divided his time between New York and Hollywood. His final screen appearance was in Warner's *Miracle in the Rain* (1956) with Jane Wyman and Van Johnson, but his final role in 1957 was that of Helen Hayes' doorman in a television episode entitled "Mrs. Gilling and the Skyscraper" on the anthology series *The Alcoa Hour*. Halliwell Hobbes passed away on February 20, 1962 in his Santa Monica home. His ashes were scattered in the Rose Garden of the Chapel of the Pines Crematorium in the West Adams district of Los Angeles. William McPeak's short biography of Halliwell Hobbes on the IMDb website ends with the following comment: "Although he was sometime uncredited in films, his roles were no less a recorded legacy of a dedicated acting talent."

MINNA PHILLIPS, who was born on June 1, 1885 in Sydney, Australia, was primarily a stage actress for the first 20 years of her career. She acted in two silent films *Forbidden Fruit* (1915) and *Daredevil Kate* (1916), shortly after arriving in the United States, but from 1920 to 1940 she appeared on Broadway in over a dozen plays. After three unsuccessful productions, she joined Basil Rathbone in *The Captive* that opened at the Empire Theatre on September 29, 1926. An original drama written by future movie executive (and husband to Myrna Loy) Arthur Hornblow, Jr. and directed by Gilbert Miller, it was a moderate success running for 163 performances. Phillips rejoined Rathbone almost immediately in another, less than successful comedy *Love Is Like That*, which closed after 24 performances. This was followed in quick succession by the Theatre Guild's production of *A Month in the Country*, in which she played Alla Nazimova's mother-in-law and was directed by Rouben Mamoulian and closed within the month, and another comedy called *After All,* starring a young Humphrey Bogart. She finally found another hit with *Autumn Crocus*, where every night for 210 performances she appeared as "The Lady with the Lost Underpants."

In January of 1940, Phillips opened in the James Thurber-Elliott Nugent comedy *The Male Animal*, playing Mrs. Blanche Damon opposite Nugent, Gene Tierney, Don DeFore and Leon Ames. Not only was the play a big success, but it turned out to be her introduction to Hollywood. When Warner Bros. bought the screen rights to *The Male Animal* the following year, she was brought out to recreate her role in the film version. After that, Phillips remained in movies for the next ten years, appearing in such films as *A Yank at Eton* (1942), *The North Star* (1943) and *Strangers on a Train* (1951). Her final screen appearance was as The Cook in the Dorothy Parker-written segment "Horsie" of *Queen for a Day* (1951). Minna Phillips died of a heart attack in New Orleans, Louisiana, on January 29, 1963 at the age of 77.

Sherlock Holmes Faces Death opened on September 17, 1943. Shortly before its release, Universal issued the following press release: "In 'Sherlock Holmes Faces Death,' the great Holmes makes further concessions to present style, giving up his baggy checked suits for quieter tweeds. And he emerges for the first time with hair combed in the conventional pompadour, discarding the picturesque but somewhat dated "windblown curls" effect of Sir Arthur Conan Doyle's conception." Apparently that did the trick, as none of the reviewers bothered to mention the change in Rathbone's appearance. *Daily Variety* proclaimed, "There's enough suspense in picture to satisfy Sherlock Holmes fans and others, too, who haven't previously caught any of the series." *The Hollywood Reporter* was more complimentary: "It all adds up to first-rate Doyle, handsomely produced and suspensefully directed by Neill...'Sherlock Holmes Faces Death' should make a very respectable showing at the box-office."

Theodore Strauss in his *New York Times* review gave the film a grudging, if somewhat amusing accolade: "Corpses and clues accumulate. Secret panels open and close, butlers and housekeepers lurk at keyholes, carrion ravens pluck at rumble-seat coverings, old family rituals are read amid thunder-and-lightning effects, unsteady old men knit in rockers and pretend to sleep, and because the camera apparently must have been quite heavy, it quite often catches only feet, not the person on them, creeping through the hallways. But through it all, Mr. Holmes moves with absolutely mathematical precision and the clipped peremptory tones of Basil Rathbone; and Doctor Watson, or rather Nigel Bruce, less brainy than brave, carries on nobly."

According to Hollywood legend, *Sherlock Holmes Faces Death* was the film that actor Dwight Frye, the unforgettable Renfield of *Dracula* (1931), was supposedly watching, while seated in a movie theatre, just minutes before suffering a fatal heart attack while returning home.

THE SPIDER WOMAN

EVEN DURING THE SPRING OF 1943, as *Sherlock Holmes Faces Death* was filming, Universal and executive producer Howard Benedict had Bertram Millhauser busily at work on another screenplay that he initially called *Sherlock Holmes in Peril*, but which was soon retitled *Sherlock Holmes and the Spider Woman*. This script would ostensibly be an original work, with only the opening sequences, with Holmes faking his death, based very loosely on the Conan Doyle story "The Adventure of the Dying Detective" that appeared in the *Strand* magazine in December 1913 (and would later appear as a chapter in *His Last Bow*). The reveal of the child's footprints to be those of a pygmy is borrowed from a chapter of *The Sign of the Four,*

which Doyle calls "The Episode of the Barrel." The film's title change was motivated by the Millhauser-created character of Adrea Spedding, a diabolical villainess to be memorably played by Gale Sondergaard and destined to inspire a second film, *The Spider Woman Strikes Back* (1946) that in fact bore no connection to the character or to Sherlock Holmes. The Millhauser screenplay was delivered to the Breen Office on May 8, 1943 and their response was quick and to the point. An example of the way the Code dealt with issues in 1943 can be observed in the letter of May 10, 1943 from Joe Breen to Maurice Pivar (assumedly the head of Universal's Story Department). "Page 26: Norman's line '…you must send me some…' with reference to perfume, seems to characterize him as a "pansy" type. Any such characterization could not be approved." In an earlier paragraph in the same letter, in reference to the relationship between Sondergaard's character and the Norman character as played by Vernon Downing, Breen had an opposing concern. "We presume," he wrote, "that there will be no hint that they are living together. This is essential." Obviously Mr. Breen was covering all the bases. The certificate of approval was forthcoming on July 22, 1943.

Sherlock Holmes and the Spider Woman began filming on May 10, 1943, just a few short weeks after *Sherlock Holmes Faces Death* had completed production. Again assuming the duties of both producer and director, Roy William Neill gets the action off to a rousing start with a body crashing through a window and a quick montage to establish a rash of suicides. After Holmes' apparent death and the touching scene between Watson and Lestrade that I described on page 49, we meet both Gale Sondergaard's Adrea Spedding and her half-brother Norman Locke played by Vernon Downing, and very soon after, Mr. Raghni Singh as played by Basil Rathbone with an atypical French accent. The action moves quickly from Raghni Singh's attempted suicide at the gambling casino and the first mention of insurance policies, to a tea-time rendezvous at Adrea Spedding's flat with each participant cunningly learning more about their opponent. Holmes and Lestrade set a trap in a rented room to find how the murders have been committed and discover that deadly spiders are the cause. The spider, actually a rather large tarantula, is described later as "a lycosa carnivora, the deadliest insect known to science, from the upper regions of the Obanga River." This mind-boggling mouthful is said with a straight face by Arthur Hohl as Adam Gilflower "from the Bureau of Entomology," following an amusing moment where Watson mistakes Gilflower for Holmes wearing another of his many disguises.

Hohl will have a chance to redeem himself quite nicely in the next film, *The Scarlet Claw*. A surprise visit from Adrea Spedding, bringing with her a strange young boy who seems to be trying to imitate *Dracula's* Renfield

Arthur Hohl as Adam Gilflower, with Basil Rathbone in *The Spider Woman.*

with his love of insects, seems at first merely to be an attempt on her part to throw Holmes off the trail of the child's footprints he found at the scene of his attempted murder, but soon turns into another murder attempt with a poisoned powder thrown into the fireplace emitting deadly fumes. The powder is called "redix pedis diabolus," another mouthful that is Latin for Devil's-foot root, borrowed by Millhauser from another of Conan Doyle's Sherlock Holmes stories, "The Adventures of the Devil's Foot."

Holmes and Watson pay a visit to Mathew Ordway, a second entomologist who originally sold the spiders to Adrea Spedding, only to find that he has also been murdered and one of Spedding's gang is impersonating him. Holmes tricks the man, played by Alec Craig, into revealing the ruse and the murderer escapes by smashing several cases of deadly spiders. Dr Watson then discovers the skeleton of what Holmes assumes to be a child, but which Watson astutely reveals to be that of a pygmy. Now aware that the footprints he discovered weren't those of a child, Holmes and Watson visit a carnival arcade in search of the mysterious pygmy, with Watson complaining, "No good, old man, it's like looking for a pygmy in a haystack." Adrea Spedding lures Holmes into the rear of the shooting gallery booth where he is overpowered and tied to one of the moving targets.

Sherlock Holmes is captured by Adrea Spedding's gang. From left, Angelo Rossitto, Vernon Downing, Gene Roth, Basil Rathbone, Alec Craig and Gail Sondergaard.

What follows is a disappointingly ineffectual climax, with Lestrade watching Watson fire at the revolving targets, unaware that Holmes is behind one of them, and Holmes working himself free of his bonds just in the nick of time. Adrea and her gang are then apprehended and Holmes and Watson wander off through the crowd—this time without Holmes' usual homily.

In an intellectual sense, Gale Sondergaard's Adrea Spedding was a formidable opponent for Basil Rathbone's Sherlock Holmes and it was enjoyable to watch the two verbally spar. This wasn't the first time that Sondergaard and Rathbone had appeared together in films; as Inez Quintero she connived with Rathbone's Captain Esteban Pasquale in *The Mark of Zorro* (1940), and again as the sinister housekeeper Abigail Doone in *The Black Cat* (1941). They were both in *Paris Calling* (1941), but had no scenes together.

GALE SONDERGAARD was born Edith Holm Sondergaard on February 15, 1899 in Litchfield, Minnesota, one of three daughters born to Hans and Christin Sondergaard. Her father, a Danish-American creamery worker, later became a teacher at the University of Wisconsin and her mother, the former Christin Holm, was a music teacher. Gale Sondergaard became interested in acting while in high school and completed her high school education at the Minneapolis School of Dramatic Art. Upon graduating she entered the University of Minnesota, earning a degree in English and public speaking. She then joined the John Kellerd Shakespeare Touring Company and spent the next few years playing a variety of roles in Shakespearean productions, appearing in a season of summer stock in Milwaukee and touring in a production of *Seventh Heaven*. She married Neil O'Malley, a fellow alumnus of the University of Minnesota, in 1922 and he followed her into acting, joining the touring company.

In October of 1928, Gale Sondergaard made her debut on Broadway in a Theatre Guild production of Goethe's *Faust*. The role of Mephistopheles was played by Irish actor Dudley Digges, and a young actor named Herbert J. Biberman was a member of the ensemble. Sondergaard would again appear as Digges' daughter, in a revival of Shaw's *Major Barbara*, immediately upon closing in *Faust*. She and Biberman would meet again when they both appeared the following year with Otto Kruger and Claude Rains in the English translation of a Russian play *Karl and Anna*, and once again immediately following, when he would direct and appear with her in another play with a Russian setting, *Red Rust*. Sondergaard would di-

Gale Sondergaard as Adrea Spedding, The Spider Woman.
With Vernon P. Downing as Norman.

vorce Neil O'Malley in 1930 and marry Herbert Biberman that same year, while they were appearing together in *Red Rust*. When the play closed in February of 1930, the couple immediately left on their honeymoon.

For the next few years, Sondergaard's career took a back seat to her husband's as he directed five plays in rapid succession, including the original production of writer Lynn Riggs's *Green Grow the Lilacs* with Franchot Tone as Curly. In February of 1933, Sondergaard returned to the Guild Theatre in a three-part play called *American Dream*. Once again Claude Rains was a fellow performer, along with Josephine Hull, Stanley Ridges and Sanford Meisner. Biberman had directed Rains in two previous plays, *Miracle at Verdun* (1931) and *The Man Who Reclaimed His Head* (1932), which Universal Pictures would film in 1934 with Rains recreating his stage role. In June of 1933 Biberman directed his wife in *Iron Flowers,* an experimental play with dance and music at the Westchester County Center, and May of 1934 saw Sondergaard opening on Broadway in the mystery *Invitation to a Murder*. The cast included Walter Abel and Humphrey Bogart (just a few months before his breakout role as Duke Mantee in *The Petrified Forest*). Sondergaard played Lorinda Channing in a manner described by the *New York Times* as "…a cross between Lady Macbeth and Queen Elizabeth."

In 1935 Biberman co-directed with John Houseman a highly praised production of Maxwell Anderson's play *Valley Forge* and Columbia Pictures signed him to a director's contract. Even though Sondergaard considered herself to be a stage actress with a successful career, she elected to join her husband in Hollywood and sat relaxing in the Southern California sun for six months, until her husband's agent Bill Shiffrin (who was my father's agent for four years) introduced her to Mervyn LeRoy and he cast her as Faith Paleologus in Warners' *Anthony Adverse* (1936). The reviews for the film singled her out, praising her performance, and she was awarded the very first Academy Award for Best Supporting Actress. Sondergaard's film career rapidly gained momentum, even as her husband languished at Columbia, directing "B" movies such as *One Way Ticket* (1935) and *Meet Nero Wolfe* (1936). Sondergaard began to establish herself as one of Hollywood's most popular villainesses in *Maid of Salem* (1937), *Seventh Heaven* (1937), *Juarez* (1939) and *The Mark of Zorro* (1940). As well as adding a menacing quality to her performances in *The Cat and the Canary* (1939), and *The Letter* (1940), about which Bette Davis wrote in her memoir, *Mother Goddam,* "Gale Sondergaard's performance … was breathtakingly sinister. I was so lucky that she was cast in the part."

After a quick return to Broadway in December of 1940 to appear in Otto Preminger's production of *Cue for Passion*, Sondergaard began what was to become a long run of films for Universal with *The Black Cat* (1941), followed by *Paris Calling* (1941) and *The Strange Death of Adolf Hitler* (1943) in which she played Anna Huber, the wife of a man who was a dead ringer for the dictator and planned to assassinate him. This was immediately followed by her co-starring role in *The Spider Woman*. Between 1943 and 1949 Sondergaard appeared in seventeen films, including *Anna and the King of Siam* (1946), for which she was again nominated for a Supporting Actress Oscar for her performance as Lady Thaing. She would lose to Anne Baxter, who won for her role in *The Razor's Edge* (1946). A small role in *East Side, West Side* (1949) would be Sondergaard's last film for the next twenty years. She would become "Mommy Gale," as she described herself in an interview, to her two adopted children Joan Kirstine and Daniel Hans. In most of the interviews that she gave in later years, Sondergaard asked that the subject of the House Un-American Activities Committee not be discussed, saying as she did to Leonard Maltin, "there is just so much to it." However HUAC, as it was called, had such an impact on her marriage and her career that I cannot leave it unmentioned.

In 1947, HUAC began its investigation into the Motion Picture industry and Herbert Biberman was subpoenaed. He appeared before the committee on October 29, 1947, and refused to answer any questions that were posed to him by the committee's chairman, J. Parnell Thomas, claiming the First Amendment of the Constitution gave him this right. Biberman, along with nine other writers and directors, including Dalton Trumbo, Ring Lardner, Jr., and Edward Dmytryk, were found guilty of contempt of Congress and sentenced to six months in jail. Known as "The Hollywood Ten," they appealed, but lost and were sent to Texarkana Federal Correctional Institute and each fined $1,000. In March of 1951, while she was appearing in a stage production of *Anastasia* in Philadelphia, Gale Sondergaard was subpoenaed to appear before the committee and wrote a letter to the Board of Directors of the Screen Actors Guild asking for their support. In it she wrote, "I most earnestly and fraternally ask the Board to consider the implications of the forthcoming hearing. A blacklist already exists. It may now be widened. It may ultimately be extended to include any freedom-loving nonconformist or any member of a particular race, or any member of a union or anyone." The Board rejected her appeal and Sondergaard appeared before the committee, refusing to answer questions and invoking the Fifth Amendment.

Blacklisted, Sondergaard's Hollywood career ended and she would not work again in a film until 1969. She and her husband moved back to New York. In October of 1965 she opened at the Gramercy Arts Theatre in a one-woman show called *Woman* that was directed by Herbert Biberman. It was a minor success and closed after 23 performances. She traveled back to Minneapolis in 1967 to appear at the Tyrone Guthrie Theatre in *The Visit* and received an Outstanding Achievement Award from her alma mater, the University of Michigan. It would be an independent film, *Slaves* (1969), co-written and directed by her husband, which would bring her back to the screen. Over the next seven years Sondergaard found work more frequently in television, appearing as a guest star on such series as *It Takes a Thief*, *Night Gallery* and *Police Story*. She guest starred in six episodes of the soap *Ryan's Hope* and appeared in a revival of *Uncle Vanya* at the Los Angeles Center Theatre. Her next film was a TV movie called *The Cat Creature* (1973), directed by Curtis Harrington in which she had a guest starring role along with John Carradine and John Abbott. It was during the production of this film that Charlton Heston made a surprise visit to the set to present Sondergaard with an Oscar to replace the plaque that was given to her in 1936 for her performance in *Anthony Adverse*.

In early 1981 the Academy of Motion Picture Arts and Sciences announced that they would be screening *The Spider Woman* and that Gale Sondergaard would make a rare personal appearance. At that time I hadn't seen any of the Sherlock Holmes films in a theatre since I first saw them when I was a boy at the Warner Beverly Theater on Wilshire Boulevard in Beverly Hills. I was anxious to go to the screening, not only to see the film, but to meet Sondergaard as well. As it turned out, a print of *The Spider Woman* wasn't available, so they ran *Sherlock Holmes Faces Death* instead, but Ms. Sondergaard did attend. After the screening and the question and answer period, I went down front and introduced myself to her. She was a bit overwhelmed by the large number of people milling about her, but she graciously shook my hand and said something nice about my father. She was 82-years-old, but her age had only faintly diminished her beauty and she stood erect and tall. I would have liked to have spoken more with her, but dozens of other people were trying to gain her attention and I backed away. Earlier, during the question and answer period, she had replied this way to someone's question about how she developed her character of Adrea Spedding: "The spider woman character as scripted had no hint of background or motivation, and I had no concept of how to play her as a three dimensional character. I mean what kind of childhood could she have had? Ultimately I chose to play her as Holmes' equal and allow their battle of wits to be played out much like a female Moriarty." (That comparison was made by Holmes himself in the film: "A female Moriarty, clever, ruthless, and above all cautious." Later he added, "Remarkable woman, audacious and deadly as one of her own spiders.")

Gale Sondergaard's daughter, Joan Biberman Compos, died in 1965 at the age of 25 and Herbert Biberman died in June of 1971. The last record of her son, Daniel Hans Biberman, was a brief article in a Eugene, Oregon, newspaper in December of 1976.

Sondergaard's final film was an insignificant quasi-horror film called *Echoes* (1983) in which she played the part of a psychic. In 1984 she retired to the Motion Picture Country Home in Woodland Hills, California, where she died from hypertension and a stroke on August 14, 1985 at the age of 86. Her ashes were scattered at sea.

Returning Roy William Neill repertory company members in *The Spider Woman* included Dennis Hoey (Lestrade), Mary Gordon (Mrs. Hudson), Vernon Downing (Norman Locke), Harry Cording (Fred Garvin) and John Burton (Announcer). New members joining the group were Arthur Hohl (Adam Gilflower), Alec Craig (Radlik) and George Kirby (News Vendor).

ARTHUR HOHL was born Arthur Edwin Hohl on May 21, 1889 in Pittsburgh, Pennsylvania, the second son of Leonard Hohl, an Austrian-Swiss engineer, and the former Christine Metzger of Germany. Within a few short years the family had relocated to Butte, California, where Leonard Hohl continued his work as an engineer and the boys their education. Arthur Hohl originally studied to be a mining engineer at Leland Stanford Junior University, but an interest in show business, which had been prevalent since childhood, finally took over and he headed to New York to try his luck at acting. "My parents were opposed to my contemplated career," he reported in a newspaper interview many years later, while he was appearing in Washington D.C. "I conceived many brilliant short cuts to fame; that is, I thought they were brilliant. Tried Vaudeville in a sketch of my own writing and was told I was too high-brow. Wrote another that I knew would please Vaudeville and tore it up before anyone saw it." In April of 1914, Hohl made his debut on

Arthur Hohl as he appeared without the beard makeup in *The Scarlet Claw*.

Broadway as young detective Chal Fisher in *The Dummy*, in which a 10-year-old Clare Boothe understudied the little girl in the cast.

Arthur Hohl left the cast of *The Dummy* in July of 1914 and sailed on the S.S. *St. Paul* to England, where in his own words, "I remained until someone started a war." He returned to New York in October and "Then it was more stock in Stamford and Waterbury." When the United States entered the War in April of 1917, Hohl enlisted, or as he put it, "Left to accept a steady job in our Uncle's army. A year in France; one bronze star. Won my commission as lieutenant in the aforementioned foreign country and returned in July 1918." Hohl joined the Washington Square Players in the Village and over the next six months opened and closed in three original plays and a revival of Shaw's *Mrs. Warren's Profession*. He finally got lucky toward the end of 1919, when he was signed by the Theatre Guild to appear in a dramatization of Tolstoy's *The Power of Darkness*. One of his cast mates was Henry Travers who would later appear in *The Invisible Man* (1933) and will always be remembered as Clarence in *It's a Wonderful Life* (1946). *The Power of Darkness* ran for three months and then Hohl went immediately into the Broadway production of *Martinique* and then back to the Greenwich Village Theatre and an original drama, *Eyvind of the Hills*. From November of 1922 to March of 1923, Hohl had a nice long run in Elmer Rice's courtroom drama *It is the Law* and then co-starred the following year in a silent film version of the play for the Fox Film Corporation. He performed in *White Cargo* at the Greenwich Village Theatre, and with Ann Harding in another courtroom drama, *The Trial of Mary Dugan*, in which he played the public prosecutor. "He gives what seems to me the outstanding single performance of the season," wrote Lucy Jeanne Price about Hohl's performance in *White Cargo* in her syndicated column, "and I've seen a good three fourths of the plays that have opened to date." A virtually indecipherable review for *The Trial of Mary Dugan* seemed to single out Hohl's performance for praise: "Being that he has in charge a long and exacting role, which he plays so well as to make of him a factor in the capitol performances of the good melodrama."

After playing another attorney, opposite Tallulah Bankhead in *The Cheat* (1931), Hohl and his wife Jesse moved permanently to Southern California and took up residence at 2172 Coldwater Canyon Drive and Arthur went back to work, again playing an attorney in *The Night of June 13th* (1932) starring one of the screen's earlier Sherlock Holmes, Clive Brook. Following this he made his first film for Cecil B. DeMille, *The Sign of the Cross* (1932); DeMille liked his work enough to bring him back in a memorable performance as Brutus opposite Warren Williams' Julius Caesar in *Cleopatra* (1934). He appeared as one of the men that Barbara Stanwyck seduces in the 1933 pre-code melodrama *Baby Face* that almost didn't get released because of its highly sexual content. Some of his other well remembered performances include Mr. Montgomery, Doctor Moreau's (Charles Laughton) unwilling accomplice in animal-to-human surgery in *Island of Lost Souls* (1932), Bassick, Professor Moriarty's henchman in *The Adventures of Sherlock Holmes* (1939) and the real estate agent in Chaplin's *Monsieur Verdoux* (1947). His telling performance as the overly protective father and café proprietor in *The Scarlet Claw* far outshadowed his cameo in *The Spider Woman*.

After appearing over 100 films, but no television productions, Arthur Hohl made his last film appearance in 20th Century-Fox's *Down to the Sea in Ships* (1949) starring Richard Widmark and Lionel Barrymore. He died on March 10, 1964 at his home on Coldwater Canyon in Los Angeles, California at the age of 75.

ALEC CRAIG was born Alexander Younger Craig on March 30, 1885. He was the second son of James C. Craig and Isabella Younger Craig who lived at 133 High Street in the village of Dunfermline in County Fife, Scotland. By the time of the 1901 Census, 16-year-old Alexander was working as a confectioner's assistant and the family had grown to include, beside brother James, sisters Ella and Jane and brothers Robert and William. Nothing is known of Alexander Craig for the next eighteen years, but one can assume that his education ended when he went to work to help support the family at age 16 and by the time of World War I, being 30 years of age, he may have served in a non-combatant capacity. At any rate, in 1919 Alexander Craig made two important decisions: first he married a young girl of his village, Margaret Carmichael Liddell, on September 24, 1919 in Edinburgh and one month later, on October 23 he and his wife boarded the S.S. *Colombia* in Glasgow and sailed for

Alec Craig as Radlik in *The Spider Woman*.

the United States. Arriving in New York on the 2nd of November, they traveled immediately to Los Angeles, California. There is no record of Alexander Craig working in films at that time and, based on his application for citizenship that he submitted some years later, his and Margaret's son James was born in Berkeley, California in December of 1922.

Alexander, now calling himself Alec, first appeared in a one-line bit in *The Little Minister* (1934), the film in which Mary Gordon, a fellow Scot, helped Katharine Hepburn perfect her Scottish dialect. The following year Craig appeared in seven films, including *Mutiny on the Bounty* in which he played McCoy, one of the *Bounty*'s crew who is flogged and mistreated by Captain Bligh and joins Fletcher Christian's mutiny. The following year Craig appeared in supporting roles in *Little Lord Fauntleroy* (1936), *Mary of Scotland* (1936) and *Winterset* (1936). After that his career took off and it never stopped for the next ten years. In 1937 he appeared in twelve films, in 1938 it was nine films and in 1939 it was twelve again. Then fourteen in 1940, thirteen in 1941 and then his banner year of 1942, when he appeared in eighteen films in one year. Sometimes he would receive screen credit and other times not; most often he would employ his Scottish brogue, as he did as Radlik in *The Spider Woman*, but he could also lose it and sound almost American if the part required him to do so, as it did when he played the Central Park zookeeper in *Cat People* (1942). Like many of his fellow repertory company members, Alec Craig contributed his services to the British War Relief film, *Forever and a Day* (1943).

In the 124 films that Craig made in his relatively short career of only eleven years, he managed to include a number of horror films, including *Dr. Jekyll and Mr. Hyde* (1941), *Undying Monster* (1942), *Calling Dr. Death* (1943), *Jungle Woman* (1944) and *The Brighton Strangler* (1945). Alec Craig died on June 25, 1945 in Los Angeles, California at the age of 60 and is buried in the Grandview Memorial Park in Glendale, California. His final two films, *Girl on the Spot* (1946) and *Three Strangers* (1946), were released after his death.

GEORGE KIRBY appears only briefly in *The Spider Woman* as a London news vendor shouting his headlines during a short montage, but he imparts such a sense of authenticity to that brief moment that you forget that it is simply an actor portraying a role and not the real thing. He returns in *The Scarlet Claw* as the village priest, Father Pierre, and again imbues the priest with a credible pastoral authority with which he guides his flock. Kirby was born George Thomas Kirby on February 18, 1879 in the Lambeth District of London, the firstborn son of George William Kirby, a furniture dealer, and the former Letitia Mary Ann Burton. He had two older sisters, another

Letitia age five (the parents apparently chose to name their firstborns after themselves), and Jeanette age four. The family would eventually grow to include two more sons, William and Joseph and two daughters, Minnie and Ivy.

Apart from these vital statistics, very little can be found about George T. Kirby's younger years as the name was quite popular. A search of the records turned up several other George Kirbys who were born around the same time in both England and America, and of course there is also the African-American comedian who bore the same name. What we do know is that at the age of 24, "our" George Kirby married Sara Lydia Potter on August 5, 1903

George Kirby as Father Pierre in *The Scarlet Claw.*

and that they eventually had three children, George, Wilen and Hector, and that George Sr. continued to live in the Lambeth district at 39 Bonham Road. He had by this time become a contract stage manager, working in London's West End, and in fact traveled with a stage company to the United States in 1905, 1906 and 1907.

At some point Kirby was apparently involved in the London production of J. M. Barrie's *Peter Pan*, most probably in 1905 when the actress Cissie Loftus (later Cecilia Loftus in the *Black Cat*, [1941]) took over the role of Peter from the original performer, Nina Boucicault. He is prominently featured in a photograph that accompanied a *Los Angele Times* article published on December 16, 1931, reporting on a gathering at the opening of a production of *Peter Pan* at the Music Box Theatre in Hollywood, honoring Cissie Loftus and others who had previously appeared in the play. The article refers to Kirby as "the inventor of the flying effects introduced in the play"; however that was incorrect as that was actually another George Kirby, the father of the inventor, Joseph Kirby. This George Kirby's company, Kirby Flying Ballets, provided the flying effects for the original production of *Peter Pan* in 1904.

When the war broke out, "our" George Kirby, now 35-years-old, joined the 2nd Rifle Brigade of the Northumberland Fusiliers, received a commission as a captain and served in Malta until his discharge on January 20, 1919. He returned to the United States in 1925 and, although there is no record of his having appeared as an actor in any Broadway productions, he most likely found work as a stage manager. In 1911 one of America's top actresses Minnie Maddern Fiske opened on Broadway in a play called *Mrs. Bumpstead-Leigh* produced and directed by her husband Harrison Grey Fiske. Eighteen years later, in 1929, Mrs. Fiske, as she was known professionally, revived the play first on Broadway and later in 1931 in Los Angeles, and George Kirby was in the cast playing the butler. From that point on, Kirby's acting career turned to the movies and in 1932 he appeared as Mr. Boots in his first film, *Cynara* starring Ronald Colman and Kay Francis, along with other Roy William Neill repertory company members Halliwell Hobbes and Ted Billings.

Over the next twenty years Kirby appeared in over sixty films, usually as a butler, a coachman, or a priest, and always uncredited. His films included *The Barretts of Wimpole Street* (1934), *The Prince and the Pauper* (1937), *The Dawn Patrol* (1938) and *The Black Swan* (1942). He also appeared in a number of Universal's horror films, including *Mystery of Edwin Drood* (1935), *Werewolf of London* (1935), *Dracula's Daughter* (1936) and *The Invisible Man Returns* (1940). In 1943 he had a particularly good year, appearing in eight films including the British War Relief film *Forever and a Day* in which he again played a news vendor. According to their website, the 447th Bomb Group that was stationed at Rattlesden Airbase during World War II viewed *Forever and a Day* in their Post Exchange theatre on March 20, 1944 and, because the cast was listed in order of appearance, George Kirby received top billing in the base's announcement. His penultimate film was *The Strange Door* (1951), one of Universal's unsuccessful attempts to bring back the horror genre starring Charles Laughton and Boris Karloff. George Kirby died at the age of 74 on December 2, 1953 in Van Nuys, California.

Universal couldn't seem to make up its collective minds as to the film's final title, so when it previewed *The Spider Woman* for the Hollywood trade papers, a week before its release on January 21, 1944, *The Hollywood Reporter* still referred to it as *Sherlock Holmes and the Spider Woman,* while *Daily Variety* called it simply *Spider Woman.* Nonetheless, the reviews were some of the best so far, with the *Reporter* announcing, "Universal rings the bell with *Sherlock Holmes and the Spider Woman,* latest in a long list of whodunit-as-if-Holmes-didn't-know thrillers…More to the point, this is one of the better films based on the tales of Sir Arthur Conan Doyle." The review went on to single out the cast, "How Miss Sondergaard can screen so beautifully and yet so menacingly is one of the delights of the film. Lesser characters are rich in color, too, particularly Dennis Hoey, who does a thick-headed cop from Scotland Yard. Vernon

Downing and Alec Craig contribute mightily to the evil of the Spider Lady's entourage." *Daily Variety* was equally effusive, writing, "Universal's new Sherlock Holmes film carries imprint of past successes plus chiller action all its own, to elevate this meller as topper of series thus far." It went on to give individual praise to several of the principals, adding "Story as worked out by Bertram Millhauser is engaging piece of writing and serves as excellent setting for realistic action on part of entire cast. Miss Sondergaard acquits herself with menacing charm, and Dennis Hoey again portrays series character of Scotland Yard Inspector Lestrade with his usual aplomb...Roy William Neill, as producer-director, must be singled out for outstandingly good piece of endeavor." According to G.E. Blackford of *The New York Journal-American*, "I don't know why they took Sherlock Holmes out of the billing. It may have been because they thought *The Spider Woman* would better attract the thrill trade...In any event, it is the redoubtable Sherlock Holmes and his friend, Doctor Watson, who are the chief item on the bill of fare...and why not? Each has grown practically letter-perfect in his characterization. Nigel's Doctor Watson continues amusing and amazingly opaque. Basil's Sherlock continues sharply delineated. There seems no end of stories and situations in which to involve them. And there seems to be no let-up in the public's response to them."

THE SCARLET CLAW

CONFIDENT THAT THEIR INVESTMENT in the Conan Doyle library of Sherlock Holmes stories would continue to produce dividends, Universal hired a team of writers to develop another screenplay and put out the following press release: "Paul Gangelin and Brenda Weisberg have been assigned by Universal to do a screenplay on *Sherlock Holmes vs. Moriarity*, which will be the third and last on Universal's "Sherlock Holmes" series for 1943-1944." As it turned out that concept never came to fruition, but would re-emerge in 1945, after a great deal of revising, as an original screenplay by Bertram Millhauser eventually titled *The Woman in Green.* In the meantime, Gangelin and Weisberg's script, with considerable rewriting by Edmund Hartmann and eventually by Roy William Neill as well, evolved into a screenplay initially called *Sherlock Holmes in Canada.*

The studio officially submitted a draft of the screenplay to the Production Code offices on December 15, 1943 and it was passed without too much objection. Some adjustments were made to a couple of the principals' paychecks, with Nigel Bruce receiving a small bump from $5,000 to $5,700 and Roy William Neill's salary rising to $5,700 as well. Universal's payment to M-G-M for Basil Rathbone's services remained at $20,000 and the film was budgeted at $177,200 for 16 days of shooting. Neill began filming on January 12, 1944 and would eventually go three days over schedule for a final cost of $189,624.54. On January 18, 1944 the studio submitted a set of lyrics to be used in the now titled *The Scarlet Claw* to the Code office. The song was from the G. Schirmer catalogue *Song of the People* and was called "Carried Off To Sea". Toward the end of the film, a group of villagers would sing boisterously, "Now raise your voice and sing along, sing till the echoes ring. Don't ever let a single soul worry 'bout anything."

The plot once again takes us to a foreign location, this time to the small village of La Morte Rouge, just outside of Quebec, Canada. The film opens with a marvelously atmospheric sequence, remindful of the opening to Neill's *Frankenstein Meets the Wolf Man* and establishing the sense of horror that permeates the entire film, as a church bell peals mysteriously and we meet the villagers of La Morte Rouge as they sit in the pub-like Journet Hotel Café and discuss the curse and the glowing monster that haunts the village. We meet the innkeeper Emile Journet (Arthur Hohl) and Potts the village postman (Gerald Hamer), as well as the village priest, Father Pierre (George Kirby), who has Potts drive him to the church where he discovers the body of Lady Lillian Penrose clutching the bell cord. From there we travel to Quebec and, in a subtle acknowledgement to Sir Arthur Conan Doyle's interest in and acceptance of the occult, to a meeting of the Royal Canadian Occult Society being attended by Sherlock Holmes and Doctor Watson, who are listening to an address by Lord William Penrose (Paul Cavanagh). Penrose is describing the existence of the supernatural monster at La Morte Rouge and the deaths that occurred 100 years before. Once Lord Penrose receives a telephone call informing him of his wife's death and Sherlock Holmes receives a letter from Penrose's dead wife pleading for help, the action shifts back to La Morte Rouge.

Holmes and Watson visit Lord Penrose at Penrose Manor and, despite Penrose's antagonistic attitude, manage to examine Lady Penrose's body, with Watson determining that the woman had been attacked by a wild animal that clawed her throat. Holmes recognizes Lady Penrose to be the former Lillian Gentry, a popular British actress who mysteriously disappeared several years before in the wake of a tragedy: an actor, who was in love with her, killed a fellow actor in a fit of jealous rage and was sent to prison, only to be killed later himself in a prison break. When Emile Journet examines the book after Holmes and Watson have registered at the Journet Hotel Café, the film cuts to an insert shot of the page and directly above Holmes' signature is the entry "Tom McKnight, New York, U.S.A." Obviously the prop man was amusing himself by using the name of the film's technical advisor to help fill the page. The source of the other name in the book, "Bertram L. Lank, Quebec" is unknown; perhaps he's the prop man's brother-in-law, or perhaps Bertram refers to screenwriter Bertram Millhauser.

Holmes discovers that Emile Journet is an ex-prison guard who moved with his daughter Marie (Kay Harding) to La Morte Rouge around the time of the phantom's reappearance. That night, as Doctor Watson settles in at a table in the café with several townspeople, including an extra (Ted Billings) who looks enough like Skelton Knaggs to be his older brother, Holmes explores the marshes where the monster is supposed to be seen and is confronted by a glowing phantom. When Watson tries to go to his aide, he finds himself trapped in a bog and Holmes has to rescue him. Discovering a piece of a torn shirt in the marsh that is later revealed to be soaked in phosphorescent paint, Holmes visits the owner of such expensive shirts, a Judge Brisson (Miles Mander). Brisson is supposedly wheelchair-bound, but through a ruse Holmes discovers that he is not disabled and is in fact in fear of his life. Brisson's housekeeper Nora (Victoria Horne) has given some of the judge's old shirts to a boatman named Jack Tanner who lives in a deserted hotel next to the river. Along with Doctor Watson and Police Sergeant Thompson (David Clyde), Holmes confronts the boatman, but he escapes by crashing through a window and diving into the water below. Watson and Sergeant Thompson fire at the figure in the water, believing they have killed Tanner. In examining Tanner's room, Holmes discovers the torn half of a photograph inscribed "To Alistair Ramson a great actor," which leads him back to Penrose Manor. In a somewhat implausible scene, he breaks into Lord Penrose's house and his safe, removes a lock box and forcing it open finds the other half of the photograph to be of Lillian Gentry before she became Lady Penrose. From Lord Penrose he learns that Alistair Ramson was the murderer who was sentenced to Talon Prison by Judge Brisson. Holmes is now certain that Tanner and Ramson are one and the same and that he is also impersonating someone else in the village.

Holmes races to save Judge Brisson, but arrives too late and discovers that Brisson has been murdered by Ramson, disguised as Nora the housekeeper. A bloody, five-pronged garden weeder is found on the floor. Holmes is later trapped by Ramson when he attempts to confront him at the deserted hotel and Ramson, feeling he has the upper hand, confesses to killing both Lady Penrose and Judge Brisson for revenge. He is about to reveal his third intended victim when Watson's arrival distracts him and he once again escapes. Holmes deduces that the third victim has to be Journet, who was a guard at Talon Prison, but when they go to speak with him they discover his daughter Marie has been murdered with her throat cut. Using Journet as a decoy and then taking his place, Holmes lures the killer, now disguised as Potts, the postman, into attacking him on the fog-filled marshes. Potts tries to escape into the marsh and in a struggle is killed by Journet, using the same murder weapon, the five-bladed garden weeder.

In the final scene, although there has been no mention of the war up to this point, the writers inexplicably have Holmes quote from another of Winston Churchill's speeches, but unfortunately, even as good an actor as Basil Rathbone cannot keep it from sounding forced and inappropriate. For some reason Rathbone's final line in reference to Churchill, "God bless him" has been scrubbed from the soundtrack. Perhaps the studio thought it might have been a bit too much for an American audience, even for a wartime audience.

On February 2, 1944 *The Hollywood Citizen News* published an article by Frederick C. Othman, detailing his day on the mist-filled marshes on Universal's back lot watching the filming of the sequence where Potts is killed. Othman colorfully described Nigel Bruce's wardrobe and the action in the scene without once mentioning the actor by name. "On this morning—the filters on the lens will make it midnight—he was clad in white shoes, brown-and-white checkered pants, a flowered vest, and the most magnificent red necktie in the wardrobe department…Underneath his haberdashery he wore rubber pants, with feet included, like a baby's sleeping garment. The idea was to keep the mud off Watson. Producer-Director Roy William Neill set up his cameras among the bogus rocks, immediately behind the New York street. There the boys used fire hoses, mud and oil to create a bog. They turned on the smoke to make fog and told the murderer to scram. He raced through the mists, with Doctor Watson behind him…In a few seconds there was a gulp-ush in the mud. Sinking slowly therein was Doctor Watson. He sank about one inch further than the mathematician had calculated and the mud began to seep in at the top of his rubber pants and we don't suppose any detective ever had an unhappier assistant." Of course it wasn't all work and no play for "Willy" Bruce, who loved a good joke. According to a news release that Universal's publicity department sent out during the filming of *The Scarlet Claw*, on the day that Nigel Bruce celebrated the 29th anniversary of receiving his wound in The Great War, he arrived on the set wearing a red-white-and-blue ribbon tied in a bow around the wounded leg. However, on another occasion he was the butt of the joke. One day Basil Rathbone brought to the set an actor who made ribbing a hobby, and introduced him to Nigel Bruce as a French critic making a lecture tour. The man began to criticize Bruce about his allegedly bad English accent, suggesting to Bruce that he associate more with his countrymen and study their speech so that he could cope with his character roles more successfully. Rathbone finally had to admit to an apoplectic Bruce that he was being ribbed.

With one minor exception, the disguises in this film are the prerogative of the villain, not Sherlock Holmes, and they are exceptionally well done by makeup artist Jack Pierce, giving Gerald Hamer an opportunity to assume several diverse characters and deliver them impressively.

Making his first and only participation as cinematographer of a Holmes film is George Robinson, who had previously earned acclaim for his work with Roy William Neill on *Frankenstein Meets the Wolf Man*. Robinson's work is outstanding; helping to create an atmosphere that is nothing short of claustrophobic, filled with shadows, mist, low-key lighting and expressionistic camera angles frequently framed by arches and candlesticks. Of course one cannot discount Neill's ability to create eerie scenes, not to mention drawing excellent performances from his actors, and in this instance even writing some of the scenes himself. The art direction by John B. Goodman and Ralph M. DeLacy and the set decoration by Russell A. Gausman and Ira Webb is worth mentioning for their excellent utilization of and dressing of existing sets, such as the lobby of the Quebec hotel, various rooms in Penrose Manor and Journet's cafe and guestrooms, plus the fog-filled marshes and the European Street, doubling for the exterior of the hotel and café. John P. Fulton's eerie special effect of the glowing phantom adds another atmospheric touch to the marsh sequences.

As an interesting side note, the dialogue director on *The Scarlet Claw* was Stacy Keach, father of actor Stacy Keach, Jr. best known for his performance as Tully in John Huston's *Fat City* (1972), and as Mike Hammer in the television series *The New Adventures of Mike Hammer* (1984-1987). Keach, Sr. was an actor as well as a writer-director and created the radio and television series *Tales of the Texas Rangers* in the early 1950s.

The returning members of the Roy William Neill repertory company who appeared in *The Scarlet Claw* were Gerald Hamer (Potts/Jack Tanner/Alastair Ramson), Arthur Hohl (Emile Journet), George Kirby (Father Pierre), Ian Wolfe (Drake), Olaf Hytten (Hotel Desk Clerk) and Ted Billings (Villager in Café). The new arrivals were Paul Cavanagh (Lord Penrose), Miles Mander (Judge Brisson), David Clyde (Sgt. Thompson) and Kay Harding (Marie Journet).

PAUL CAVANAGH was born William Griggs Atkinson in Durham, England on December 8, 1888. He was the second child of Mathew Atkinson, a former Army officer who was now a shopkeeper in the village of Felling, and his wife Margaret. His sister Annie was three years older; a second sister, Elsie, would be born seven years later. Young Atkinson was educated at the Royal Grammar School in Newcastle and later at Cambridge University, where he studied law. After graduation, Atkinson traveled to Western Canada, working several odd jobs before joining the Royal Northwest Mounted Police, soon to become in 1920 the Royal Canadian Mounted Police, the national police force of Canada. After nine months with the Mounties, Atkinson began practicing law in Edmonton, Alberta and in 1914 he married, shortly before joining a Canadian Regiment and serving in France. Receiving shrapnel wounds about the head and shoulders, he recuperated in a British hospital and after his discharge joined a London law firm. He and his wife separated in 1922 and E. Jean Atkinson returned to live in Toronto, Canada. In 1924, Atkinson, now as-

Paul Cavanagh as Lord Penrose in *The Scarlet Claw.*

suming the professional name Paul Cavanagh, left the law profession and began his career as a stage actor, appearing in a revival of Victor Herbert's *The Enchantress* and *The Constant Wife* with Fay Compton. In February of 1928 Cavanagh appeared in the musical comedy *Lady Mary* that had a successful run of 181 performances.

Paul Cavanagh made his first film in 1928, a silent based on Walter Howard's play about two boys in the Crimean War called *Two Little Drummer Boys.* Later that same year he co-starred in Victor Saville's *A Woman in the Night* and in 1929 he co-starred in Anthony Asquith's *The Runaway Princess* with Mady Christians. Shortly thereafter, Cavanagh sailed to the United States to appear on Broadway in *Scotland Yard.* The play had a relatively short run (September to October of 1929), but it was long enough for a Paramount talent scout to spot Cavanagh's performance as Capt. John Leigh, D.S.O. and sign him to a contract. Over the next five years Cavanagh alternately starred in Paramount's "B" films and supported the major stars in the studio's important films, with loanouts to every other studio in town as well. His one big claim to fame during this period was co-starring with Mae West in *Goin' to Town* (1935).

Although they were living apart, with E. Jean Atkinson still remaining in Toronto, Cavanagh and his wife were sued by the Internal Revenue Service in 1935 for back taxes. The IRS's position was that Cavanagh did not have the right to claim that half of his earnings were community property under California law and not subject to taxation. Because Cavanagh and E. Jean Atkinson were still legally married at that time, the court ruled in his favor, although it took until January of 1942 for the decision to be rendered.

His contract with Paramount Pictures having expired in 1935, Cavanagh returned to England in 1936 to star with Margot Grahame and American actor David Burns in *Crime Over London* (1936) and would remain there for two years, starring in two more films, *Danger in Paris* (1937) with Greta Nissen and Sally Gray and an early Alistair Sim film, *A Romance in Flanders* (1937). He then returned to Hollywood and to M-G-M studios to play a supporting role in one of the studio's lesser productions, *Within the Law* (1939). From 1941 onward until 1950, like most of his contemporaries, Cavanagh alternated between playing British earls, lords and military officers in over 35 films. He also appeared in his share of horror films, such as *The Strange Case of Doctor RX* (1942), *The Man in Half Moon Street* (1944) and *House of Wax* (1953).

For some reason, every time that I would see Paul Cavanagh in a film he would remind me of my father. To my eye there is a strong resemblance between the two of them and it has something to do with set of the chin and the mouth. Of course both of them frequently wore moustaches, which would increase the similarity. Generally speaking, Cavanagh's roles were more often higher up the pecking order than the butlers, Nazi of-

Paul Cavanagh as a young man.

Dennis Hoey as a young man.

ficers and police inspectors that my father played, and he wasn't as bulky or as tall as my father. Whenever I would mention this to someone else, they would always disagree with me, but never-the-less I still think they look enough alike to be brothers, particularly if you compare photographs taken of them when they were younger. I'm not implying that they are, merely that they look alike.

In 1946, having divorced his first wife some years before, Cavanagh married Katherine Layfield Luhn and they had one child. In later years, Cavanagh would appear in numerous television series, including a recurring role as the Secretary General in one of the first live TV science fiction shows, *Space Patrol* (1950-1955), and another as Commissioner Morrison in the Johnny Weissmuller series *Jungle Jim* (1955-1956). His final appearance was in an episode of the television series *Have Gun Will Travel* in 1960. Paul Cavanagh died of a heart attack on March 15, 1964 in Baltimore, Maryland and is buried in the Lorraine Park Cemetery in Woodlawn, Maryland.

MILES MANDER was born Lionel Henry Miles Mander in Wolverhampton, Staffordshire, England on May 14, 1888, the second son of Samuel Theodore Mander and the former Flora Saint-Claire. Mander's father was a member of the prominent Mander family, industrialists and public servants who built a varnish and paint business into the largest manufacturer of varnish, paint, and printing ink in the country. Mander's older brother Geoffrey would one day become chairman of Mander Brothers and a Member of Parliament and would take the title Sir Le Mesurier Mander upon being made a Knight Bachelor in 1945. His younger brother Alan would in later years marry the Princess Sudhira of India. Miles Mander's father, who was at one time mayor of Wolverhampton and built Wightwick Manor where the young Manders grew up, died when Miles was 12, and his mother died three years later. Young Mander, who had been attending Harrow School in Middlesex, was shipped off by the family trustees to McGill University in Quebec, Canada. Unfortunately, Mander spent more time across the border in New York City pursuing chorus girls for pleasure than studying for his exams, so the trustees sent him packing to New Zealand in 1908 to work on his uncle Martin Bertram Mander's sheep station.

Considering Miles Mander's physical appearance, he hardly seemed the type to pursue the boisterous, action hero-type existence that he in fact did. Inheriting $350,000 on his twenty-first

Miles Mander

birthday, he spent the next seven years spending it. He owned a stable of racehorses, among other endeavors, and on October 11, 1911 promoted the 20-round rematch between Jack Johnson and Sam Langford in Paris, France. He married an Indian princess, Pratavia Devee, the daughter of Sir Nripendra Narayan Bhup Bahadur, the Maharajah of Cooch Behar, known to her friends as "Pretty." Manders had met her in London in May of 1911 when she came with her family to the coronation of King George V and Queen Mary and they were married in Calcutta the following year, after her father's untimely death. Mander began flying an early Louis Bleriot monoplane and in 1914 won a cup for his first official flight at Brooklands, a 2.75-mile motor racing circuit and aerodrome built near Weybridge in Surrey, England. He competed in long distance balloon racing with members of the Royal Aero Club and served as a captain in the Royal Army Service Corps in World War I. He was gassed in 1916 in France.

After the War, Mander's opportunities began to diminish along with what was left of his inheritance. He began drinking heavily and only after his doctor told him that further drinking would kill him did he finally give up liquor. "And there I was," he was quoted as saying, "28-years-old and broke, untrained for any worthwhile business and ready for the ash heap." Mander's marriage to "Pretty" was fraught with trouble and fodder for the gossip mills when Mander discovered "Pretty" in bed with South African diamond merchant Reginald De Beer. She returned to India and Mander partitioned for divorce in 1922. In 1923 he would marry Kathren Bernadette French of Sydney, Australia, and they would have a son, Theodore. Mander would write a book of memoirs and advice to him, *To My Son—In Confidence* (1934).

Desperate for a job, Mander managed to get himself hired as an extra at a London movie studio and his career in films began. Within four years he was playing the third lead in a silent comedy called *The Temporary Lady* (1920) and the following year he portrayed Godfrey Norton opposite Eille Norwood's Sherlock Holmes in a two-reel version of *A Scandal in Bohemia* (1921). In 1925 he played the male lead in Alfred Hitchcock's first feature film, *The Pleasure Garden*, and it was here that he undoubtedly met Alma Reville with whom he would later write the screenplay for *The First Born* (1928), one of the films that he also produced and directed. Mander had begun writing plays and short stories as early as 1927 and two of his plays were produced in London. There is some confusion regarding whether he was the author of the original play *Conflict* that became the basis for his film *The Woman Decides* (1931), or whether Miles Malleson, an established playwright who plays a small uncredited role in the film, was actually the author.

Mander's career as a writer-director-producer lasted from 1923 to 1936, during which time he directed eight short silent films and wrote and directed one feature silent film and three sound features. In *The First Born* (1928) he discovered and co-starred with Madeleine Carroll and John Loder and, just to prove that he wasn't afraid of being accused of nepotism, his own son Theodore played his young son in the film. In his next film, *Fascination* (1931) he would again star Madeleine Carroll and a young actor who had just co-starred with my father and Fay Compton in Anthony Asquith's *The Battle of Gallipoli* (1931). His name was Carl Harbord and he would later play Inspector Hopkins in *Dressed to Kill* (1946). Making their first appearances in the film was a very young boy and a young actress by the name of Queenie Thompson. Years later, Mander spoke about this in a newspaper interview. "I had to have a six-year old blonde boy and I made tests after tests. Finally there came to my office a woman with a youngster whose hair was so dark I didn't even want to hear his story. But the woman was so insistent that I finally had the boy read some lines. He did so well that I put him in the picture and let the audience wonder how he turned blonde by the time he grew up. His name was Freddie Bartholomew." Mander went on to talk about the young actress as well. "I needed some chorus girls. Among them was Queenie Thompson, who had been dancing in a cabaret. I changed her name to Merle O'Brien. She did fine too, now she's known as Merle Oberon."

In 1935, Mander was put under contract to 20th Century-Fox as a writer-director and he and his family sailed for the United States and moved into a home at 725 North Rodeo Drive in Beverly Hills, California. For the next six months, Mander sat in his office waiting for an assignment and at the end of that time his contract was revised and he went back to acting for a living. His first film for Fox was a "B" movie starring the German mezzo-soprano Mme. Ernestine Schumann-Heink, *Here's to Romance* (1935), in which he had a small supporting role. But in his next film, *The Three Musketeers* (1935), the role of King Louis XIII gave him an opportunity to be noticed and more important roles started coming his way. In 1938 he was appearing in *Kidnapped*, playing the role of Ebenezer Balfour, the evil uncle of young David Balfour, when he suffered his first heart attack. The studio would have replaced him, but for the intervention of the young actor playing David Balfour, Freddie Bartholomew, who was repaying a debt to the man who first hired him as an actor. The studio kept his role open until Mander could recover and resume work.

The following year Mander revisited the Dumas classic twice more, playing Cardinal Richelieu in the Ritz Brothers' comedy version *The Three Musketeers* with Don Ameche, and as Aramis in *The Man in the Iron Mask* with Louis Hayward and Joan Bennett. In between he played Lockwood, the traveler who is told the tragic story of Cathy and Heathcliff, in *Wuthering Heights* (1939). Some of the other important films in which he appeared were *That Hamilton Woman* (1941), *To Be or Not to Be* (1942), *This Above All* (1942), *Phantom of the Opera* (1943) and *The Picture of Dorian Gray* (1945). His two most memorable performances in later years were as Giles Conover in *The Pearl of Death* (1944) and as Mr. Grayle, Claire Trevor's cuckolded husband, in *Murder My Sweet* (1944).

Mander's health had always been a problem for him and for the studios as well, since they generally required that their actors be covered by cast insurance. From the time of his first heart attack in 1938 onward he suffered from high blood pressure and an enlarged heart, as well as an ailment known at the time as "knotted type veins," which doctors described as the result of a heart or kidney condition. When he was signed to appear in *The Pearl of Death*, the studio's insurance department questioned whether he was physically able to take on the role of Giles Conover. An inter-office communication from Katherine M. Brooker of Universal Pictures' insurance department pointed out that Lloyd's of London had refused to cover him and that the physician's report advised, "That there is a possibility if Mr. Mander would run or be hurried, that he might have a fatal collapse." As it turned out, the studio went ahead and hired him and Mander completed the film without incident, but two years later he suffered a fatal heart attack at the age of 57 while having lunch at the Brown Derby restaurant in Beverly Hills. According to an AP dispatch on March 14, 1945, he left the following message in his will: "I wish to take this last opportunity to express gratitude to the American people and their Government for permitting me to spend the last years of my life in their marvelous country, enjoying the American way of life." Miles Mander was buried in the Ocean View Burial Park in Burnaby, British Columbia, Canada.

DAVID CLYDE came from a theatrical family. His father was the renowned Scottish actor John Clyde who was famous for his portrayal of Scottish hero Rob Roy on the stage and was known as Scotland's first film star for portraying Rob Roy in a silent film in 1911. David Clyde's younger brother was Andrew Clyde, who as Andy Clyde became a Mack Sennett comedian in two-reel comedies in the United States and ultimately made his name as a western character actor who played California Carlson to William Boyd's Hopalong Cassidy in films, radio and television. Clyde's younger sister was Jean Clyde, who would become a prominent British stage actress in England, Australia, South Africa, the United States and Canada. David Clyde, who was born in Glasgow, Scotland on May 27,

1887, was the third of six children of John Clyde and the former Mary Allan. His older brother John Clyde, Jr., who also aspired to be an actor, was killed in World War I. As a young man David traveled with John, Andrew and Jean in his father's repertory company throughout Scotland and, like his siblings, developed a passion for the stage.

By 1924 David Clyde was in London, a member of the Garrick Theatre Company and married to a young actress whose birth name was Dorothy Fay Hammerton, but who was appearing under the name of Gaby Fay. She would lat-

David Clyde as Police Sergeant Thompson in *The Scarlet Claw*.

er change her name once again to Fay Holden and in 1937 would appear as Mrs. Emily Hardy in *You're Only Young Once* at M-G-M and from that point on forever be remembered as Mickey Rooney's mother in the 15 films in the Andy Hardy series.

In 1926, David and Dorothy Clyde traveled to the United States to appear at the Copley Theatre in Boston, and the following year David Clyde and "Gaby Fay" were both appearing on Broadway—David in *The Adventurous Age* at the Mansfield Theatre, and Gaby in *Murray Hill* at the Bijou Theatre. The writer and star of the latter was Leslie Howard. After Gaby (Dorothy) appeared the following year in another comedy, *Dinner is Served*, written and directed by its star Alan Mowbray (who in 1946 co-starred in *Terror by Night*), the Clydes moved to Vancouver, Canada where David bought a part interest in the Empress Theatre and formed a repertory group called the British Guild Players. From 1929 to 1931 the company presented current London and Broadway hits, often with Gaby Fay as the leading lady. One of the members of the company was Basil Radford, who appeared with the British Guild Players until his return to England in 1931. Radford would be remembered for his pairing with actor Naunton Wayne in Hitchcock's *The Lady Vanishes* (1938) as one of the two cricket-obsessed Englishmen on the train. They would reprise these roles in Carol Reed's *Night Train to Munich* (1940).

In 1934, Clyde appeared in the first of the 87 films that he would make in Hollywood, *Molly and Me*. The following year, Dorothy made her rather inauspicious debut as one of the villains in a low-budget exploitation film about drug dealers called *The Pace That Kills* (1935) and David made his first film with Roy William Neill, a romantic adventure called *Eight Bells* (1935) starring Ann Sothern and Ralph Bellamy. Clyde and Neill would ultimately make three more films together, *Frankenstein Meets the Wolf Man* (1943), *The Scarlet Claw* (1944), and *The House of Fear* (1945). David and Dorothy bought a ranch in the San Fernando Valley and the two settled down to a steady routine of film work. In 1937 they both appeared in *Bulldog Drummond Escapes* starring Ray Milland at Paramount. In 1939 they celebrated their twenty-fifth wedding anniversary and several newspaper articles made note of the event, including Louella Parsons: "Fay Holden, Mickey Rooney's ma in the Hardy movies, has a Mr. Hardy in real life. His name is David Clyde and Sunday they will celebrate their twenty-fifth wedding anniversary." Obviously, as far as Ms. Parsons was concerned, Mrs. Clyde had more star power than her husband as she didn't bother to mention that David Clyde was also an actor.

David Clyde met Alan Ladd on the set of *Rulers of the Sea* (1939), an adventure film starring Douglas Fairbanks Jr. David had a featured role and Ladd had a small part that paid him $250. They would work together again in the Clark Gable-Rosalind Russell adventure *They Met in Bombay* (1941), where both played British soldiers dragooned by Clark Gable into one of his disreputable schemes. David apparently helped Ladd with his career in the early days and when Ladd and his wife Sue Carol had their second child a son in 1947, they named him David in Clyde's honor. Ladd would also arrange that Clyde would appear in two of his films, *Salty O'Rourke* (1945) and *Two Years Before the Mast* (1946).

1944-1945 was a busy time for Clyde; apart from appearing in *The House of Fear*, and *Salty O'Rourke*, he also appeared in *Love Letters* with Jennifer Jones, in which he played the postman who brings the eponymous letters, and *The Lost Weekend* with Ray Milland. However, Clyde's health was failing and he died on May 17, 1945 at his ranch in the San Fernando Valley at the age of 60. His final two films, *Two Years Before the Mast* and *Devotion* were released in 1946 after his death. David Clyde is buried in the Forest Lawn Memorial Park in Glendale, California. Fay Holden died of cancer on June 23, 1973 and is also buried at Forest Lawn Memorial Park.

TED BILLINGS' physical appearance made him a natural for horror films and he ultimately made fifteen of them during his 25-year career in films. Most were for Universal Pictures, starting with *Franken-*

stein (1931) and including other classics such as *The Invisible Man* (1933), *Bride of Frankenstein* (1935) and *Tower of London* (1939). He also appeared in the 1932 Fox Films production *Sherlock Holmes* starring Clive Brook and the second of the Rathbone-Holmes films at 20th Century-Fox, *The Adventures of Sherlock Holmes* (1939), in addition to three of the Rathbone/Bruce films at Universal. He was also lurking around in *Hangover Square* (1945) starring Laird Cregar and

Ted Billings as a Villager in the pub in *The Scarlet Claw.*

The Body Snatcher (1945) starring Boris Karloff, Bela Lugosi and Henry Daniell.

Billings, whose real name was Edwin Theodore Billington, was born in London, England on April 8, 1880, the eldest son of Edward J. and Emily Billington. Apart from the record of the births of his brother, Edward T. Billington in 1888 and his sister, Emily (Minnie) Billington in 1890, there is little known about Ted Billings's early life, other than his physical appearance as an adult, which he described on his naturalization papers in October of 1918 as 5'2", 110 lbs., with a fair complexion, brown hair, blue eyes and a broken nose. We do know that Billings immigrated to Canada some time around the turn of the century and then entered the United States by way of the Great Northern Railroad, arriving in Washington State on November 27, 1903. He then made his way to Los Angeles, where he eventually found work in the nascent motion picture industry as a prop man.

With the exception of one screen appearance in 1917 as "The Witch" in a charming children's silent film entitled *The Babes in the Woods* that was filmed in Hawaii, Billings continued working as a prop man for at least the next five years and then alternated for another eight years between the prop department and bit roles in films such as *The Prisoner of Zenda* (1922) and *Robin Hood* (1922). His 1918 draft registration stated that he was employed as a prop man at the Fox Studios on Western Avenue in Hollywood. The *Daily Record* in Ellensburg, Washington on June 3, 1929 featured a syndicated column, "Screen Life in Hollywood" by Robin Coons, which spoke about Ted Billings. "In Hollywood," wrote Coons, "if a man isn't a celebrity, he usually is at least related to one. Ted Billings, diminutive prop man at Warners who seems to carry a whole warehouse of small props in his bulging pockets, claims Josh Billings, the noted American humorist, as his great grandfather." Apparently Billings was embellishing his credentials somewhat because his real last name was Billington and Josh Billings was simply a pen name for the 19th century humorist, whose real name was Henry Wheeler Shaw. Still, you can't blame a man for trying.

In 1919, Billings and Margaret Ludwick were married and moved into a home in Sherman Oaks, California. Margaret had been married previously and had three children, Richard, Elmo and Benny by her first husband, Benjamin Ludwick. The children continued to live with Ted and Margaret until they matured and moved out on their own. By 1931 Ted Billings had given up being a prop man to work full time as an extra and a bit player in films. His first big role (with no dialogue) was in *Bride of Frankenstein* (1935), in which he played Ludwig, helper to Dwight Frye's Karl and to Colin Clive's Henry Frankenstein. Over the years he would work as an extra in crowd scenes in many big films, such as *A Christmas Carol* (1938), *Abe Lincoln in Illinois* (1940) and *Shine on Harvest Moon* (1944). He even played a studio grip in *The Goldwyn Follies* in 1938. Although he very seldom spoke a line of dialogue in any of his films, Billings's unique appearance kept him working in films until he eventually made his 100th screen appearance in a small bit in *Forever Amber* in 1947. Ted Billings died on July 5, 1947 in Sherman Oaks, California and is buried in Pierce Brothers Valhalla Memorial Park in North Hollywood, California.

KAY HARDING's film career encompassed seven films in thirteen months, all for Universal Pictures. She was born Jackie Lou Harding in Cushing, Oklahoma on January 5, 1924 and by the time she was 20-years-old she was in Hollywood playing a small role in her first film, *Weird Woman* (1944), one of Universal's *Inner Sanctum* series starring Lon Chaney. She then did uncredited bit parts in two more Universal films, a musical comedy starring Harriet Hilliard (Mrs. Ozzie Nelson) called *Hi, Good Lookin'!* (1944) and a wartime morale booster titled *Follow the Boys* (1944) that had every star on Universal's contract list in it. Then, given a new first name of Kay by the studio, she played the featured role of Marie Journet in her first Sherlock Holmes film *The Scarlet Claw*, followed by another uncredited role in the Olsen and Johnson comedy *Ghost Catchers* (1944). Based on her performance in *The Scarlet Claw* Universal decided to give her a more prominent role as the ingénue lusted over by Martin Kosleck's character in their final mummy incarnation *The Mummy's Curse* (1944). After that it was a very brief appearance (don't blink or you'll miss her) in the opening sequence of *The Woman in Green* (1945) as the fourth victim and then her career was over. We must assume that, like so many

Kay Harding as Marie Journet, with Nigel Bruce as Doctor Watson in *The Scarlet Claw*.

other young starlets, once she left the business she married and started raising a family; however no record exists of such a romantic climax. We do know that Kay Harding passed away at the age of 60 in Santa Clara, California on March 15, 1984.

The Scarlet Claw was released on May 26, 1944 and the reviews were somewhat mixed, with Bosley Crowther of the *New York Times* still heaping scorn on everyone's efforts with comments such as, "So what have we here but another in a series of B mystery yarns so inferior to Conan Doyle's originals that it isn't even mentionable any more." His compatriot Howard Barnes of *The New York Herald Tribune* was of a similar mind as he wrote, "*The Scarlet Claw* makes much of Sir Arthur Conan Doyle's celebrated sleuth and puts a clown's cap again on Doctor Watson. As a horror film, it is a generally dreary pipedream." At the same time, John T.

McManus of *PM* rather liked Nigel Bruce's efforts writing, "Nigel Bruce, particularly, is certainly as felicitous an incarnation of the fuddly Doctor Watson as anyone could ask, and the little asides and 'businesses' scripted for him seem invariably to be the best parts of any given Sherlock Holmes episode." *The New York World-Telegram's* headline stated its position quite clearly: "Sherlock Holmes Returns as Good Old Hawkshaw," and the Alton Cook review added, "This is Sherlock Holmes in the good old style for a change—instead of his recent reincarnations in the comic strip spirit." The Hollywood trade papers were also more complimentary, with the *Motion Picture Herald* stating, "Ingeniously contrived and tailored to thrill-and-suspense pattern, 'The Scarlet Claw' is one of the tops of Universal's 'Sherlock Holmes' series, swell entertainment for double bill ingredient." And the *Hollywood Reporter* claimed, "The picture is a top line credit for Roy William Neill, who in addition to producing and directing it, also contributed to the screenplay. On all counts, it is a demonstration of ability which should lead to bigger assignments." As a reward for his efforts, Neill would be given the dubiously "bigger assignment" of directing Maria Montez and Jon Hall in *Gypsy Wildcat*, for which he brought along some of his repertory company for support, including Nigel Bruce, Gale Sondergaard and Harry Cording. But first Neill would produce and direct another Sherlock Holmes film, *The Pearl of Death*.

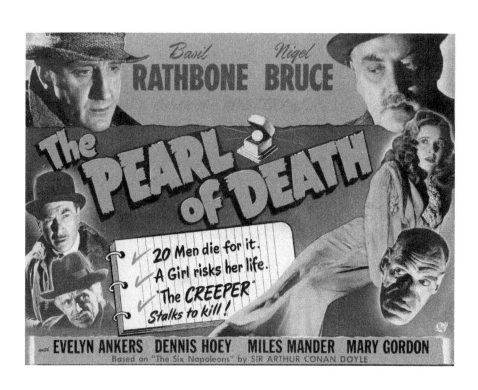

THE PEARL OF DEATH

THE SEVENTH FILM in the Sherlock Holmes cycle, *The Pearl of Death* was a return to the Moriarty formula, although it wasn't the cunning professor who challenged our intrepid detective, but an equally cunning adversary by the name of Giles Conover (Miles Mander) aided by his female assistant Naomi Drake (Evelyn Ankers) and "The Oxton 'Orror," as Inspector Lestrade dubbed him, as played by Rondo Hatton. Bertram Millhauser's screenplay, for which he was paid $7,150, was a loose adaptation of Sir Arthur Conan Doyle's "The Adventure of the Six Napoleons" from *The Return of Sherlock Holmes*, with Millhauser taking the six plaster busts of Napoleon and adding "The Creeper" to commit the murders in Conover's search to reclaim the Borgia Pearl. Millhauser completed a revised draft of the screenplay and it was submitted to the Breen Office on March 1, 1944. The initial response was a "strong concern for repeated references to violence—particularly in regard to the 'Creeper's' character." As Millhauser worked to accommodate the censor's concerns, Roy William Neill began filming on April 11, 1944, with a scene involving Basil Rathbone, Nigel Bruce and Dennis Hoey on the set of Holmes's Baker Street flat on Universal's Stage 14. According to the assistant director's report they completed the sequence at 12:55 and broke for lunch. Neill would finish filming on April 20, two days over schedule and just slightly under the original $192,225 budget, which reflected a sizable raise in Nigel Bruce's salary (from the $5,700 he'd made on the previous film to $12,000). The budget continued to allocate $20,000 for Basil Rathbone's salary and also $3,500 for Evelyn Ankers, who was under a term contract to the studio. Dennis Hoey again received $1,000 a week, Miles Mander $750 a week and Rondo Hatton $350 for one week's work.

The Pearl of Death seems to miss the dynamic presence of a Moriarty, presenting instead the lethargic Giles Conover as played by Miles Mander. It is however, bolstered by Evelyn Ankers' performance and the many disguises she assumes. We first meet her in her glamorous Naomi Drake mode, on board the Dover Ferry as she enters the cabin of James Goodram (Holmes Herbert) and steals the Borgia Pearl that has been concealed in his specially constructed suitcase, and then rejoins an elderly clergyman in one of the deck chairs. This is of course Sherlock Holmes in one of his many elderly disguises and before the ferry docks he has taken possession of the pearl, now hidden in Naomi Drake's camera. Because Naomi has used the ruse of not wanting her photographs ruined by being exposed and has asked the clergyman to carry the camera through customs for her, we must assume that the Dover Ferry is arriving from a foreign port—but since it is 1944 and Cherbourg, (the ferry's usual port of departure) was in Nazi occupied France, where in fact are these travelers coming from?

James Goodram identifies himself to the customs officer (Leyland Hodgson) as a courier for the Royal Museum, bringing in the Borgia Pearl, only to discover that the pearl has been stolen from his suitcase. Upon retrieving the camera from Holmes's clergyman, Naomi hurries to a car and finds Giles Conover waiting for her. In conversation he reveals to the terrified Naomi the presence of "The Creeper," who he has found prowling around her room, "making wistful little noises like a dog." She is perfectly safe, he assures her; "I have him under lock and key." When Conover opens the camera he finds it empty, save for a note signed "S.H." He informs Naomi, "You've been *had*, my dear, properly *had*." The note is from "Sherlock Holmes of Baker Street."

At 221 Baker Street, Holmes removes his disguise and shows Watson the Borgia Pearl, revealing the pearl's worth of fifty thousand pounds and its history of violent deaths down through the centuries. He informs Watson of his newest adversary. "In his whole diabolical career, the police have never been able to pin anything on him. And yet show me crime without motive, robbery without a clue, murder without a trace and I'll show you Giles Conover." Lestrade arrives to escort the Borgia Pearl to the Royal Regent Museum, where the curator, Frances Digby (Charles Francis), demonstrates the security precautions. In a nice change of pace for Holmes's character he is made to look the fool: In an attempt to show the curator that the pearl is not really safe, he inadvertently enables Conover to steal it. (This was the scene I observed them filming in 1944.)

When Conover is quickly captured by Police Sergeant Murdock (Leslie Denison) and the pearl is missing, Holmes has Lestrade arrange to hold him for two days and allow his food to come from a nearby café in the hopes that he will attempt to contact his accomplices. An amusing scene between Dennis Hoey's Lestrade and Billy Bevan's police constable fails to turn up the expected clue, but the dishes lead us to Naomi Drake, posing as a Cockney dishwasher, who finds the message at the bottom of a plate of thick soup.

The murder of a retired Major Harker, whose spine has been broken, is the clue Holmes has been waiting for: A visit to the murder scene reveals a great deal of broken pottery and dishes scattered about the room. Watson's examination of the body discloses that the victim's spine was crushed at the third lumbar vertebrae, from which Holmes deduces that the murderer must be "The Hoxton Creeper," the only murderer to kill in that fashion. Holmes's and Watson's discussion out on the street of the connection between Giles Conover and the "Creeper" is overheard by Naomi Drake, now posing as an old match woman, and a moment later some of Conover's gang try to shoot them. The film has a tendency to stop the action several times for a comedy moment, such as the scene between Lestrade and the police constable, and now it does it again with a slightly less amusing routine involving Watson's glue pot and a newspaper clipping. This moment is interrupted by a visit from a disguised Giles Conover, carrying a booby-trapped book intended for Sherlock Holmes. Roy

Giles Conover (Miles Mander, right) confronts Basil Rathbone as Sherlock Holmes and Dennis Hoey as Inspector Lestrade. With Charles Francis' Francis Digby and Nigel Bruce's Doctor Watson looking on. In *The Pearl of Death*.

William Neill manages to create a good deal of tension as Watson toys with the book without opening it, while we the audience squirm, knowing that death awaits the person who does.

Several more deaths of a similar nature, with broken china and pottery covering the bodies, lead Holmes to conclude that the china has been broken to cover up some other motive for the murders and that it would happen again. And sure enough, our very next image is that of the "Creeper," a shadowy, hulking figure, committing another murder that ends with more broken china and blaring newspaper headlines. In examining the broken shards, Holmes and Watson discover several pieces from identical shattered plaster busts of Napoleon Bonaparte, all recovered at separate murder sites. This leads them to the pottery shop of George Gelder (Harry Cording) where they learn from Police Sergeant Murdock that Giles Conover was alone in the shop for a few moments before Murdock captured him. Gelder informs Holmes that six copies of the Napoleon bust were sold to a dealer named Amos Hodder (Ian Wolfe) and that a woman had also inquired about them. "Naomi Drake," exclaims Holmes as they rush from the shop. A visit to Amos Hodder's shop reveals Naomi Drake, impersonating a bespectacled saleswoman, who eavesdrops on Holmes's conversation with Hodder. The trail now leads to Doctor Boncourt, the one remaining owner of a Napoleon bust who is still alive, and to the climax of the film.

Roy William Neill was clever to never show the "Creeper's" face until the very end of the film, using shadows and close-ups of his latex-covered hands to establish his presence. Neill knew that once he revealed Rondo Hatton's face to the audience, any future attempt to create a sense of dread would be anticlimactic. And so the "Creeper" continues to move in the shadows until Conover confronts Doctor Boncourt only to find that he is in fact Sherlock Holmes in disguise. When Conover calls upon his fearsome accomplice to finish the job, we see Rondo Hatton for the very first time and it is indeed a shocking moment, with Neill and cinematographer Virgil Miller placing their camera and lights below eye level to enhance Hatton's startling features. Holmes, playing on the "Creeper's" infatuation for Naomi Drake, deceives him into believing that Naomi will hang for the murder of Doctor Watson. This infuriates the "Creeper" and he turns on Conover, snapping his back and killing him.

The Borgia Pearl is found inside the last Napoleon bust and as Lestrade and his men literally go in to pick up the pieces, Holmes recites another of his closing epigrams. This time at least it doesn't deal with the War, but with mankind's greed, cruelty and lust for power, "That has set men at each other's throats down through the centuries. And the struggle will go on, Watson, for a pearl, a kingdom, perhaps even world dominion, until

Rondo Hatton as "The Creeper" killing Giles Conover (Miles Mander) in *The Pearl of Death*.

the greed and cruelty are burned out of every last one of us. And when that time comes, perhaps even the pearl will be washed clean again."

The Roy William Neill repertory company was well represented in this film, what with the regulars Dennis Hoey (Lestrade) and Mary Gordon (Mrs. Hudson), plus Miles Mander (Giles Conover), Evelyn Ankers (Naomi Drake), Ian Wolfe (Amos Hodder), Holmes Herbert (James Goodram), Leslie Denison (Police Sergeant Murdock), Harry Cording (George Gelder), Harold De Becker (Café Boss) and Leyland Hodgson (Customs Officer). The new additions were Billy Bevan (Police Constable), Charles Francis (Francis Digby), Lillian Bronson (Major Harker's Housekeeper), Colin Kenny (Museum Guard), Wilson Benge (Second Ship's Steward), Charles Knight (the bearded man at the Museum) and of course Rondo Hatton (the Creeper).

RONDO HATTON appeared in only one of the Sherlock Holmes films and was supposedly shot and killed by Sherlock Holmes in *The Pearl of Death*, but that didn't stop Universal from bringing the "Creeper" back in two more films, *House of Horrors* (1946) and *The Brute Man* (1946).

Rondo Hatton as "The Creeper" in a publicity photo for *The Pearl of Death*.

Rondo K. Hatton was born in Hagerstown, Maryland on April 22, 1894, the eldest son of Stewart and Emily Hatton. The parents were both school-teachers who had traveled to Maryland from Missouri in the years be-fore Hatton's birth. Soon the Hatton family was moving again, by way of Hickory, North Carolina and Charles Town, West Virginia, finally arriving in Tampa, Florida where, after Hatton's father's death, the family lived with his grandmother and Hatton graduated from Hillsborough High School. A good-looking young man at the time, Hatton was supposedly voted handsomest boy in his class. After graduating, Hatton went to work for the local newspaper as a sportswriter and joined the Florida National Guard. In March of 1916 his unit was activated and he was sent to the Mexican border to help General "Black Jack" Pershing pursue Pancho Villa. After nine unsuccessful months of pursuit, Villa remained at large and President Wilson recalled the troops in preparation for The Great War.

While serving in France, Hatton was exposed to mustard gas and received a medical discharge and a pension. He returned to Florida and joined *The Tampa Tribune* as a reporter and eventually married Elizabeth Immell James on April 15, 1926. The first signs of the disease acromegaly began appearing around this time; the disease is initially hard to diagnose and was probably present for many years before changes in Hatton's face and hands became noticeable. Acromegaly results when the pituitary gland produces excess growth hormones and is often associated with gigantism. Other victims of the disease are actor Richard Kiel (*The Spy Who Loved Me* [1977]) and wrestler-actor Andre the Giant (*The Princess Bride* [1987]).

Hatton was divorced from Elizabeth in 1930 and that same year, while assigned by his newspaper to cover the making of the motion picture *Hell Harbor* (1930) that was filming on location in Rocky Point, Hatton interviewed Henry King, who was producing and directing this, his first sound film for Inspiration Pictures starring Lupe Velez and Jean Hersholt. King talked Hatton into portraying a dance hall bouncer in the film and suggested that he should come out to Hollywood and try acting as a profession. Hatton arrived in Hollywood in early 1937, managing to make contact with Henry King who gave him a fairly substantial supporting role, with several lines of dialogue, as Brian Donlevy's bodyguard, also named Rondo, in the 20th Century-Fox film *In Old Chicago* (1937). From that point on most of Hatton's roles were non-speaking bits that took advantage of his appearance, such as one of the contestants in the ugly-man contest in *The Hunchback of Notre Dame* (1939) and the leper in *The Moon and Sixpence* (1942). He can be seen as one of the cowboys in the bar, listening as Henry Fonda reads Dana Andrews' letter to his wife in *The Ox-Bow Incident* (1943).

In 1944 Hatton was signed by Universal Pictures to appear in *The Pearl of Death* as the Hoxton Creeper and his appearance caused enough of an audience reaction to warrant the studio casting him in its production of *The Jungle Captive* (1945) and putting him under contract. They promoted him in the press, saying his appearance was caused by his wartime exposure to mustard gas, and cast him in their serial *The Royal Mounted Rides Again* (1945). Subsequently he played a character henchman to Gale Sondergaard in *The Spider Woman Strikes Back* (1946) and The Creeper in *House of Horrors* (1946). In his final film *The Brute Man* (1946) he is the title character, a man disfigured and turned into a monster by an accident during a college chemistry lab experiment. His acting in this film leaves a great deal to be desired and one wonders how much longer his career might have lasted had he not died of a heart attack on February 2, 1946. In fact Universal didn't release *The Brute Man*, but sold it to Producers Releasing Corporation (PRC) as the studio was changing hands and being merged with International Pictures to become Universal-International Pictures. Rondo Hatton is buried in the American Legion Cemetery in Tampa, Florida and his legacy is perpetuated by the Classic Horror Film Board with their Rondo Award that honors all forms of the horror media.

BILLY BEVAN, with his droopy walrus mustache and Cockney accent, is arguably the most recognizable of all of the Roy William Neill repertory players, and yet he only appeared in two of the Sherlock Holmes films. In fact Bevan, whose real name was William Bevan Harris, never set foot in England. He was born on September 29, 1887 in Orange, New South Wales, Australia. Bevan, whose career lasted over 46 years, began on the Australian stage at the age of 17 with the Australian Light Opera Company. Bevan was only 5'5" tall, so he was a perfect choice for the Pollard's Lilliputian Opera Company, a light opera company made up mostly of children who performed Vaudeville skits and musical comedies

Billy Bevan as he appeared as the passenger car attendant in *Terror By Night*.

on tour in Australia and New Zealand. In 1912 when the Pollard Opera Company divided into two sections, Bevan crossed the Atlantic to tour with them in Canada and the United States. According to the *Blue Book of the Screen*, published in 1923, Bevan played Blinky Bill in *The Belle of New York*, Koko in *The Mikado* and leading roles in the *Geisha, Floradora* and *Santoy*. It was during this period with the Pollard Opera Company that Bevan undoubtedly came to know fellow Australian actor Harold Fraser, later to change his name to Snub Pollard and become one of silent films' leading comics. Although both Bevan and Pollard sported large, droopy mustaches and made hundreds of silent film comedies, they both appeared in only two films in the early 1940s, *The Earl of Chicago* (1940) and *Confirm or Deny* (1941).

In February of 1914 Bevan resigned from the Pollard Opera Company and traveled on the S.S. *Princess Victoria* from Vancouver, British Colombia to Seattle, Washington to join the Isobelle Fletcher stock company. Bevan's first film appearance was in 1916 for Henry Lehrman's company L-KO (Lehrman Knock Out) in the comedy short *Dad's Dollars and Dirt Doings*. Within months he was starring in his own short films, such as *A Wise Waiter*, or supporting L-KO stars such as Alice Howell and Lehrman's answer to Fatty Arbuckle, Fatty Voss. Over the next three years Bevan appeared in twenty film shorts for Henry Lehrman's company and in 1918 he was signed to a long-term contract by Mack Sennett. From then until sound came in in 1929, Bevan played alongside such Sennett stars as Mabel Normand, Ben Turpin and Edgar Kennedy, finally starring in his own shorts starting in 1921.

Billy Bevan and a bevy of bathing beauties from one of his silent comedies.

In 1917 Bevan married Leona Roberts, a New York native of Hungarian ancestry, and bought a home in Beverly Hills at 919 Roxbury Drive. They had two daughters, Edith, born in 1919, and Joan, born in 1922. Bevan continued making sound shorts during the early 1930s (occasionally for Mack Sennett), such as a two-reel sound short with Andy Clyde called *Scotch* (1930), and starring in *Who's Who in the Zoo* (1931), and *The Spot on the Rug* (1932) and the RKO short, *Frozen Face* (1931). By 1933 he had become a character actor and was playing supporting roles in features, such as Hale in John Ford's *The Lost Patrol* (1934), Jerry Cruncher in *A Tale of Two Cities* (1935) and one of the English Bobbies, along with Halliwell Hobbes, who discover Dracula's grave in *Dracula's Daughter* (1936). His other horror film roles were in *The Invisible Man Returns* (1940), *The Return of the Vampire* (1944) and *The Lodger* (1944).

In 1950 Bevan appeared as Will Scarlett in his penultimate film, Columbia Pictures' *Rogues of Sherwood Forrest* starring John Derek and Diana Lynn, along with fellow Roy William Neill repertory company members Paul Cavanagh, Harry Cording, Leslie Denison, Olaf Hytten, Guy Kingsford and Gavin Muir.. On November 26, 1957, after appearing in 141 short films and 114 feature films, Billy Bevan died in Escondido, California at the age of 70.

CHARLES FRANCIS was born in Burton Upon Irwell, Lancaster, England on July 23, 1885, the fourth of six children of the Reverend Albert E. Francis and his wife, Emily. Reverend Francis was the vicar of St. Catherine's Church in Burton Upon Irwell and the large household was waited upon by several servants. Another child, a daughter named Mary, was born in 1893. In 1901 Reverend Francis died of illness along with two of his children, Beatrice and Edward.

Charles A. Francis began his acting career in repertory in the small town of Nelson in Lancaster County, but was soon making the transatlantic crossing to appear in Broadway productions. His first roles on Broadway were in a repertory company's revival of two Henri Bernstein plays, *The Thief* and *The Whirlwind* at Daly's Theatre in October and November

Charles Francis as Francis Digby, with Nigel Bruce and Basil Rathbone in *The Pearl of Death*.

of 1911. Shortly thereafter he was signed to appear in two original plays at the Hudson Theatre, in the second of which, *The Lady of Dreams*, one of his co-players was Margaret Wycherly, later to be remembered as Gary Cooper's mother in *Sergeant York* (1941) and Jimmy Cagney's mother in *White Heat* (1949). Francis became a member of the Players Club near Gramercy Place and remained in New York until July of 1916 when he returned to England and was recruited into the British Army, serving until the end of the war.

While still in the army, Francis returned to the United States in March of 1918 in an original play with music called *Getting Together* that was cast with veterans of the British Army and received quite stunning reviews. The *New York Times'* review had the following headline: "*Getting Together* is the real thing; Rousing melodrama, with real war heroes and a tank in action." The reviewer went on to write, "*Getting Together*, which was produced last night at the Lyric, in a generous effort to persuade the British and Canadians among us to enlist before they are nabbed by the draft, is melodrama of a new sort. The result is by far the most moving and the most thrilling war melodrama that has yet been seen here." A real army tank was indeed featured in a trench scene, pushing its way through barbed wire. Private Charles Francis portrayed a British soldier, a British surgeon and the character of Death.

On May 30, 1930, Francis married Louise Reinhardt of Delaware and they had a daughter, Rosemary, born in Wilmington, Delaware on August 31, 1931. From that point on, Charles Francis continued to commute regularly with his family between London and New York, appearing in more than twenty Broadway productions until Universal Pictures signed him to a two-picture contract in 1938. After appearing in two "B" dramas, *The Jury's Secret* (1938) and *Strange Faces* (1938), Francis returned to New York for a featured role in *The Flying Gerardos,* which had a short run at the Playhouse Theatre, and then back to Hollywood to appear in Frank Lloyd's *The Howards of Virginia* (1940) with future Roy William Neill repertory company players, Vernon Downing, Leyland Hodgson and Olaf Hytten, as well as an unknown bit-player named Alan Ladd. One more play, *The Wookey* starring Edmund Gwenn and Heather Angel, which ran from September of 1941 to January of 1942, and Francis was back in Hollywood to pursue his brief film career. From 1942, starting with the Tyrone Power adventure film *The Black Swan*, until 1944, when he completed Roy William Neill's, *The Scarlet Claw* and *The Pearl of Death*, Francis appeared in only four films, including a wonderful bit in Warner's *Thank Your Lucky Stars* (1943) when Bette Davis sang Arthur Schwartz and Frank Loesser's "They're Either Too Young or Too Old" to him in an amusing night club sequence.

In 1946, my father took his play *The Haven* to New York, along with a group of his fellow actors from Hollywood including Melville Cooper and his wife Elizabeth Sutherland, Valerie Cossart, Dennis King and Charles Francis, who played the pivotal role of Inspector Ramsey. Unfortunately the play closed after three nights and everyone except Francis returned to Hollywood. Francis remained in New York and continued to perform in theatre for the next eight years, retiring to Connecticut in 1954 after playing the sea captain in the original production of *The King and I* for its entire run of 1,246 performances. He returned from retirement briefly in 1958 to appear in an episode of a short-lived television series called *Adventures of the Sea Hawk,* starring John Howard. Charles A. Francis died in Litchfield, Connecticut in October of 1968 at the age of 83.

LILLIAN BRONSON is another perfect example of an unrecognized, but talented performer. In the latter part of her life she appeared quite regularly on television and I remember seeing this handsome woman with white hair and a soft voice, most times playing someone's relative—usually the leading lady's mother or aunt—and being enormously impressed with the quiet strength that she displayed. And at the time, I don't think I ever knew her name.

Lillian Bronson was born on October 21, 1902 in the town of Lockport, New York, the third of three daughters of Sylvester Marvin Bronson and the former Emma Huber. The Bronson family was well known in Lockport: In 1851, Sylvester's grandfather Ira founded the Ira Bronson Carriage Company, later to be known as Bronson & Son. Their carriages were considered the best in the country and several were displayed at the Paris World Exposition in 1889. By 1919 Sylvester Bronson had an automobile repair business and his daughter Lillian was about to graduate from Lockport Union High School. She went on to study drama at Bryn Mawr in Pennsylvania and then on to the University of Michigan. After graduation, Lillian moved to New York and by December of 1930 she was appearing in her first Broadway production, an original melodrama called *Five Star Final.* The play had a nice run of six months and soon after Lillian was again performing on Broadway at the Forrest Theatre in *Lean Harvest,* a drama directed by and starring British actor Leslie Banks (*The Man Who Knew Too Much* [1934]) and another actor with whom she would work again several times in films, Nigel Bruce.

Bronson would appear in one more production, a 1932 revival of *Camille* starring Lillian Gish, before taking a break from the Broadway stage. She returned in 1947 in a new play by John Van Druten starring Leo G. Carroll called *The Druid Circle.* Considering that she didn't arrive in Hol-

lywood until the early 1940s, one might assume that she found employment in off-Broadway and road productions and in the numerous radio
programs that were being produced in New York at that time. Her first film
was *Happy Land* (1943), as Mattie Dyer, one of the denizens of a small Mid-
western town who suffer with Don Ameche, the town's druggist, the loss
of his son in the war. Bronson appeared in ten films in 1944, including *The
Pearl of Death*, *Gaslight* and *The Invisible Man's Revenge*. By 1953 when she
made her first television appearance she had performed in over sixty motion pictures. Her first foray into television was with fellow Roy William
Neill repertory company member Hillary Brooke in *The Abbot & Costello
Show* in 1953 and from that point on, with a few exceptions such as *So This
Is Love* (1953), *The McConnell Story* (1955) and *Spencer's Mountain* (1963),
she worked exclusively in television. Her performance in *Spencer's Mountain* earned her the following from reviewer Bruce Elder: "There's also a
good bit of human drama here, and some especially nuanced performances
by Donald Crisp and Lillian Bronson, as Fonda's aging parents."

Lillian Bronson as Major Harker's housekeeper in *The Pearl of Death*.

The Kent Twitchell mural of Lillian Bronson.

Bronson would ultimately guest star in 109 separate television productions; sometimes reappearing in a continuing role such as Grandma in *King's Row,* or a judge on *Perry Mason,* or in a variety of roles in different episodes, as was the case with Jack Webb who liked her work enough to hire her eight times in three different series, *Dragnet, Adam-12* and *Emergency!* In 1973, the Los Angeles Inner City Mural Program commissioned muralist Kent Twitchell to paint a giant mural on the side of a building near the Hollywood Freeway's downtown interchange. After spending hours poring over photographs in the Screen Actors Guild directory, Twitchell chose Lillian Bronson as the model for his mural because she reminded him of his grandmother and painted her with a flowing afghan streaming out behind her. The mural was painted over with a billboard in 1986 and Twitchell won an out-of-court settlement to pay for restoring the mural and a smaller version now exists. I personally don't see that strong a resemblance with the likeness of Lillian Bronson, since the woman in the mural wears a worried expression that belies the inner calm that Bronson always conveyed.

Bronson's last appearance as an actress was as Fonzie's grandmother in an episode of *Happy Days* in 1975, after which she retired to Laguna Beach, California where she lived until her death on August 1, 1995 at the San Clemente Hospital of complications from a stroke. Her legacy lives on with the Lillian Bronson collection at the University of Southern California's Doheny Library and at DeFlippo's Bed and Breakfast in her hometown of Lockport, New York, where the Lillian Bronson Room has been named in her honor.

CHARLES KNIGHT's appearance as the bearded man in the Royal Regent Museum sequence suggests that Roy William Neill had originally intended to make more of his presence, even awarding him a close-up at one point, but as it stands it's hard to fathom why he is there at all, except to briefly become a red herring who ends up going nowhere and is never explained. Knight, an Englishman, whose full name was Charles William Knight, was born on March 23, 1879 and made his screen debut in a John Wayne *3 Mesquiteers* western called *Pals of the Saddle* (1938) at Republic Studios, ultimately appearing in 22 films. He frequently played the role of a butler in a number of Three Stooges shorts and it was in these films that he would receive his only on-screen credits. In 1943 he appeared briefly on Broadway in an original comedy called *Try and Get It!* that closed after eight performances. His other films included *The Lodger* (1944), *Enter Arsine Lupin* (1944) and *Two Guys from Milwaukee*

Charles Knight as he appeared as the baggage car guard in *Terror by Night*.

(1946) in which he was once again a butler. He would appear in two more films in the Sherlock Holmes series, *The Scarlet Claw* (1944) in which he appeared briefly as the assistant police inspector and in *Terror by Night* (1946) in which he was the sinister-looking guard in the train's baggage car. Charles Knight died on January 24, 1979 at the age of 93 in Panorama City, California.

COLIN KENNY, who appears briefly as the museum guard who lets Holmes, Watson and Lestrade out of Francis Digby's office after Giles Conover had locked them in, was an Irish actor who began acting in films in the early silent era. Born Oswald Joseph Collins in Dublin, Ireland on December 4, 1888, Kenny was educated in England and established himself on the British stage before coming to the United States in 1917. His first film was the Elmo Lincoln starrer *Tarzan of the Apes* (1918) and for the next eleven years, until the advent of sound, he was featured in over thirty films. Kenny made his first screen appearance for Universal (then known as Universal Film Manufacturing Company) in *The Triflers* (1920). In 1928 he returned briefly to London to appear in featured roles in a silent film for British International Pictures, *Honeymoon Abroad* (1928), and then a sound film for British Lion Film Corporation, *The Clue of the New Pin* (1929). By 1930 Kenny and his French actress wife Mathilde had returned to the United States, where with both being in their 40s they were more suited for character roles and the parts grew smaller with fewer screen credits. Kenny still managed an average of six films a year, appearing in such classics as *Clive of India* (1935), *Captain Blood* (1935), *The Adventures of Robin Hood* (1938) and *The Sea Hawk* (1940). In later years he would frequently appear as a military officer or a policeman in such films as *Dr. Jekyll and Mr. Hyde* (1941), *Mrs. Miniver* (1942) and *Ministry of Fear* (1944). He also appeared in his share of horror films, both at Universal and elsewhere, including *Tower of London* (1939), *The Invisible Man Returns* (1940), *The Leopard Man* (1943), *The Lodger* (1944) and *The Brighton Strangler* (1945). His role of the bogus constable in *Terror by Night* who goes to bring Alan Mowbray to the dining car would mark

Colin Kenny as the Museum Guard in *The Pearl of Death*.

his final appearance in the Sherlock Homes series. Colin Kenny would ultimately appear in over 200 film and television roles before his death, two days before his 80th birthday, on December 2, 1968 in Los Angeles, California.

The Pearl of Death opened at the Rialto Theatre in New York on August 25, 1944 and this time the reviews were all on the positive side with *the New York Daily News* proclaiming, "All murder mystery fans have a soft spot in their hearts for Arthur Conan Doyle's ace sleuth, Sherlock Holmes. They will be gratified to know that 'The Pearl of Death,' latest in the series, is one of the best." The *New York World-Telegram* singled out Rondo Hatton's performance writing: "The Creeper himself is shown mostly as a shadowy smudge moving eerily on walls and floors; You don't get a look at his pan till the very end. Then you'll wish you hadn't. This lad doesn't need a Frankenstein mask. Boris Karloff is a Greek god beside him." Even the *New York Times* had good things to say, announcing, "The picture builds up suspense and, of course, holds a good share of thrills and horror-chills. The Rathbone-Bruce team turns in a good, solid performance, as does Miles Mander, who plays the role of a nefarious and

My autographed photo of Nigel Bruce and Basil Rathbone.

clever jewel thief. Dennis Hoey, as scowling detective Lestrade, plays his part broadly but effectively." The *New York Journal-American* even singled out Bertram Millhauser for anonymous praise, saying, "With Basil Rathbone once again impersonating Sherlock Holmes and with Nigel Bruce carrying on as Doctor Watson, this one emerges as better-than-average in the Holmes series, chiefly because the scenarist in 'adapting' Doyle, retained as much of the original story as possible."

I have fond memories of my visit that day to the set of *The Pearl of Death* and the excitement it created in me that would one day influence my decision to choose motion pictures as my career, a decision that I have never regretted. For a long time after that visit, I kept two autographed photographs on my bedroom wall—the first was of Basil Rathbone and Nigel Bruce in their familiar pose standing side by side, and the second was a head shot of Nigel Bruce upon which he had inscribed the following: "To Michael, who is a nice boy in spite of his father." One day that photo just disappeared from its place on my bedroom wall and I never saw it again. I suppose that my father grew tired of the sentiment, even though it was written in jest. The other autographed photo remains a treasured part of my film memorabilia connection.

THE HOUSE OF FEAR

WRITER ROY CHANSLOR WAS HIRED by Universal and paid $3,750 to create a script based on Conan Doyle's story "The Five Orange Pips" from *Adventures of Sherlock Holmes.* He came up with a suspenseful tale that the studio dubbed *The House of Fear,* borrowing the title from a 1939 film they had made with the same name starring William Gargan and Irene Hervey. The studio was again emphasizing the horror aspects of the film, later proclaiming on one of their lobby posters, "HORROR Stalking its halls!" Chanselor finished a first draft in early April of 1944 and it was sent to the Production Code Administration offices on the corner of Beverly Boulevard and La Cienega Boulevard in West Hollywood. The studio received initial

qualified approval, subject to removal of references to prussic acid, which the code felt would be found objectionable by Political Censor Boards. At this time there were still individual censor boards in many states, including Pennsylvania, Massachusetts, New York, Ohio and Kansas and even Ontario, Canada. The Production Code would attempt to coordinate with these boards and would frequently advise the studios on items in their scripts that they thought might be found objectionable by the local boards. The Code would refer to these boards as "Political Censor Boards." As it turned out, the references to prussic acid remained in the film.

Aubrey Mather was signed by the studio to play the pivotal role of Bruce Alastair in *The House of Fear* and his contract called for him to be paid the flat sum of $3,500. Dennis Hoey's contract called for him to be paid the usual $1,000 a week for 1 5/6 weeks work, a total of $1,834. Rathbone and Bruce continued to receive their usual salaries of $20,000 and $12,000 respectively and Roy William Neill his $5,700. Technical Advisor Tom McKnight received $500 as authorized by Howard Benedict, who was still the executive producer receiving $2,750, although he no longer received screen credit. Prior to their beginning filming both Aubrey Mather and Dennis Hoey were subjected to a physical examination for cast insurance and both were passed by the studio physician. The studio's initial budget called for 16 shooting days at a cost of $192,250. Director Neill began filming on May 9, 1944 and finished on May 26, 1944, which was three days over schedule for a final cost of $197,568.

Screenwriter Chanslor took the Conan Doyle original story "The Five Orange Pips," with its bizarre mystery involving the Ku Klux Klan and slavery in America and its somewhat unsatisfactory resolution and, after borrowing a plot device from Agatha Christie's *Ten Little Indians*, the title from a 1939 Universal film and some creative rewriting on his part, turned it into a basic whodunit. The film begins with a highly atmospheric introduction to the seven members of the Good Comrades seated at their dinner table, narrated by a Mr. Chalmers (Gavin Muir), who describes the deaths of two of The Good Comrades and the curse of Drearcliff House where "No man ever goes whole to his grave." We then find ourselves in Sherlock Holmes's flat as Chalmers, who represents an insurance firm, expresses his concern that the deaths are suspicious. The Good Comrades have established an investment plan involving mutual insurance policies with each member naming the others as beneficiaries. Now that two of the original seven Comrades have died violent deaths, Chalmers is concerned that there may be a plot by one of the survivors to kill the others. Holmes, intrigued to learn that each death is preceded by the delivery of an envelope containing a certain number of orange pips, accepts the case.

Drearcliff House, which is supposedly on the west coast of Scotland, is a dreary mansion situated high on a cliff, as established by a distant matte shot of the house and cliffs—the same shot that was used to establish the bombed out church housing the Nazi spies in the finale of *Sherlock Holmes and the Voice of Terror*. The interior is in fact a redress of the Musgrave Manor set from *Sherlock Holmes Faces Death*, complete with oak staircase and paneled windows with lots of lightning effects. Once again, Roy William Neill and his director of photography Virgil Miller use the camera imaginatively to achieve an excellent sense of foreboding over the ensuing action.

Holmes and Watson arrive at the village of Ingramere in time to witness a funeral procession. Afraid that they may be too late and another of the Good Comrades has died, Holmes learns from shop owner Alex MacGregor (David Clyde) that it is actually the village blacksmith, "Cut down in the flower of his manhood," he declares. Watson solicitously asks his age and MacGregor replies, "Just 72." Upon entering the village pub they are observed by Doctor Simon Merrivale (Paul Cavanagh) as they follow Bessie the barmaid (Doris Lloyd) to the desk to sign the register. Merrivale returns to Drearcliff House to inform his fellow Comrades, Bruce Alastair (Aubrey Mather), Captain John Simpson (Harry Cording)

The Good Comrades toast their missing member. From left, Cyril Delevanti, Harry Cording, Paul Cavanagh, Wilson Benge, Aubrey Mather and Holmes Herbert.

and Alan Cosgrave (Holmes Herbert) that Sherlock Holmes has arrived to investigate the deaths of their fellow Comrades, Ralph King (Richard Alexander) and Stanley Raeburn (Cyril Delevanti). The fifth member of the Good Comrades, Guy Davis (Wilson Benge), is ominously missing from the group and only Bruce Alastair seems genuinely pleased to hear the news of Holmes's arrival.

Holmes and Watson question MacGregor, while plying him with whiskey, and learn the history of the Alastair clan and their horrible deaths. David Clyde gives a most amusing performance as the sodden MacGregor, pilfering his host's glasses and downing their whiskey while proclaiming that Drearcliff House is haunted by the "memory of evil." The Good Comrades' housekeeper Mrs. Monteith (Sally Shepherd) enters the pub to announce to the local police sergeant (David Thursby) that another murder has occurred. Holmes and Watson accompany the sergeant to Drearcliff House where they are greeted by Bruce Alastair, who upon recognizing Holmes chatters excitedly, "Oh, this is excellent, most excellent!" Guy Davis's body is found in the furnace, burnt beyond recognition. After learning that Mrs. Monteith has been keeping a letter for him that contains five orange pips, Holmes suggests that Scotland Yard be notified. The following morning Captain Simpson discovers a needle in his chair and Holmes, after testing it with chemicals, reveals that the pin contains a deadly poison. Later that evening, another attempt appears to be made on Simpson's life when he halts in the middle of a toast to their departed friend Guy Davis and declares that his wine has a peculiar odor. Holmes explains that the odor of bitter almonds suggests the presence of prussic acid, a form of cyanide. Simpson is visibly upset and, after accusing his fellow Comrades of trying to kill him, storms out of the room, leaving the others to complete the toast, but only after Doctor Merrivale exchanges glasses with a nervous Bruce Alastair. A somber Mrs. Monteith arrives, bearing a letter for Alan Cosgrave that contains four orange pips.

After the Good Comrades have retired for the evening, with Doctor Merrivale offering to stay in Cosgrave's room overnight, Holmes and Watson return to the study and discuss the mysterious events. This is the second time in this film that screenwriter Chanslor uses this rather static device of reviewing past events and Roy William Neill is called upon to use all of his directorial skills to keep the audience involved in the story. During this lengthy discussion we the audience learn that the needle in Capt. Simpson's chair was undoubtedly placed there by Simpson himself and the "poison" in Simpson's wine was actually nothing more than almond concentrate placed there by Holmes to judge his reaction, which, in the second instance, was genuine fear. After Holmes interrupts an attempt on Watson's life, Inspector Lestrade (Dennis Hoey) and Sergeant Bleeker (Leslie Denison) arrive just in time to hear Alastair proclaim that the door to Cosgrave's room is locked and he's been unable to elicit a response. Doctor Merrivale is found unconscious on the floor and Cosgrave is missing. Lestrade attempts to take over the investigation, but is interrupted by a huge explosion and ends up blustering "Suffering cats, what is going on here?" What's left of Cosgrave's body is found amidst the rubble of the storage shed, where Alastair explains dynamite was stored to "blow up some cumbersome rocks." Footprints show that the body was brought to the shed and as Lestrade retraces the trail he comes upon Capt. Simpson watching from a distance. Lestrade shows him the rope used to tie up Doctor Merrivale with a bowline knot and Simpson bristles at the implication that a seafaring knot should point the finger of guilt at him. As the group disperses, Holmes wonders out loud which of the Good Comrades will be the next to receive the orange pips. "Orange Pips," bellows Lestrade, "Won't someone please tell me what's going on here?" It seems that poor Lestrade's role is to fumble and fume his way through this film, in Chanslor's feeble attempt to generate humor. I have to confess that I've had a terrible time referring to the group as the Good Comrades as I insist on writing Good Companions, the title of a film that my father appeared in many years before in 1933 in England, and which may well have been the inspiration for Chanselor's choice of a name for his group.

As it turns out, it is Capt. Simpson who is the next recipient of a letter containing the orange pips, but Lestrade assures him that he will be well protected by Scotland Yard and the local police. Holmes discovers a pair of muddy shoes that match the size of the footprints found at the storage shed. He and Watson leave Lestrade to his vigil as they go off to explore the beach. More footprints in the sand lead them into a trap, where they are nearly killed by a boulder pushed from the cliff above. Returning to the house they find Lestrade has been locked in the closet and Capt. Simpson is missing. A quick investigation reveals Sgt. Bleeker recovering from a blow to the head and a broken window in one of the French doors which, because there is no glass on the carpet, Holmes deduces was broken from the inside. Lestrade is certain that Simpson is the murderer and has attempted to escape, but Mrs. Monteith solemnly proclaims, "You'll find him like the others…a corpse." Simpson's body is soon discovered on the beach, mutilated in such a way that his arms, head and legs are missing. Holmes determines from Sgt. Bleeker that the mutilation was very neat, just as if it were done by the…"the skilled hands of a surgeon?" queries Holmes. Director Neill follows this declaration with a nice bit of morbid humor, a close shot of Doctor Merrivale's hands carving a turkey.

Mrs. Monteith arrives with a letter addressed to Inspector Lestrade that almost gives him apoplexy, until Holmes opens it to find merely a note and no orange pips. The note is from Alex MacGregor, asking Lestrade to come to his shop in the village to discuss the Drearcliff mystery. When Holmes and Lestrade arrive at the shop, they find that MacGregor has been murdered. Holmes now believes that MacGregor saw something at Drearcliff that caused his death. The solution is at Drearcliff House and they must quickly return there.

In a sequence that really goes nowhere, but is a lot of fun, full of suspense and atmospheric effects, Doctor Watson, hearing the sound of glass breaking upstairs, wanders through the house, while a ferocious rainstorm and lightning flashes outside, finding a series of empty bedrooms and open French doors. As a prowler's feet hide from view behind drapes, Watson is lured outside by someone knocking on the front door and of course gets himself locked out in the driving rain. Watson is thoroughly soaked, not to mention unnerved by the time he finds the French doors that he had previously locked now open. He ends up taking a shot at what appears to be a menacing figure, but turns out to be a suit of armor. The whole sequence is beautifully staged by Roy William Neill and is an entertaining if totally superfluous five minutes of padding. And of course when Watson goes to show Holmes and Lestrade that Merrivale and Alastair aren't in their rooms, there they are in bed as if nothing had happened. Upon questioning Mrs. Monteith, Holmes learns that she saw a fisherman running from the house just after the letter for Lestrade was pushed under the front door.

Holmes and Watson are waiting at the pub when the fishermen return and Holmes learns from one of them (Alec Craig) that he delivered the note for Alex MacGregor and that MacGregor had asked him if he believed in ghosts. When the fisherman replied in the negative, MacGregor answered "No more do I." Holmes is certain that he now has the key to the crime as he and Watson visit the graveyard to dig up Macgregor's coffin, only to find it is empty. This gives Watson another chance to play the fool, in a ridiculous conversation with an owl as he shovels dirt from the grave. The empty coffin causes Holmes to fear that another murder is about to occur at Drearcliff. Upon their return, Lestrade informs them that Doctor Merrivale has been killed, crushed by a rock on the beach. Lestrade is now certain that the surviving member of the Good Comrades, Bruce Alastair is the murderer. Watson goes to the library to keep an eye on Alastair, who plaintively declares, "I didn't kill anybody, really I didn't." Suddenly noticing something strange about Capt. Simpson's tobacco urn, Watson leaves to inform Holmes of his discovery only to be attacked. Hearing Watson's cry for help, Holmes and Lestrade discover a

Holmes and Lestrade apprehend The Good Comrades. From left, Harry Cording, Paul Cavanagh, Holmes Herbert, Richard Alexander, Wilson Benge, Basil Rathbone and Dennis Hoey.

secret passageway in the fireplace and follow it down into what Alastair describes as "The old smuggler's cave down below," and it is there that they find all of the other Good Comrades alive and well. Holmes explains their plan to fake their deaths and collect the insurance money and declares that Alastair was an innocent dupe.

In the final scene in Holmes' flat, in which Holmes finishes spelling out the plot to people who by rights should already possess this information, we learn that the six members of the Good Comrades have been convicted for the murder of Alex MacGregor and that they arranged their deaths by substituting the bodies of recently expired villagers. The tag, with Holmes thanking Alastair for supplying the clue that helped to save Watson's life, ends with a line of dialogue from Holmes that clearly implies that there will be more filmed adventures to come, "Thereby enabling us to continue our long and happy association together."

The House of Fear's large cast permitted Roy William Neill to utilize a great many of his repertory company, including Paul Cavanagh (Dr. Simon Merrivale), Holmes Herbert (Alan Cosgrave), Harry Cording (Captain John

Simpson), Gavin Muir (Mr. Chalmers), David Clyde (Alex MacGregor), Alec Craig (Angus, the fisherman), Leslie Denison (Sergeant Bleeker), Wilson Benge (Guy Davies) and of course Dennis Hoey (Inspector Lestrade). The new additions were Cyril Delevanti (Stanley Raeburn), Aubrey Mather (Bruce Alastair), Sally Shepherd (Mrs. Monteith), Doris Lloyd (Bessie, the Barmaid) and David Thursby (Police Sergeant), who had a minor role in *The Pearl of Death*, but who is more prominently featured in this film.

AUBREY MATHER was born in 1885 in Minchinhampton, Gloucestershire, England, the youngest child of the Reverend Frank A. Mather and Jessie C. Mather. He had three sisters, Emily 14, Janet 8 and Una 5, and a brother James 10. Aubrey attended Trinity College, Cambridge University where he became interested in theatrics. He made his dramatic debut as Bernardo in *Hamlet* in 1905 and then toured for several years with a Shakespearean repertory company before making his debut in London's West End in *Brewster's Millions*. On September 23, 1919 Mather arrived for the first time in New York City on board the S.S. *Nieuw Amsterdam* to make his Broadway debut on October 14 at the Manhattan Opera House in *The Luck of the Navy*. The play was not a success and closed in early November and Mather went on tour in Canada in a play that had previously had a short run at the Gaiety Theatre in 1917 called *General Post*. He would not return to the United States until 1936 when he appeared as Polonius in a revival of *Hamlet* with Leslie Howard.

In 1930, Mather appeared in a featured role in his first British film, *Young Woodley* starring Madeleine Carroll. In the *New York Times'* review, Mordaunt Hall reported, "Aubrey Mather is quite good as Woodley's sympathetic and tolerant father." Mather appeared in four more films in 1932, including *Aren't We All* starring Gertrude Lawrence and *Be Mine Tonight*, a musical starring tenor Jan Kiepura. In the West End, Mather appeared in a series of plays, including *A Pair of Sixes*, *Nightie Night* and *The Rattlesnake*, and in 1934 opened at the Shaftesbury Theatre in *Admirals All*, which ran for 192 performance. He continued acting in films as well, appearing in three films in 1934 and seven more in 1935-36, including a film version of Shakespeare's *As You Like It* starring Laurence Olivier and his first of three films for Alfred Hitchcock, *Sabotage*, in which he played the greengrocer who suggests that saboteur Oscar Homolka has been showing films in his theatre that are "a little too 'ot!" After that, he appeared in two more Hitchcock films, *Jamaica Inn* (1939) and *Suspicion* (1941).

Mather began a steady commute back and forth to the United States, appearing on Broadway in a comedy called *Bachelor Born* in 1938 along with another member of the Roy William Neill repertory company, Gavin

Muir. Then he returned to London to star in several BBC television productions and in Kurt Weill's *A Kingdom for a Cow* at the Savoy Theatre; it opened on June 25, 1938, and closed after three weeks. Then it was back to Broadway for another comedy starring Estelle Winword, *Good Hunting,* that also had a limited run, then back to London to appear in another BBC television production, John Van Druten's *London Wall.* Four months later Britain declared war on Germany and Italy and Mather left for a temporary exile in the United States that ultimately lasted until 1950.

Aubrey Mather as Bruce Alastair in *The House of Fear.*

His first Hollywood film was a potboiler for Hal Roach studios called *Captain Caution* (1940) that starred Victor Mature, who had just finished running around in a loincloth for Roach's *One Million B.C.* (1940). Over the next ten years, Aubrey Mather appeared in 42 films and gave some memorable performances, including Professor Peagram in Howard Hawks' *Ball of Fire* (1941), Mayor Lacade in *The Song of Bernadette* (1943) and an amusing performance in *The Secret Garden* (1949) as Dr. Griddlestone who has his ill-fitting wig stolen by a recalcitrant pet crow. Over the years Mather managed to play his share of butlers in five films including *A Yank at Eton* (1942), *Wilson* (1944), *The Hucksters* (1947) and perhaps his most memorable butler, Merriman in *The Importance of Being Earnest* (1952). Before returning to England, Mather revisited Broadway in three more productions starting in December of 1944 with a mystery thriller directed by down-on-his-luck film director James Whale, *Hand in Glove,* and followed in 1945 by Philip Barry's *Foolish Notion* starring Tallulah Bankhead, and finally in January of 1950 a revival of *As You Like It* starring Katharine Hepburn, in which he played the banished Duke, and which had a respectable run of 145 performances. Upon his return to England in July of 1950, Mather appeared in several television productions and five more films as well as recording an album of *The Importance of Being Earnest* at the Abbey Road Studios in 1953 with John Gielgud, Roland Culver and Dame Edith Evans. A review of the album mentioned the following, "Jean Cadell does a fine job as a batty old spinster in love with the local vicar Canon Chasuble (Aubrey Mather). This couple does well in their parts, particularly when they must compete with the memory of Margaret Rutherford and Miles Malleson in the 1952 film."

Mather's final performance was in September of 1955 in Terence Rattigan's *Separate Tables* at the St. James Theatre in London's West End with Margaret Leighton and Eric Portman. He died on January 15, 1958 after a long illness at the age of 72.

The name Aubrey comes from the German meaning noble and bright and Aubrey Mather always seemed to possess these attributes in his performances, whether playing a mild-mannered innocent or a conniving villain.

SALLY SHEPHERD was born Sara L. Hillhynes on June 19, 1896 in Bishopbriggs, East Dunbartonshire, Scotland, not far from the city of Glasgow. She apparently first came to the United States in 1928 at the age of 32, arriving in New York onboard the S.S. *California* on January 17, 1928. She went to live with a cousin, Margaret Cumming in Maspeth, Long Island, a small neighborhood located in the borough of Queens. The first indication of her working as an actor came when she appeared as a ballet dancer in a revival of Rudolf Friml's *The Vagabond King*. The next

Sally Shepherd as Mrs. Monteith, with Nigel Bruce and Basil Rathbone in *The House of Fear*.

came when she moved to Southern California in the early 1940s and began appearing in films. She played a nurse in her first film at Universal, *Enter Arsene Lupin* (1944) along with practically the entire Roy William Neill repertory company; Gale Sondergaard, Miles Mander, Holmes Herbert, Leyland Hodgson, Lillian Bronson, Gerald Hamer, David Clyde, John Burton, Leslie Denison and Arthur Stenning. The following year would bring her the two most important roles in her career and the only ones in which she would receive a screen credit, Mrs. Monteith in *The House of Fear* and Crandon, Hillary Brooke's maid in *The Woman in Green*.

1945 saw her touring with Reginald Denny and Lillian Harvey in a production of Noel Coward's *Blithe Spirit* that was produced by Russell Lewis and Howard Young, a couple of very nice chaps that I would come to know quite well many years later when they were running the Sacramento Music Circus and they hired me to write and direct an original revue called *The Heyday of Burlesque*. Sally Shepherd's film career was relatively short, only five years, and in that time she appeared in just twelve films. Roy William Neill would use her again in a smaller role in *Dressed to Kill* (1946) and then she would move to 20th Century-Fox to appear in three films, *Moss Rose* (1947), *Thunder in the Valley* (1947), and *The Snake Pit* (1948), and two films at M-G-M, *If Winter Comes* (1947) and *Hills of Home* ((1948). Her final screen appearance would be in William Dieterle's *The Accused* (1949) with Loretta Young and Robert Cummings. Sally Shepherd apparently never married and she died in Los Angeles on August 26, 1982 at the age of 86.

DORIS LLOYD, whose full name was Hessy Doris Lloyd, was born on July 3, 1891 in Liverpool, Lancashire, England, the eldest daughter of Edward Franklin Lloyd, an "organ builder," and the former Hessy Jane McCappin. Lloyd had an older brother, Norman (not the actor Norman Lloyd) and a younger sister, Milla. In 1911, when Doris was nine years old, the family was sharing a home with her mother's sister's family at 38 Eaton Road, West Kirby. Lloyd's

Doris Lloyd as Bessie, the Barmaid in *The House of Fear.*

acting career began on the London stage and by 1920 she was starring in silent films, beginning with *The Shadow Between* (1920). In 1921 she co-starred with Basil Rathbone in the play *The Edge O' Beyond*, which had a successful run of 150 performances at the Garrick Theatre. The following year she starred in the silent film *Love's Influence* (1922).

By 1923, Lloyd's younger sister Milla, now Mrs. Milla Brest, was living in Hollywood and on September 25, 1923, Lloyd and her mother sailed on the S.S. *Pittsburgh* for New York and then on to Hollywood to join Milla. Lloyd's first Hollywood film was *The Lady* (1925) starring Norma Talmadge and the following year she co-starred as Limehouse Polly, Lon Chaney's lover in *The Blackbird* (1926). For the next few years she continued to play top featured roles in such films as George Arliss' *Disraeli* (1929), the early sound version of *Charley's Aunt* (1930) starring Charles Ruggles and Halliwell Hobbes, Universal's version of *Waterloo*

Doris Lloyd and Basil Rathbone in the 1921 play *The Edge O' Beyond*.

Bridge (1931) starring Mae Clarke and directed by James Whale and *A Study in Scarlet* (1933) with Reginald Owen as Sherlock Holmes and Alan Mowbray as Inspector Lestrade. In 1930, Lloyd was asked to take over the second lead in the play *Among the Married* that was then playing at the Majestic Theatre in Los Angeles starring Florence Eldridge. (Mary Astor, who had been playing the role, left the play when her husband director Kenneth Hawks was killed in a plane crash.) Lloyd would divide her time between films and theatre, appearing in a number of productions at the Pasadena Community Playhouse, including *Queen Victoria* in which she played the title role. She would also appear in several episodes of CBS' *Lux Radio Theatre.*

The 1930 census shows that Lloyd was still living with her mother in Beverly Hills, along with a 5 year old girl named Gene Arthur who was described as a "granddaughter." This might indicate that Doris' sister Milla had died and that she and her mother were raising Milla's daughter, or that perhaps it was Doris' child. Either way, there was no mention of the father, other than a notation that he was born in England.

By the beginning of the 1940s, Lloyd was playing character roles in films, though still with featured billing, such as in *The Letter* (1940) starring Bette Davis and Gale Sondergaard and *Shining Victory* (1941) with James Stephenson and Geraldine Fitzgerald. By the mid-1940s the parts had grown smaller, sometimes without screen credit, but she continued to work steadily in such diverse films as *Keep 'Em Flying* (1941) with Abbott and Costello and *Journey for Margaret* (1942) with Robert Young and a very young Margaret O'Brien. She also had her share of horror films, including *Dr. Jekyll and Mr. Hyde* (1941), *The Wolf Man* (1941), *Night Monster* (1942) and *The Lodger* (1944). Doris Lloyd was a good friend of my father's and they appeared in scenes together in Roy William Neill's *Frankenstein Meets the Wolf Man* (1943) and *The House of Fear*, as well as in *This Above All* (1942), *Forever and a Day* (1943), *Kitty* (1945) and *Tarzan and the Leopard Woman* (1946).

In 1950 Lloyd went to New York to co-star in the original Broadway production of J. B. Priestley's *An Inspector Calls*, starring Thomas Mitchell and directed by Sir Cedric Hardwicke. She then went on tour with the play until returning to Hollywood to appear in M-G-M's *Kind Lady* (1951) with Ethel Barrymore and Maurice Evans. When Lloyd retired in 1967, after playing a small role in the Rosalind Russell comedy, *Rosie!* (1968), she had appeared in over 190 films and television episodes. Lloyd moved to Santa Barbara, California, where she died on May 21, 1968 of a heart ailment. She is buried in the Wee Kirk Churchyard of the Forest Lawn Memorial Park in Glendale, California.

DAVID THURSBY, probably one of the more familiar faces in the pantheon of Hollywood's character actors, was born David Johnson Thursby in Cockermouth, Cumberland, in the English Lake District, on February 28, 1889. He was the sixth of ten children of village tailor John Thursby and Sarah Bowe Thursby. Like several of the other members of the Neill Repertory company, very little is known of Thursby's early career. What is known is rather confusing, considering the first record of his traveling to America is August 6, 1920, yet he apparently was in New York City in June of 1918 when he signed a Draft Reg-

David Thursby (r) as the Police Sergeant, with Aubrey Mather in *The House of Fear.*

istration card giving his age as 30. There are no records of David Thursby working in any Broadway plays, but by 1920 he is declaring his profession as an actor on his arrival at the Port of New York and staying with his sister Jennie Thursby in the town of Manchester in upstate New York.

By 1929, Thursby had applied for U.S. citizenship and moved to Southern California. He went to work in films, playing a carnival barker in the early sound film *Smiling Irish Eyes* (1929) starring Colleen Moore. He apparently didn't appear again in films until 1934 when he began working full time and appeared in six films that year, beginning with G.W. Pabst's *A Modern Hero* (1934) and including *The Little Minister* (1934) along with Olaf Hytten, Alec Craig, Ted Billings, Reginald Denny and Mary Gordon. The following year his count grew to fourteen films with appearances in such major productions as *Mutiny on the Bounty* (1935) and *Captain Blood* (1935) in which he played sailors on both ships, and *Cardinal Richelieu* (1935) and *I Found Stella Parish* (1935) with Kay Francis. Ten films over the next year, including another film with Errol Flynn, *The Charge of the Light Brigade* (1936) followed by two more films with Spencer Tracy, *San Francisco* (1936), and *Captains Courageous (1937)*. As the years went by, Thursby would average between ten and fourteen films a year, working with such varied stars as Shirley Temple in *The Little Princess* (1939), Errol Flynn again in *The Adventures of Robin Hood* (1938) and *The Sea Hawk* (1940), Tyrone Power in *A Yank in the R.A. F.* (1941), *Son of Fury* (1942) and *The Black Swan* (1942), even Lassie, in *Challenge to Lassie* (1949). He served Gene Kelly a beaker of ale as an innkeeper in *The Three Musketeers* (1948), and as a London Bobby during Princess Elizabeth's wedding, he sang with Fred Astaire in *Royal Wedding* (1951).

He even managed to appear in eight horror films at various studios, including both *Werewolf of London* (1935) and *She-Wolf of London* (1946) at Universal and *The Undying Monster* (1942) and *The Lodger* (1944) at 20th Century-Fox.

In 1951 he played a helmsman in *Sealed Cargo*, a film that I remember well because it was one of the few interviews I went on as an actor. My agent took me out to the old Selznick Studios in Culver City, then called RKO Culver, to meet the director Alfred Werker. My recollection is that we went onto the set where a full-scale reproduction of a schooner was set up on rollers (to simulate the motion of the sea); the cast and crew were working in a small cabin set off to one side. We waited until they finished filming the scene with Dana Andrews and then the casting director, Ruth Burch, took me over to say hello to Alfred Werker. The next thing I knew I was back on the street, all in a matter of minutes. Needless to say I didn't get the part, it went to Skip Homeier who had already beaten me out of two other roles and was probably already cast in this role by the time I showed up. I gave up acting shortly after that and became an assistant film editor.

Apart from his acting, David Thursby was also a playwright, having written at least two plays. The first was called *Fresh as a Daisy*, which he wrote in 1945 and described as "an engaging comedy in three acts," and *Vim, Vigor and Vitality*, which he wrote in 1952 and which he described as "a gay comedy in three acts." Thursby had a home at 8333 Lookout Mountain Drive in Hollywood just off Laurel Canyon, one of the main arteries between Hollywood and the San Fernando Valley, and it was there that he retired in 1965, after having played a featured role in *Starr of the Yankees*, a TV movie directed by Arthur Hiller. He died on April 20, 1977 at the age of 88, having appeared in 133 films and television productions.

CYRIL DELEVANTI, appears briefly in *The House of Fear* as one of the conspirators, but had a much more memorable role in Roy William Neill's *Frankenstein Meets the Wolf Man* (1943) as Freddy Jolly, the grave robber who desperately begs his accomplice for help when the newly revived Lawrence Talbot reaches out of his coffin and seizes his arm in a death grip. This happens to be one of my favorite scenes in a film that I greatly admire for Neill's excellent staging throughout. Harry Cyril Delevanti was born in the Paddington District of London, England on February 23, 1889, the eldest son of Edward P. Delevanti, a professor of music, and the former Mary Elizabeth Rowbotham. He was 22-years-old when he first traveled to America, arriving on October 10, 1911 on the German liner *Kronprinzessin Cecile*. His travel documents showed that he was traveling to Chicago, where he would join an acting troupe. By 1912, Delevanti had returned to England, and on January 20, 1913 he married Eva Kittie Peel in London. They would ultimately have two children, a daughter, Kitty Winifred, and a son, Cyril Harold.

Although Delevanti never appeared on Broadway, he still commuted several times to the United States for acting jobs and was here again when England declared war on Germany on August 4, 1914. He made his way to New York and booked passage to return to England. On February 4, 1915 Germany declared the seas around the British Isles a war zone, announcing that after February 18, allied ships in the area would be sunk without warning. Many of the large liners were laid up, due in part to declining passenger travel across the Atlantic, but the RMS *Lusitania*, the fastest first-class passenger liner, was still in commercial service. On April 5, 1915, Delevanti sailed on the *Lusitania* for Liverpool, arriving on April 11. Less than a month later, on May 7, 1915, the *Lusitania* would be sunk by a single torpedo fired from the German submarine U-20. She sank in 18 minutes, just 11 miles off the Irish coast, and 1,198 people died with her, including almost 100 children.

For a man who would eventually appear in over 140 films and television episodes, Cyril Delevanti's career was slow in getting started. After moving his family to California he made his film debut playing a reporter in the Ann Harding—Leslie Howard starrer *Devotion* (1931), but wouldn't work again in films until 1938. Delevanti made his living during these years as a drama coach, giving lessons to aspiring actors such as a young James Craig (*The Human Comedy* [1943]). In 1938 Delevanti was hired by director Ford Beebe to play Wing Fu in the Universal serial *Red Barry* starring Larry "Buster" Crabbe. Beebe, a prolific writer-director who specialized in Universal serials, also directed two of Universal's horror films, *Night Monster* (1942) and *The Invisible Man's Revenge* (1944). Beebe would eventually become Delevanti's son-in-law, marrying Delevanti's daughter Kitty, who was 25 years his junior. Jerry Blake's web page honoring the Serials of the 1930s and '40s had this comment on Delevanti's performance in *Red Barry*: "Cyril Delevanti is brilliant as Wing Fu, seeming very reserved and aloof when dealing with strangers or enemies, but revealing real warmth and emotion when dealing with his friends or with his son (Philip Ahn)." Delevanti would play another Asian character for Universal in the Tom Brown-Marjorie Lord-Edgar Barrier serial *The Adventures of Smilin' Jack* (1943).

Delevanti worked frequently for Universal during the 1940s in films such as *Two Tickets to London* (1943), *Phantom of the Opera* (1943), *Phantom Lady* (1944), and for Ford Beebe again in *Night Monster* and *The Invisible Man's Revenge* (1944). He played a clown in Charles Chaplin's fi-

Cyril Delevanti (r) as the doomed Grave Robber, with Tom Stevenson in
Frankenstein Meets the Wolf Man.

nal American film *Limelight* (1952) and shortly thereafter appeared in his
first television series *I Led Three Lives* starring Richard Carlson. From that
point on he appeared in over seventy different television episodes, plus an
occasional film performance, before he was given his most important and
personally satisfying role as Nonno, Deborah Kerr's elderly poet grandfather, in John Huston's film of the Tennessee Williams play *The Night of
the Iguana* (1964). Delevanti won a coveted Golden Globe nomination as
Best Supporting Actor for his performance. His final screen appearance,
at the age of 85, was in African-American actor Fred Williamson's detective thriller *Black Eye* (1974). Delevanti died the following year and is
buried at Forest Lawn Memorial Park in Glendale, California.

The House of Fear was released in New York on March 16, 1945 and
Bosley Crowther, who seemed to have developed an avid dislike for any
part of the Universal films, said in his *New York Times* review, "…[N]either
the mystery nor the solution are anything to get nervous about, and Mr.
Rathbone's performance of the detective is as pedestrian as a cop on patrol.
Sherlock Holmes has certainly gone to the bow-wows in the clutches of

Hollywood." Crowther wasn't the only one who seemed to find fault with this endeavor; another was Otis L. Guernsey of the *New York Herald Tribune* who wrote, "No one could quarrel with Basil Rathbone's characterization of Sherlock Holmes, Nigel Bruce's of Watson, or Aubrey Mather's of the doddering Scottish laird of the castle. But the script writing and directing of this Universal series will have to improve before Sherlock once again rises magnificently to a criminal occasion." Not all of the New York critics shared that opinion, with Alton Cook of *the New York World-Telegram* saying, "The latest of the Sherlock Holmes stories, 'The House of Fear,' gets closer to the old Sir Arthur Conan Doyle spirit than any of this series has the past couple of seasons. They have been throwing Sherlock in among monsters and Nazis lately, but not in this new one at the Rialto—The opportunity to slip back into the mood of preoccupation and elaborate talk of the original is just the thing for Basil Rathbone's florid style of acting, of course. If one of your main interests in the series has been the way he played Sherlock, this will be among the very best." And Kate Cameron's *New York Daily News* review echoed this praise; "This is one of the better pictures in the series…With producer-director Roy William Neill at the helm, and Basil Rathbone, Nigel Bruce and Dennis Hoey in their accustomed places, Universal maintains the high standard it set for itself with other pictures in this entertaining series of detective puzzles. Other members of the cast who help to make this a good picture for mystery fans include Aubrey Mather, who is currently playing an important part in the Theatre Guild production of Philip Barry's "Foolish Notion" at the Martin Beck Theatre."

The reviewers on the West Coast shared this positive opinion, with *Daily Variety* calling it "better than average." And the *Hollywood Reporter* declaring, "a well-conceived tale, ably produced and directed by Roy William Neill, it offers plenty of opportunity for the drawing of colorful characters, and affords stars Basil Rathbone and Nigel Bruce, as Holmes and Watson, a chance to operate adequately in their somewhat fantastic roles." The *Reporter* went on to heap more praise on Roy William Neill and Virgil Miller; "Direction by Neill is clever, and cannily designed to reap the greatest harvest of suspense from the script. His function as a producer is performed more than adequately. The photography by Virgil Miller does much to heighten the eerie quality of the background against which the story is played." The public chose to ignore Bosley Crowther's negative opinion and continued to flock to the films. Once again Universal made a handsome profit and once again the creative team was set to work preparing another adventure for Sherlock Holmes and Doctor Watson.

THE WOMAN IN GREEN

TOWARD THE END OF OCTOBER, 1944, Bertram Millhauser was once again signed to create the next Holmes script and developed a blackmail-themed idea he called *Invitation to Death*. Millhauser received $7,583, a slight increase from his previous salary on *The Pearl of Death*. The character of Inspector Lestrade appeared in Millhauser's initial draft as did another character named Wade, a blackmailer. In the next draft Professor Moriarty became the culprit and Wade disappeared from the script. When he turned in his first draft dated 12/21/44, the Breen Office flatly turned it down. Their heated objection was to Millhauser's plot device of having the Moriarty character murdering little girls of eight or nine years

of age and their bodies being mutilated by the severance of a finger as a basis for blackmailing the victims. Millhauser went to work to address the Breen Office's demands, primarily by increasing the age of the victims, and on January 10, 1945 the censor board okayed the revised draft of 1/4/45, complimenting the studio on the "excellent manner in which suggestions made in our letter of December 27, 1944, have been followed in this revision. We appreciate your splendid cooperation in this connection." Having secured the Breen Office's blessings, the studio set about casting their film, with their first choice being to bring back character actor Henry Daniell to portray arch-villain Professor Moriarty, paying him $1,500 a week with a three week guarantee. On January 6, 1945, studio contractee Hillary Brooke was signed for $750 a week with a two week guarantee to play the role of Moriarty's accomplice Lydia Marlowe. On January 11, 1945, the day before Roy William Neill began filming, Universal's script department issued a memo stating: PLEASE NOTE: Throughout the script the name of "Inspector Lestrade" has been changed to "Inspector Gregson".

Millhauser incorporated several popular filmic devices into his screenplay, including the use of narration and flashbacks. His decision to have the disembodied voice of Inspector Gregson, rather than Dr. Watson, narrate the opening sequence was somewhat disquieting, particularly to fans of Sir Arthur Conan Doyle's creation who expected Watson to always be his storyteller. In fact Watson, who doesn't appear until well into the first act, has a more subdued and thoughtful persona in this film, less inclined to act the buffoon, except for one forced scene with a hypnotist.

Film historian David Stuart Davies surmises that the grim nature of the film was reason enough for Millhauser to create these changes and also to replace the ubiquitous Lestrade with the no-nonsense Gregson, played with low-key restraint by Matthew Boulton. Although my father was busy filming the Cornel Wilde-Evelyn Keyes comedy *A Thousand and One Nights* for Columbia Pictures until late January of 1945, I don't believe that this was why he didn't appear in *Woman in Green*. Whatever the reason, it is interesting to note that for the most part, Inspector Gregson's dialogue is identical to what had been written originally for Inspector Lestrade.

The film begins with the aforementioned narration played over stock shots of uniformed Bobbies marching out of the "Yard," as Inspector Gregson (Mathew Boulton) sets the scene with his description of the three murders of young women, called the "Finger Murders" because of the grisly severing of each victim's forefinger. We then meet Gregson and a disagreeable fellow officer (Boyd Irwin) as they await the commissioner (Alec Harford), who upon his arrival berates his staff for not solving the murders before a fourth girl has been killed. Gregson calls on Sherlock

Holmes to ask for help and after viewing the corpse of the fourth young woman (Kay Harding), whose right forefinger has also been surgically removed, (a fact that causes Gregson to momentarily lose his composure) Holmes suggests they go for a drink. The restaurant scene opens with a stock shot from some obscure Universal film of a dance specialty act, which hardly seems the appropriate spot for Holmes and Gregson to stop by for a nightcap, but it does give Holmes the opportunity to observe Sir George Fenwick (Paul Cavanagh) seated at a table with an attractive woman (Hillary Brooke). When they leave Pembroke House, we follow them to her flat where her housekeeper Crandon (Sally Shepherd) is waiting to help drug Sir George. Holmes and Doctor Watson visit the flat of the murdered girl and Holmes announces that he is certain that the murders are only incidental to a larger scheme. Gregson arrives to report the murder of a fifth young woman in Edgeware Road who has also had her finger removed. The following morning Fenwick awakens in a strange rooming house on Edgeware Road and discovers a severed finger in his pocket, while hearing a newspaper vendor shouting about another "Finger Murder!" Fenwick returns to Lydia Marlowe's apartment to inquire about the missing ten hours in his memory and is confronted by Professor Moriarty (Henry Daniell) who shows him his cigarette case that fell, according to Moriarty, from Fenwick's coat pocket while he was bending over the body of a young girl with a knife in his hand.

A young woman comes to visit Holmes and while he is watching her getting out of her car he notices a cab pull up next to an empty house across the street. Holmes recognizes the young woman as Maude Fenwick (Eve Amber), Sir George's daughter. Through the means of a flashback, again narrated in awkward fashion, she describes an incident that took place the previous evening when she witnessed her father burying an object in his flower garden. The object, which she has brought with her, is a woman's finger. Holmes and Watson accompany Maude back to her father's home where Gregson joins them. When they enter his library they discover Fenwick lying on the floor, dead from a bullet wound to the back. Holmes notices Fenwick's hand is clutching a crumpled Pembroke House matchbook and remembers that he and Gregson saw him there with a woman. "Someone didn't want me to speak with Sir George," he declares.

A report from Sir George's bank reveals that he drew out his entire balance in cash, nearly £10,000, just after the last girl was murdered, which suggests to Holmes that he was being blackmailed. Watson scoffs at Holmes's declaration that Professor Moriarty is behind the blackmail scheme, reminding him that Moriarty was hanged in Montevideo over a year ago. "I know someone was hanged in Montevideo under that name," Holmes replies. "But I'll stake my reputation that Moriarty is alive and here, now, in London." A phone call for Doctor Watson interrupts the debate with a request for his aid for a fat woman who has fallen and fractured her leg. Watson pulls his dust-covered medical valise from a cupboard and rushes off, as Holmes begins to play his violin. He soon becomes aware of Professor Moriarty's presence, standing in the shadows watching him. The ensuing conversation between the two adversaries is beautifully played by both Rathbone and Daniell, as they duel with words, testing to find each other's vulnerability. When Holmes threatens Moriarty with arrest he is stopped by the threat of never seeing Watson again. Obviously the phone call was a ruse to get Watson into a trap. Moriarty assures Holmes, "No harm will come to Doctor Watson this time, but I can't answer for the future." He warns Holmes to drop the case, threatening Holmes' life if he doesn't, and then leaves the flat. Watson returns, grumbling about the practical joke that has been played upon him and is shocked to hear that Moriarty has just left. Why did he let him go? When Holmes explains that he was bluffed into believing harm would come to a good friend, Watson realizes he was the potential victim. Holmes now knows the motive for the finger murders, but still needs to find out the method used on the blackmail victims. At this point, Millhauser creates a scene suggested by an incident in Conan Doyle's short story "The Adventures of the Empty House." As they talk, Holmes notices that the first floor front window in the vacant house across the street is now open, but wasn't a half an hour ago. He asks Watson go over to check on it and, grumbling all of the way, Watson complies. As he searches the house, another figure stealthily climbs the stairs behind him carrying a rifle. The figure goes to the open window and fires at the silhouette of Holmes, seated in his chair reading a book, shattering the glass. Holmes appears by Watson's side and explains the figure is a bust of Julius Caesar. The assassin turns out to be Corporal Williams (Tom Bryson), a recently discharged soldier who appears to have been placed in a trance with a hypnotic suggestion to kill Holmes. Inspector Gregson is called to Holmes' flat. Holmes believes that he knows who the woman is that has hypnotized Corporal Williams. Gregson leaves with Williams, and Holmes and Watson discuss the means by which Moriarty and the woman trap their victims into believing they are murderers. A phone call brings word that Williams is missing. As they hurry to Scotland Yard, they find Williams' dead body propped against their front door.

Moriarty and Lydia plot to lure Sherlock Holmes to her flat to destroy him. She will go to the Mesmer Club where Holmes and Watson are going to learn more about hypnotism and arrange to meet him. Meanwhile Doctor Onslow (Frederick Worlock), the head of the Mesmer Club, arranges for Holmes and Watson to observe a session of hypnotism, which Watson dismisses as "mumbo-jumbo." A further demonstration, where Onslow puts Watson under, finally convinces the good doctor that there might be something to the science of hypnotism. Lydia Marlowe arrives and strikes up a conversation with Holmes, who quite obviously recognizes her as Sir George's companion from Pembroke House. After joining her for a drink at Pembroke House, Holmes allows her to bring him back to her flat.

Setting the mood with low lights and soft music, Lydia then suggests that Holmes take a sedative to make him more susceptible to being hypnotized. After first demurring, Holmes agrees and takes the pill, as Lydia draws his attention to a single white flower in a bowl of water on the coffee table. When Holmes appears to have been hypnotized, Moriarty has him sign a suicide note, walk out onto the terrace and step up onto the ledge.

After several missteps and loss of balance, Watson and Gregson burst into the flat and arrest all of the culprits. Holmes reveals that he was pretending to be hypnotized, having substituted Lydia's drug with a pain killer so that he could withstand the test of a sharp knife. As Moriarty is being led away he breaks free and leaps across to the neighboring terrace, but misses his footing and falls to his death. There is no homily at the end of the film, merely a comment from Holmes that he is "thinking of all the

The improbable climax to *The Woman In Green*.

women who can come and go in safety in the streets of London tonight. The stars keep watch in the heavens, and in our own little way, we too old friend are privileged to watch over our city."

In my opinion, *The Woman in Green* is not one of Roy William Neill's better endeavors, perhaps because Millhauser's script doesn't give him much to work with. Other than the marvelously performed scene in Holmes' flat between Rathbone and Henry Daniell's Moriarty there isn't much suspense in the film and the finale, with Holmes supposedly hypnotized and stumbling along the terrace ledge, totally lacks suspense and believability. Film historians have commented that Rathbone was growing tired of the character and it was beginning to show, but frankly it seems to me that it was Neill who needed inspiration.

Once again, Neill uses many of his repertory company in *The Woman in Green,* including Hillary Brooke (Lydia Marlowe), Henry Daniell (Professor Moriarty), Paul Cavanagh (Sir George Fenwick), Frederick Worlock (Onslow), Sally Shepherd (Crandon), Mary Gordon (Mrs. Hudson), Leslie Denison (Barman), John Burton (Waring), Harold De Becker (Pencil Seller) and, in a very brief role as Sir George Fenwick's butler, Olaf Hytten. I will add some further comments on Hillary Brooke and Henry Daniell, as well as discussing Matthew Boulton (Gregson), Alec Harford (Commissioner), Boyd Irwin (Disagreeable Officer) and Arthur Stenning (Porter).

HILLARY BROOKE's haughty elegance and cultivated accent made her the "B" picture's version of Agnes Moorehead and she was a delight to watch on the screen. Whether playing a comic foil to Bob Hope as Madame Pompadour in *Monsieur Beaucaire* (1946) or the vindictive rival to Hedy Lamarr as Meg Saladine in *The Strange Woman* (1946), her caustic delivery gave every performance a wonderful lemony twist. In *The Woman in Green,* in which she played the title role and received top billing after Rathbone and Bruce, she softened her persona to add to the seductiveness and hypnotic quality of Lydia Marlowe. Brooke apparently didn't care for Henry Daniell, saying in one interview that Daniell kept complaining about working late and was cold and very distant.

Hillary Brooke's career began to build after this film and she would go on to play many well-remembered roles, such as the mother in *Invaders from Mars* (1953) and Doris Day's best friend in *The Man Who Knew Too Much* (1956). Brooke had been married briefly to dancer Alan Shute while still in New York and later to assistant director Jack Voglin while in Hollywood. Voglin was the son of noted theatrical scenic designer Arthur Voegtlin and would later become a production manager who worked for my nemesis Jack Broder in 1966. (Read the whole story in my book *Elvis,*

Sherlock and Me.) According to Hollywood columnist Jimmie Fidler's reporting in a 1948 column, the Brooke- Voglin divorce hit a snag when the couple couldn't agree on custody of their German sheep dog.

Brooke would in later years become a practiced comedienne in several television series, most notably *My Little Margie* (1952-1955) and *The Abbott and Costello Show* (1952-1953). In 1960 Brooke appeared in her final role as Greta Morgan in an episode of the television series *Michael Shayne* starring Richard Denning and soon after married Raymond A. Klune, who had been David O. Selznick's production manager for many years on pic-

Hillary Brooke as Lydia Marlowe in *The Woman in Green*.

tures like *Gone With the Wind* (1939) and *Since You Went Away* (1944) and was at the time of their marriage vice president and general manager of M-G-M studios. Klune's son Donald Klune was an assistant director at M-G-M while I was there writing the Elvis Presley films in the late 60s. When Ray Klune retired, he and Brooke moved to San Luis Rey, San Diego County, California, where he died in 1988. Hillary Brooke died on May 25, 1999 from undisclosed causes at a hospital in Fallbrook, California at the age of 84. There is a star in her honor on the Hollywood Walk of Fame.

HENRY DANIELL, who like the characters he portrayed on the screen was indeed cold and distant, took advantage of that personality trait to invest many memorable characters both on the screen and the stage; with unforgettable performances on the Broadway stage as Henry Abbott in *Kind Lady* (1935) and Eilert Lovburg in *Hedda Gabler* (1942) and in films such as Henry Brockelhurst in *Jane Eyre* (1944) and Doctor Wolfe (Toddy) MacFarlane in *The Body Snatcher* (1945). As for his performance as Professor Moriarty in *The Woman in Green*, Basil Rathbone had this to say in his autobiography *In and Out of Character*: "There were other Moriartys, but none so delectably dangerous as that of Henry Daniell's masterly Moriarty." Daniell continued working in films and when live television began he appeared frequently as a guest star in popular programs such as *The Philco-Goodyear Television Playhouse*, *Armstrong Circle Theatre* and *Kraft Theatre*. His later films included *The Egyptian* (1954), *Lust for Life* (1956) and *Witness for the Prosecution* (1957). In 1962 he made his seventh film for director George Cukor, *The Chapman Report*, and indirectly gave a major boost to my career. *The Chapman Report* was

Henry Daniell as Professor Moriarty in *The Woman in Green.*

based on a novel by Irving Wallace that took its inspiration from Doctor Alfred Kinsey's surveys of Sexual Behavior in the Human Male and Female, published during the late 1940s and early 1950s. The central part of the film was comprised of interviews by a research team of four disparate housewives, played by Claire Bloom, Glynis Johns, Shelley Winters and Jane Fonda, dramatizing their personal lives and sexual history. I was the assistant film editor until the editor, on loan from 20th Century-Fox, finished the initial editing and returned to Fox to start another picture and I was moved up to editor. At that point the only thing left to be done was to send the film to the Production Code Administration (now called the Shurlock Office after its new boss Geoffrey Shurlock) and to the Legion of Decency, the organization of Catholic bishops set up in 1934 to keep a watchful eye on immorality in the movies and supervised by Monsignor Little in New York City. The two censor boards found plenty to object to, but the Legion particularly hated the film and in fact wanted the studio to shoot a new ending in which the main researcher, played by Efrem Zimbalist Jr., would confront Doctor Chapman, played by Andrew Duggan and denounce the whole idea of the survey. At a screening that was held with Jack Warner to go over the censor notes I piped up with a suggestion for a different scene that would have Zimbalist and a character played by Henry Daniell, who in previous scenes had objected strenuously to the survey, meet briefly in a shot that had been lifted from the picture and then exit into a smaller set that we would construct and film a conversation where Zimbalist would defend the survey and give his reasons. Warner liked my idea so much that he had me write the scene and the next thing I knew he promoted me to producer and gave me a film of my own to produce, which became *Palm Springs Weekend* (1963). The following year George Cukor cast Henry Daniell as the Prince of Transylvania, a diction expert and once again a villain in the musical *My Fair Lady* (1964). Daniell had appeared briefly in several master shots in the dress ball sequence and was preparing to go to the studio the next day to continue filming when he suffered a massive heart attack at his home in Santa Monica and died on Halloween morning October 31, 1963. He was survived by his wife Anne and his actress daughter Allison. I will always owe Henry Daniell a debt of gratitude for having been there when I needed him.

MATTHEW BOULTON made his only appearance in a Sherlock Holmes film as Inspector Gregson in *The Woman in Green*; however, this would mark his thirteenth portrayal of a British police inspector in films starting with his first role in *To What Red Hell* (1929), a British silent film starring Sybil Thorndike and Bramwell Fletcher.

Boulton was born on January 20, 1883 in Lincolnshire County, England. By the time he was 28years-old he was married and working as an actor in London where he and his wife Ruth, a fellow actor, were living in a Notting Hill boarding house. In 1921 he traveled with a theatre troupe to Quebec, Canada and then on to Detroit. Michigan. Boulton also dabbled in writing and one of his plays, *The Brass Doorknob*, was given a trial performance at the Manhattan Little Theatre Club in New York City in 1926. In May of 1931 John Gielgud had a big success in a stage adaptation of J.B. Priestley's novel *The Good Companions* at His Majesty's Theatre in London and shortly after Boulton was signed to appear in the Broadway production with Hugh Sinclair taking over Gielgud's role. (Gielgud had gone off to make the film version with Jessie Matthews and Edmund Gwenn.) Arriving in New York on September 7, 1931 aboard the S.S. *Samaria*, the cast went immediately to the 49th Street Theatre to begin rehearsals and opened on October 1. The play had only a limited success, closing after 68 performances, and Boulton was back in London looking for work. He found it in England's burgeoning film industry, playing various roles in five films for British International Pictures, including three police inspectors.

In 1935, Boulton was cast as Inspector Belsize in Emlyn Williams' stage play *Night Must Fall*. The play, which starred Williams and Dame May Whitty and was directed by Williams, was a smashing success when it opened at the Duchess Theatre on May 31, 1935 and the following year

Mathew Boulton as Inspector Gregson in *The Woman in Green*.

the entire cast traveled to the United States to present it on Broadway. Unfortunately, New York audiences were turned off by the violent nature of the play, where a psychopathic killer conceals his victim's head in a hatbox, and it closed after only 64 performances. Boulton returned once again to London, but this time an offer was waiting for him, Alfred Hitchcock wanted him to play a police officer in his upcoming film *The 39 Steps* (1935). Hitchcock liked his performance and signed him to play the more important role of Superintendent Talbot in his next thriller *Sabotage* (1935). When M-G-M made their film adaptation of *Night Must Fall* (1937), again starring Dame May Whitty with Robert Montgomery in Emlyn Williams' role, they brought Boulton over from England to recreate his role of Inspector Belsize. He stayed on to join Dame May Whitty and Henry Daniell in another drama for M-G-M, *The Thirteenth Chair* (1937) in which he played another police officer, Commissioner Grimshaw. From that point on, Boulton's career kept him in Hollywood and he would eventually make over 65 films, playing police inspectors and commissioners in fourteen of them, before his death in Los Angeles, California on February 10, 1962.

ALEC HARFORD had previously appeared in a small role as a patron of the seedy pub where Sherlock Holmes finds Kitty (Evelyn Ankers) in *Sherlock Holmes and the Voice of Terror*, but he is featured prominently as the little C.I.D. Commissioner in the opening sequence in *The Woman in Green*. Harford, whose full name was George Alexander Harford, was born September 8, 1888 (another Virgo like Hillary Brooke and me) in

Leyton, East London, England. Harford's father died when he was quite young and his mother, Annie Eliza Harford, ran a Wine and Spirit store in the Lewisham district of South London. In his youth, Harford worked as a company clerk, but soon found his way into the acting profession, traveling to Australia and Canada. In 1916, while Harford was working in Winnipeg, Canada, he enlisted in the Canadian Army and served for two years in World War I.

On June 30, 1926, Alec Harford married Esther Alden from Pawtucket, Rhode Island and they moved to Brooklyn, New York, where on January 26,

Alec Harford as he appeared as the pub patron in *Sherlock Holmes and the Voice of Terror*.

1927 their daughter Betty was "prematurely" born. Soon after, Alec and his family returned to England where he continued pursuing his career as an actor. The only film on record that he made in England was a 1933 drama called *Doss House* (the British term for flop house), but by 1934 Harford was in Hollywood and appearing in his first American film, *Sylvia Scarlett* (1935) starring Katharine Hepburn. He also left the country briefly in 1934 to return via Mexicali, Mexico and apply for his United States citizenship. Throughout the 1930s, '40s and early '50s, Harford worked steadily in mostly uncredited roles in such films as *The Adventures of Robin Hood* (1938), *A Dispatch from Reuter's* (1940) and even a Laurel & Hardy comedy, *A Chump at Oxford* (1940). In all of the 44 films that Alec Harford made in Hollywood he received screen credit in only two, the first being an anthology film that A&P supermarket heir Huntington Hartford produced to feature his then wife Marjorie Steele called *Face to Face* (1952); Harford had a featured role in the first episode, based on a story by Joseph Conrad, "The Secret Sharer" that starred James Mason. The following year, Harford received his only other screen credit in the Alan Ladd starrer *Botany Bay* (1953). For many years Alec Harford was featured on a number of Hollywood radio programs such as *Lux Radio Theatre*, *Escape* and *Crime Classics*. He made his final film in late 1954, *Lady Godiva of Coventry* (1955) in which he played the original Peeping Tom, spying on Maureen O'Hara as she rode naked through the streets. Alec Harford died in Los Angeles on March 31, 1955.

BOYD IRWIN, who plays the rather unpleasant fellow police officer complaining to Mathew Boulton's inspector about the open window in the first scene of *Woman in Green,* was born John Boyd Irwin on March 12, 1880 in the beach resort of Brighton, England. He was the second of two sons of John Irwin and the former Jessie Janet Merrick; his brother John Merrick Irwin would eventually become a Vaudeville performer in the United States. Boyd Irwin began his acting career in Australia, performing in both theatre and films. He may be the first member of the Roy William Neill repertory company to appear in Sherlock Holmes-related dramas, when in February of 1904 in Sydney, Australia he played "a man about town" in the Sherlock Holmes mystery play *The Bank of England*, and in 1911, when he traveled to Auckland, New Zealand to appear in *The Speckled Band*, both original plays by producer J.C. Williamson. In 1905, Irwin married Madeline B. Shorter in Sydney, and their son Berne Boyd Irwin was born there on April 22, 1907. Irwin would spend fifteen years appearing in theatrical productions in both Australia and New Zealand, and, beginning in 1915, starring in some of Australia's earliest silent films.

On April 23, 1919, Irwin arrived in San Francisco from Australia on the S.S. *Sonoma,* and after briefly exploring the town's theatrical possibilities travelled on to Los Angeles, where Madeline and Berne would join him a few months later. Irwin's first Hollywood film was *The Luck of Geraldine Laird* (1920), in which he co-starred with actress-producer Bessie Barriscale. In 1921, he joined the cast of Douglas Fairbanks' *The Three Musketeers* as the villain, Comte de Rochefort. In 1923, he played Muriarc in one of Universal Pictures' earliest serials *Around the World in Eighteen Days* and the following year he was Levasseur in the silent version of Rafael Sabatini's *Captain Blood.*

Boyd Irwin as he appeared in *Dressed to Kill.*

By 1930 Irwin, who was now fifty-years-old, was playing character roles in films. In one of his first sound films, he played the captain of the giant Zeppelin in Cecil B. DeMille's M-G-M extravaganza *Madame Satan* (1930) starring Kay Johnson and Reginald Denny.

Irwin's son Bern and his wife Isabella had married the previous year, and Bern was also trying his hand at acting. In between film roles, Irwin returned to the stage in 1932, starring in *The Apple Cart* in Oakland, California, and the following year he traveled to New York to star on Broadway opposite Ethel Barrymore's daughter in an original comedy called *Under Glass.* The play closed after eight performances, but Irwin remained in New York until January of 1934, appearing in two more plays, neither of which lasted more than a week and a half. On his return to Hollywood, one of his first films was Universal's *The Man Who Reclaimed His Head* (1934), followed soon after by *Werewolf of London* (1935). During the next few years, Irwin supported such stars as Ronald Colman in *A Tale of Two Cities* (1935) and *The Prisoner of Zenda* (1937), Jimmy Stewart in *You Can't Take It with You* (1938), Basil Rathbone and Nigel Bruce in *The Adventures of Sherlock Holmes* (1939) and Charles Chaplin in *Monsieur Verdoux* (1947). He would return to the Sherlock Holmes repertory company once more in *Dressed to Kill* (1946). Boyd Irwin's final film (he never appeared on television) was the Glenn Ford-Terry Moore starrer *The Return of October* (1948). He died on January 22, 1957 at the age of 76 in Los Angeles.

ARTHUR STENNING was making his fourth and final appearance in the Sherlock Holmes series as the porter at the Mesmer Club in *The Woman in Green*. He had previously appeared as a British officer in the finale of *Sherlock Holmes and the Voice of Terror*, as a plainclothes policeman in *The Spider Woman* and a ship's steward in *The Pearl of Death*. Arthur Nathan Stenning was born on February 6, 1883 in the London borough of Islington, the third son of George Charles Stenning, a fruit

Arthur Stenning as he appeared as the ship's steward in *The Pearl of Death*.

and green merchant, and the former Marian Scott. As he grew, Stenning aided his father in the grocery business, but when World War I broke out he became an officer in the British Army and in 1919 traveled to Australia. In 1920 he came through Vancouver, British Columbia, Canada on his way to enter the United States. Eventually Stenning found his way to New York and made his Broadway debut in a revival of John Galsworthy's play *The Silver Box* along with fellow Roy William Neill repertory company member Halliwell Hobbes. Between 1930 and 1935 Stenning appeared in five more plays, including two with a young Basil Rathbone and Henry Daniell. He was also a member of Walter Hampden's repertory company, appearing in both *Cyrano de Bergerac* in 1932 and a revival of Shakespeare's *Hamlet* in 1934 along with another repertory company member, Thomas Gomez.

By 1935 Stenning was back in Canada appearing in a featured role in silent screen star Ruth Roland's final picture, *Nine to Nine* directed by Edgar G. Ulmer. In 1939 he was in Hollywood, playing a small role in Universal's *Tower of London* (1939) starring Basil Rathbone and Boris Karloff and then rejoined Rathbone in *Sherlock Holmes and the Voice of Terror* (1942). He stayed on at Universal to appear in *Two Tickets to London* (1943), (a film for which Roy William Neill wrote the original story), and the Charles Boyer episode in *Flesh and Fantasy* (1943). Stenning appeared in only 14 films and in 1952 he made his final appearance in an episode of the *Hallmark Hall of Fame* entitled "Joan of Arc", with Winston Churchill's daughter Sara portraying the French heroine. In 1953 he returned to Broadway once again to join Basil Rathbone in the role of Inspector Gregson in Rathbone and his wife Ouida Bergere's unsuccessful production of *Sherlock Holmes*. Arthur Stenning died on Christmas Eve of 1972 at the age of 89. He is buried at the Hollywood Memorial Cemetery in Hollywood, California.

The Woman in Green opened at its usual stand at the Rialto Theatre on the corner of Broadway and 42nd Street in New York on June 15, 1945 and the *New York Times* took its usual swipe at the film. Only this time it wasn't Bosley Crowther, but Thomas M. Pryor who singled out the screenwriter for most of his scorn: "A Hollywood script writer named Bertram Millhauser takes full responsibility for what transpires on the screen of the Rialto, and it's just as well, for Sir Arthur never perpetrated a disappointment such as *The Woman in Green*." Most of the other reviews were lukewarm at best, including the *New York World Telegram's* Alton Cook who said, "If you have never seen one of them, this one is worth a try on an idle evening. Or if you have seen any of the others, don't be surprised if you find yourself wondering whether you haven't already seen this one." Irene Thirer of the *New York Post* put it this way: "The new Sherlock Holmes whodunit at the Rialto has to do with hypnotism which, in effect, may lead to all sorts of weird situations, but which is definitely more fascinating in the flesh than when perpetrated in directed fashion for the screen." However the *New York Herald Tribune's* Otis L. Guernsey, Jr. did have some nice things to say for Basil Rathbone and Henry Daniell: "Rathbone's performance is always equal to the breadth of the script, which in this case allows him to approach very near to the character of the Sir Arthur Conan Doyle detective. Henry Daniell makes a perfect Professor Moriarty—suave, self-possessed and confronting Holmes in Baker Street in a coolly audacious duel of wits. No doubt the series would benefit from Daniell's continued presence as an opponent for the Rathbone characterization."

Undeterred by the reviews, the public continued to plunk down their money at the box office and Universal was already working on the next production. This is taken from an *AP* news release that appeared on July 25, 1945: "Basil Rathbone and Nigel Bruce have started working with Producer-Director Roy William Neill on the story for their next Sherlock Holmes starrer at Universal, *Red Dawn*. Latest of the cycle, produced and directed by Neill, was recently finished under the title *The Woman in Green*." Whether there was any truth to this press release or not, there was a new film in the works and it would eventually be titled *Pursuit to Algiers*.

PURSUIT TO ALGIERS

FOR ITS NEXT HOLMES FILM, Universal reached out to a new writer Leonard Lee, a journeyman who had earlier written the original story for 20th Century-Fox's *Bomber's Moon* (1943), the second film at Fox where my father switched personas to become a really nasty Nazi Gestapo officer. Lee's first draft of his original screenplay, initially titled *The Fugitive*, was delivered to the Breen Office on June 16, 1945 and once again they were concerned that the drinking be "held to an absolute minimum." They also asked the studio to delete the mention of "Cyamic Acid" although they probably meant cyanic acid. Lee continued to revise his script, still titled *The Fugitive*, through August when the title was changed to *Pursuit to*

Algiers. Much of the film's action takes place onboard a cargo-passenger ship named the S.S. *Friesland*—a name borrowed from Conan Doyle's "The Adventure of the Norwood Builder", first published in the *Strand* in October of 1903. Morton Lowry, who had earlier played the killer John Stapleton in Fox's *The Hound of the Baskervilles* (1939) and the sadistic schoolteacher in John Ford's *How Green Was My Valley* (1941), was signed at $500 per week for 2 2/3 weeks to play Prince Nikolas, disguised as the ship's steward. Marjorie Riordan, who had just been released by Warner Bros., was signed to play Sheila Woodbury for $500 a week with a 2 1/6 week guarantee. Once Universal saw how she registered on film they immediately signed her to a term contract for 6 months at $200 a week, but then never used her in another film. Which is a shame, as Riordan was a very attractive young performer with a good singing voice, and her acting abilities could have been properly developed with the right guidance. As it was, Riordan only appeared in three more feature films and an episode of the television series *Racket Squad* before leaving films altogether in 1951 to study to be a clinical psychologist. She died in 1984 at the age of 63. Nigel Bruce received another raise, with his salary rising to $15,000 Howard Benedict, who had continued to receive a salary throughout, suddenly began receiving credit as the executive producer after having been missing from the screen since *Sherlock Holmes Faces Death*, which probably meant that he was again taking a more active interest in developing the films. Benedict would continue to receive the executive producer credit for the remainder of the series.

The film was initially budgeted for 18 days of filming at $232,435 and (most likely because of the extensive use of process film backgrounds for the ship set, a procedure that habitually takes a great deal of time to prepare and shoot) went three days over budget for a final cost of $240,603.51, making it the most expensive film of the entire series up to that point. Another reason for the overage was the ship set that art directors John B. Goodman and Martin Obzina designed. The S.S. *Friesland's* extensive interior and exterior sets were constructed on the Phantom Stage at a cost of $18,185 This would be the first of two films in a row where modes of transportation were the settings for Sherlock Holmes' adventures; perhaps Roy William Neill was seeking that much needed inspiration and if not in this film, then in the next one, the new settings seemed to do the job.

With what at first appears to be another plot dealing with a stolen jewel, this time the Duchess of Brookdale's emerald collection, *Pursuit to Algiers* actually begins rather promisingly with a marvelously conceived and directed sequence that leads Holmes and Watson, through a series of obscure clues, to a meeting with the prime minister of Rovenia (Frederick Worlock) and several of his cabinet members. The prime minister explains to Holmes and Watson that their king has been assassinated by a group of insurgents trying to take control of the country and that they need Holmes' help to return the king's son, Prince Nikolas, who has been living incognito in London, safely to Rovenia. Over Watson's vociferous objections, Holmes agrees to help. Later that night they meet the prince (Leslie Vincent) as they are about to board a small plane to fly them to Rovenia. Watson is told that he cannot accompany Holmes and Nikolas as the plane is only a three-seater. Holmes and Watson devise a plan for Watson to travel to the Mediterranean by ship as a decoy and to meet Holmes later in Algiers.

Pursuit to Algiers utilizes stock footage very imaginatively in several sequences aboard the S.S. *Friesland*, starting with a montage of preparations at the docks and later the ship's leaving port and traveling at sea. The initial montage is followed by Watson's boarding the ship and our meeting several other characters, the first being Johansson, the Purser (Sven Hugo Borg) and including Sheila Woodbury (Marjorie Riordan) an American singer from Brooklyn, with no trace of a Brooklyn dialect, whose manager (George Leigh) rushes up the gangplank at the last moment to return her portfolio of musical arrangements to her. As Watson is being led to his cabin by Sanford the steward (Morton Lowry), they pass a couple of very suspicious looking men speaking in whispers, Childre (John Abbott) and Kingston (Gerald Hamer), who are later overheard by Watson speaking about "kings and bodies" in a very suspicious manner. In the ship's lounge, Watson meets Agatha Dunham (Rosalind Ivan), a totally obnoxious and slightly masculine lady who wears a monocle and dominates every conversation, and Mr. Arnold (Wilson Benge), a quiet little minister who wears a hearing aid. When Watson inadvertently knocks Miss Dunham's purse to the floor, a pistol is revealed. However, nothing is ever made of it or ever explained, which makes it one of the many red herrings artificially inserted into the plot.

A news release is posted on the ship's bulletin board announcing the crash of a three-seater plane with three occupants all presumed killed in the crash. Watson has only a moment to mourn the presumed death of Sherlock Holmes when he is summoned to a cabin to treat a sick passenger. The passenger turns out to be Prince Nikolas, and Holmes is with him. He informs Watson that the plane was shot down and that they were never on board. Watson is upset to find out that the entire plot was engineered by Holmes from the start and that he wasn't informed, but Holmes quickly assuages his hurt pride and enlists him in the subterfuge to pass off Nikolas as his nephew until they can safely hand him over to his people in Algiers.

Everyone is gathered in the ship's lounge listening to Sheila Woodbury singing "There Isn't Any Harm in That," written by Everett Carter and Milton Rosen (who also wrote another original if not particularly memorable song for the film called "Cross my Heart"). Watson asks Sheila to sing "Flow Gently, Sweet Afton" and she admits that she doesn't know it and asks for her music case. When Watson introduces Nikolas and Holmes to her, she grows visibly upset and rushes out of the lounge clutching her case. The next morning, she seems fully recovered as she joins the others in the lounge, even inviting Nikolas for a stroll on the deck, which Holmes finds suspicious. Watson goes looking for them and gets lost in the thick fog that has enveloped the ship. He bumps into Childre and Kingston, again discussing "bodies and contacting somebody in authority," then finds himself walking briskly with Miss Dunham. Holmes interrupts a *tete-a-tete* between Sheila and Nikolas just as she appears to have deliberately dropped her compact next to an opening in the railing that has been carelessly left unlocked.

The arrival of three suspicious new passengers, Mr. Mirko (Martin Kosleck), Mr. Gregor (Rex Evans) and Mr. Gubec (Wee Willie Davis), when the ship stops unexpectedly off the Lisbon coast, adds a little spark to the proceedings, but the film has begun to lose steam at this halfway point, resorting to various forms of padding, including two songs, admittedly performed quite satisfactorily by Marjorie Riordan. Another red hearing is inserted into the mix with Watson's repeated references to his "not trusting" Sanford the steward, but it is quickly made clear that the new arrivals are in fact the assassins sent to kill Nikolas. An attempt is made to poison Nikolas' coffee, but Watson notices that the cream has curdled and Holmes grabs the cup out of Nikolas' hand, declaring that the coffee is laced with cyanic acid. Apparently the studio didn't acquiesce to the Breen Office's request to remove the reference to cyanic acid. Another unnecessarily padded scene of deck-side shuffleboard between Holmes, Watson, Gregor, and Mirko, filled with presumably clever double-entendres, seems to go on forever and is followed by another scene in the lounge with more "clever" allusions to "losing and winning the game." After everyone has retired, Mirko and Gregor attempt to kill Holmes by throwing a knife through his porthole, but Holmes thwarts their efforts and slams the porthole on Mirko's wrist, breaking it. A reason for the shuffleboard game is at last explained when Holmes reveals that he recognized Mirko's accurate hand and remembered "…the circus of Medlano, in Paris, and your amazing exhibition of knife throwing."

The following morning Sheila's mysterious behavior is explained when Holmes confronts her on the deck and tells her that her actions when they first met led him to believe that she had just discovered something in her music case that upset her—something that had to be small enough to fit in the case—something like jewels. Holmes then explains that the owner of the café, where she has been retained as an entertainer, has been suspected for years of being the largest receiver of stolen goods in the Near East. Holmes will see that the Duchess of Brookdale's emeralds are returned and that Sheila will receive the reward. A relieved Sheila informs Holmes that she "won't have to carry this briefcase around with me anymore." Watson observes her kissing Holmes on the cheek as she leaves and comments, "Extraordinary sight." To which Holmes replies, "Elementary, my dear fellow, and very pleasant."

As Sheila sings "Flow Gently, Sweet Afton" for Doctor Watson, followed by a version of "Lock Lomond" sung by Nigel Bruce (not a bad voice at that), Agatha Dunham prepares her dinner party, placing favors with each passenger's name on them at each setting, as had been suggested by Mr. Gregor. After Miss Dunham and Sanford leave, Gregor replaces Nikolas's favor with one that contains explosives, commenting that the two weigh almost the same. Holmes then reveals that Childre and Kingston are in fact archaeologists on their way to Egypt to excavate

Marjorie Riordan as Sheila Woodbury accompanies Nigel Bruce's Dr. Watson, as he sings "Lock Lomond"

a tomb. At the dinner party, another overly padded and talky scene, Watson delivers a long, drawn-out dissertation of screenwriter Leonard Lee's version of the "Giant Rat of Sumatra," a tale that Conan Doyle correctly referred to in "The Adventures of the Sussex Vampire" as "a story for which the world is not yet prepared." Borrowing a classic routine from Zoltan Korda and R.C. Sherriff's *The Four Feathers* (1939), where Sir C. Aubrey Smith uses fruits and table settings to illustrate his story, director Neill has Watson begin his tale, as Sheila and Nikolas start to open their favors to retrieve the hats inside. Holmes notices something strange about Nikolas' favor and replaces it with his own. He then goes out on deck and is spotted by Gubec. The trio of assassins, who are beginning more and more to resemble the Three Stooges, follow Holmes on deck and watch him throw the favor overboard just as it explodes harmlessly in the sea.

When the ship drops anchor in Algiers harbor, Holmes sends Watson to meet the prince's entourage as he and Nikolas prepare to leave the ship. Imitating Doctor Watson's voice, Gregor gains entry to the room and captures Nikolas. Holmes is subdued and tied up by Gubec and they leave the ship with Nikolas as their hostage. Watson returns to find Holmes locked in his cabin, only to discover that the real Prince Nikolas is actually Sanford the steward, and that the assassins have been captured and the other Nikolas released. Once again Watson is piqued that Holmes didn't inform him of Sanford's true identity, but Holmes explains that he was afraid Watson couldn't keep from giving the Prince's identity away. "Yes, Watson, let me advise you," he says with a smile, "if you ever consider taking up another profession, don't even think of becoming an actor." I'm sure that most of the audience laughed at that inside joke, and it was certainly better than another homily from Holmes.

Leonard Lee's rather talky screenplay didn't give Roy William Neill much of an opportunity to display his craft; in fact the blocking of the actors and the camerawork were for the most part quite pedestrian. The well-lit ship interiors gave him virtually no chance for low-key lighting or interesting camera movement and only the fog-bound decks had any sense of tension to them. He did however successfully utilize the process screen to tie in the ocean and the ship's decks whenever possible, thereby effectively creating the illusion that his characters were playing their scenes on a real sea-going vessel. When I was at M-G-M, working on the screenplays for the Elvis Presley films with director Norman Taurog, in particular one called *Double Trouble* (1967), I came up with the idea for a sequence on a fog-shrouded Channel Steamer with several mysterious characters stalking Elvis that was admittedly borrowed from *Pursuit to*

Algiers. I don't know how it went on their set, but we had severe problems with the "bee's smoke," the mixture of a special oil and heat that created the look of fog. In order to photograph fog or smoke, you had to fill the set with five times as much as you actually see on the screen, so our effects men kept pumping more and more smoke into the set until it was so thick you couldn't see anything. After several hours of this, people were coughing and gasping and we had to open the big stage doors and let everyone step outside for a breath of fresh air. In spite of all the hardships, the scene looked great on the big screen.

For a change there were only four members of the repertory company working in this film and two of them appeared only in the opening sequences and not on the ship. Olaf Hytten makes a brief appearance as the sporting goods store proprietor in the opening sequence and Frederick Worlock has a few scenes as the prime minister of Rovenia. The other two were Gerald Hamer as the archaeologist, Mr. Kingston, all dolled up in a false beard and cigarette holder, and Wilson Benge as the hard of hearing minister, Mr. Arnold.

The new members of the cast included Marjorie Riordan (Sheila Woodbury), Morton Lowry (Sanford), Leslie Vincent (the false Prince Nikolas), Rosalind Ivan (Agatha Dunham), Martin Kosleck (Mr. Mirko), Rex Evans (Mr. Gregor), Wee Willie Davis (Mr. Gubec), John Abbott (Mr. Childre) and Sven Hugo Borg (Johansson, the Purser).

MARJORIE RIORDAN's brief film career was by her own doing, as she chose to leave Hollywood after appearing in only eight films, one short and one television episode to pursue a more challenging career in clinical psychology. Marjorie Jane Riordan was born on January 4, 1920 in Washington D.C. to John K. Riordan and the former Rose Shoresman. By the time Marjorie was 10-years-old the family had moved to Milwaukee, Wisconsin, where both her parents worked as clerks for the U.S. government. While attending Washington High School, Marjorie became a finalist in a state-wide forensic tournament, but was eliminated in the third round of the humorous declamation event. After graduating from Wisconsin University, Marjorie did some modeling and was quickly discovered by a talent scout and brought to Hollywood, where she was given a featured role in Columbia Pictures' *Parachute Nurse* (1942). After she appeared as Lon McCallister's love interest in the all-star *Stage Door Canteen* (1943), producer Sol Lesser signed Marjorie to a term contract, but transferred her contact to Warner Bros. the following year. Marjorie's first role at Warners was as Bette Davis' daughter in *Mr. Skeffington* (1944) and she followed that with a leading role in a Warner Bros. short entitled *Navy Nurse* (1945).

Marjorie Riordan as Sheila Woodbury
in *Pursuit to Algiers.*

Marjorie Riordan spent most of her time during 1944 and 1945 posing for pin-up photographs and entertaining at the Hollywood Canteen. It was there that she met Marine Major George Lumpkin, a decorated hero with a Navy Cross and the Air Medal for his actions in the battle for Guadalcanal. Riordan and Lumpkin were secretly married for several months before she finally broke the news to the columnists and posed for more photographs. Her role as Sheila Woodbury in *Pursuit to Algiers,* in which she sang three songs, was a pleasant break in her routine. By 1951 she had made up her mind to quit movies and go back to graduate school to study speech therapy. From this she developed an interest in clinical psychology and eventually opened her own practice in this field in North Carolina. Marjorie Riordan and George Lumpkin were divorced in January of 1958 and shortly after she married Alan Schlaff in Nevada on February 21, 1958. The couple moved back to Los Angeles, where a son, John, was born on March 1, 1959. Marjorie and Alan would remain married until his death in May of 1972. Marjorie would succumb to breast cancer in Los Angeles on March 8, 1984 at the age of 64. She is buried alongside her husband at the Westwood Memorial Park in Westwood Village, Los Angeles, California.

MORTON LOWRY, whose birth name was Edward Morton Lowater, was born in the town of Barton-Upon-Irwell in Manchester, England on February 13, 1914, the son of Edward M. Lowater and the former Bertha Holmes. Lowry did some acting on the British stage before sailing to the United States on the S.S. *Berengaria* in December of 1937. After arriving in New York on December 22, he went on directly to Hollywood, where he stayed with a girlfriend, Virginia Barrato, at her apartment at 1825 Ivar Avenue. A few weeks later Lowry crossed the U.S.-Mexican border at Calexico, California and re-entered as a legal immigrant and shortly thereafter landed his first film role as David Niven's younger brother in Warner Bros remake of *The Dawn Patrol* (1938), also starring Errol Flynn and Basil Rathbone. Lowry made four more films in 1939, including M-G-M's *Tarzan Finds a Son!,* in which he and Laraine Day played Johnny Sheffield's parents, who are killed at the beginning of the film in a plane crash.

It would appear that Lowry was then signed by 20th Century-Fox to a term contract, as over the next few years he appeared in a number of films for the studio, including his role as the murderous John Stapleton in 20th Century-Fox's first Basil Rathbone-Sherlock Holmes film *The Hound of the Baskervilles* (1939). In 1941 he played one of his more memorable roles as Mr. Jonas, the sadistic schoolteacher who is given a beating by Rhys Williams in John Ford's *How Green Was My Valley*. My father's name appears in the closing credits for the film play-

Morton Lowry as the real Prince Nikolas, with Basin Rathbone in *Pursuit to Algiers*.

ing a character named Mr. Motschell, but he doesn't appear in the film and for years I had wondered what had happened. When I was writing my first book, Tom Weaver solved the mystery for me by sending me a copy of Philip Dunne's screenplay. According to the script, after Mr. Jonas had received his comeuppance for thrashing young Roddy McDowell's Huw Morgan, the scene continued with my father as Mr. Motschell, the headmaster, angrily entering the schoolroom. After reading this portion of Dunne's screenplay it was obvious to me that this moment was anticlimactic and it is my guess that it was appropriately cut from the final print after a preview.

Lowry finished his long run of films for 20th Century-Fox with a featured role in the World War II film *The Immortal Sergeant* (1943) starring Henry Fonda, although he did return for two more films in 1944 and 1945. His final Hollywood film was Paramount's *Calcutta* (1947) with Alan Ladd and Gail Russell. In 1950, Lowry married English actress Lilian Bond, a former showgirl in the *Ziegfeld Follies* and *Earl Carroll's Vanities*, who had played Lily Langtry in *The Westerner* (1940). The couple returned to London, where Lowry began appearing on British television, including a BBC production of the Edna Ferber-George S. Kaufman play *The Royal Family* that was called *Theatre Royal* (1952). In 1959, he was signed by the Incorporated Television Company to play a recurring role in their Richard Greene series *The Adventures of Robin Hood*, as well as for several episodes in another of their series, *The Four Just Men* starring Richard Conte and Dan Dailey. Morton Lowry and Lilian Bond returned to the United States a few years later and settled in San Francisco, where Lowry succumbed to a heart attack on November 26, 1987.

LESLIE VINCENT, whose real name was Leslie Fullard-Leo, was born in New York on September 6, 1909 and grew up in Hawaii, the son of wealthy industrialist Leslie Fullard-Leo. Vincent's mother, Ellen Fullard-Leo, had been born in Capetown, South Africa and would later become well-known for her activities with the U.S. Olympic Association. In 1922, Vincent's family purchased the Palmyra Atoll, one of a series of islets located due south of Hawaii, (roughly halfway between Hawaii and American Samoa) from Judge Henry Ernest Cooper and established the Palmyra Copra Company to harvest the coconuts growing there. In 1974,

Leslie Vincent (r) as the false Prince Nikolas, with Marjorie Riordan,
Nigel Bruce and Basil Rathbone in *Pursuit to Algiers*.

the atoll would be the setting for the infamous double murders, known as the "Sea Wind Murders," of a wealthy San Diego couple, Malcolm "Mac" Graham and his wife Eleanor "Muff" Graham. The murderers were later arrested in Honolulu on board the Graham's sailboat the Sea Wind and convicted of the crime. Vincent and his two brothers, Dudley and Ainsley, grew up on Oahu and graduated from the Punahou School in Honolulu. Vincent later studied acting at the Royal Academy in London and it was here that he most likely developed his slight British accent that served him well as an actor.

In 1940, Vincent arrived in Hollywood and was soon appearing in films. Right from the start, directors saw him as a young Englishman and cast him in roles such as a British army lieutenant in *They Met in Bombay* (1941) and a British pilot in *A Yank in the R.A.F.* (1941), none of which garnered him any screen credit. After similar roles in ten more films over the next four years, Vincent finally got his chance at a featured role as the downed British pilot smuggled to freedom by Constance Bennett and Gracie Fields in *Paris Underground* (1945) and shortly after that he was cast as the faux prince in *Pursuit to Algiers*. Then it was back to smaller uncredited roles until he gave up films in 1948, returning to Hawaii to enter the hotel business. He and his brothers sued the U.S. government to return Palmyra Atoll to them, after it had been taken over as a military base during World War II, and after several years of litigation the U.S. Supreme Court ruled in their favor. In 1972 Leslie Vincent made a guest appearance on Jack Lord's *Hawaii Five-O*, using his full name of Leslie Vincent Fullard. He died in Hawaii on February 1, 2001.

MARTIN KOSLECK made his one appearance in a Sherlock Holmes film in *Pursuit to Algiers*, but he was no stranger to Universal's horror films. Starting with *The Mummy's Curse* (1944), he then appeared in *The Frozen Ghost* (1945), *House of Horrors* (1946) and *She-Wolf of London* (1946). He was born on March 24, 1904 in Barkotzen in Pomerania, Germany; some records claim that his real name was Nicolaie Yoshkin, the son of a Russian-Jewish forester, but there is no listing of the surname Yoshkin in any genealogical site and his mother appears as Alice Kosleck on a ship's manifest in 1939. What is clear is that Martin Kosleck studied for six years with the Max Reinhardt Dramatic School and worked in musical revues in Berlin. He once appeared with a young Marlene Dietrich in a production of Shakespeare's *The Taming of the Shrew* at the Grosses Schauspielhaus in Berlin. He also developed a self-taught talent as a painter and would later paint a portrait of Dietrich that she greatly admired. He also appeared with his future wife, Eleonora von Mendelssohn in the play *The Tribute*.

In 1927, at the age of 23, he had his first screen role in a silent film starring Walter Slezak called *Der Fahnentrager von Sedan* and would appear in another silent film and two sound films including the science-fiction thriller *Alraune* (1930) starring Brigitte Helm, who played Maria in Fritz Lang's *Metropolis* (1927). By 1931, Kosleck, who had been speaking out against the rising Nazi Party and Adolf Hitler, decided to leave Germany for Britain and then on to the United States, arriving in New York aboard the S.S. *Westernland* on November 18, 1931. He continued on to Los Angeles and supported himself with his painting while he tried to break into films. In 1934 he was appearing at the Pasadena Playhouse in Dostoyevsky's *The Brothers Karamazov* with Hobart Bosworth.

Martin Kosleck as Mr. Mirko in *Pursuit to Algiers.*

1934 also brought Kosleck his first Hollywood screen role as a dance director in fellow expatriate William Dieterle's *Fashions of 1934* starring William Powell and Bette Davis. No more films roles presented themselves until Anatole Litvak cast him in *Confessions of a Nazi Spy* (1939), the first of several films in which he portrayed German Propaganda Minister Joseph Goebbels. After this somewhat controversial film was released, Kosleck found himself being sought for more Nazi roles, including *Espionage Agent* (1939), *Underground* (1941), *Berlin Correspondent* (1942), *Bomber's Moon* (1943) and *The Hitler Gang* (1944) in which he again played Goebbels. In 1938, Kosleck followed many other immigrants' tactic to enter the United States, by walking across the border from Mexicali to Calexico. The following year he applied for his American citizenship and brought his mother over from Europe. They lived at 5423 Blackoak Drive in Los Angeles.

Kosleck worked constantly throughout the war years, even appearing as Basil Rathbone's fanatical assistant in Paramount's *The Mad Doctor* (1941). In 1943, while playing a Gestapo officer in *The Fighting Guerrillas* for 20th Century-Fox, he came very close to losing his sight when in a scene where he is supposedly shot at, pieces of glass and particles of lead pierced his eyes. The incident was written about by Hollywood columnist Erskine Johnson, who described it this way: "For 10 days his eyes were blacked out in a hospital room while doctors fought to save his sight. The doctors were successful, but he still has to take treatments. And then, typically Hollywood, the scene in which he was injured was cut from the picture. Why? 'Oh,' says Kosleck, 'the studio thought it slowed down the action.'" By 1946, the sort of roles Kosleck was noted for were no longer in demand and he found himself working less and less, so in 1948 he moved to New York. A short time later he became the fourth and final husband of Eleonora von Mendelssohn, the German émigré, actress and theatrical society grande dame.

Kosleck appeared on Broadway as The Deaf Mute in Jean Giraudoux's *The Madwoman of Chaillot*. The play, which opened on Broadway in December of 1948 starring Estelle Winwood and John Carradine, was a big success and played 368 performances, closing in January of 1950. An attempt was made to revive the play in June of 1950 with most of the original cast, but with Kosleck's wife, von Mendelssohn replacing Doris Rich as Mme. Josephine (The Madwoman of La Concorde). Unfortunately the play ran for only 17 performances and in January of 1951, von Mendelssohn died under supposedly mysterious circumstances. This claim was exploited in 2007 when Alfred A. Knopf published the personal memoir of Leo Lerman, a writer and editor for over 50 years for Conde Nast Publications. In *The Grand Surprise: The Journals of Leo Lerman* that is a collection of rather florid prose, Lerman, who died in 1974 and was an admitted homosexual, wrote about his infatuation for Eleonora von Mendelssohn and claimed that although her death was listed as a suicide, several unreported clues pointed to murder, including the fact that a pillow was found over von Mendelssohn's face and a bath mat had been soaked in ether. The unspoken implication was that Martin Kosleck was responsible. The police never brought charges against anyone and the ruling of suicide remained the official cause of death. A year later, according to further entries in Lerman's published journals, Lerman himself came to accept the fact that von Mendelssohn's lengthy drug addiction had caused her to commit suicide, but he never retracted his accusations that Martin Kosleck was responsible for his wife's death.

In 1952 Kosleck began working in live television productions in New York including *Robert Montgomery Presents* and *The Motorola Television Hour*. In 1954 he returned to Los Angeles to appear in a number of the early filmed series. In 1962 he once again portrayed Joseph Goebbels in *Hitler* with actor Richard Basehart in the title role. His work slowed down after he suffered a heart attack during the early '70s and he appeared in his final film, *The Man with Bogart's Face,* in 1980. Kosleck continued with his painting, his work being exhibited in both New York and Los Angeles; both Marlene Dietrich and Bette Davis purchased his portraits of them. Martin Kosleck died at a Santa Monica convalescent home, after having had abdominal surgery, on January 15, 1994.

REX EVANS, whose full name was Reginald Llewellyn Evans, was born on April 13, 1903 in Southport, a seaside town just north of Liverpool in North West England. Evans' father was a well-to-do solicitor in Southport and he and his wife Gertrude had been married for only a year when Evans was born. As an only child, Evans grew up in a ten room house on Rawlinson Road in Southport, attended to by a nurse and several servants. By the mid-1920s, Evans was appearing in London cabarets and music hall reviews and becoming a favorite of café society as a nightclub pianist. He made a cameo appearance in the early sound film *Comets* (1930) a musical revue that featured well-known vaudevillians and cabaret artists in songs, dances and dramatic sketches. This film also included an early screen appearance by Charles Laughton and his wife Elsa Lanchester singing a duet of "The Ballad of Frankie and Johnny," which was not well-received by the critics. Evans completed several trips to the United States before making his first feature film appearance in a musical comedy starring British slapstick comedienne Cicely Courtneidge, *Along Came Sally* (1933). His first Broadway appearance was in the original North American production of the Bertolt Brecht -Kurt Weill *Threepenny Opera* at the Empire Theatre in April of 1933. Unfortunately, despite great successes in Europe, American audiences failed to appreciate the artistic style of Brecht and Weill and the play closed after 12 performances.

Evans returned to London to try his hand at films, but had only one small role in *Rembrandt* (1936). Returning to the United States on the S.S. *Berengaria,* he landed in New York on January 28, 1936, and

Rex Evans as Mr. Gregor in *Pursuit to Algiers.*

traveled on directly to Los Angeles. His luck improved, mostly because of his friendship with director George Cukor, who hired him for a small role in his production of *Camille* (1936). A frequently quoted story that is still worth repeating tells of Greta Garbo noticing Evans on the set and going to Cukor to ask, "Who is that big man, and what part is he playing?" Cukor answered, "He's playing the part of a friend who needs a job." Ultimately, Evans would appear in nine Cukor films over the next eighteen years, including *The Philadelphia Story* (1940), *Adam's Rib* (1949) and *A Star Is Born* (1954). He also played his share of butlers, including the running role of J.H. King's butler in all three of the *Five Little Peppers* films in 1939 and 1940 and he appeared as Vazec, the surly innkeeper in Roy William Neill's *Frankenstein Meets the Wolf Man* (1943) before taking on his role as Mr. Gregor in *Pursuit to Algiers*. In 1946, shortly after appearing in a small role in M-G-M's all-star musical *Till the Clouds Roll By*, Evans returned to Broadway to portray Sir Augustus Lorton in a revival of Oscar Wilde's *Lady Windermere's Fan* starring Cornelia Otis Skinner and Estelle Winwood. The play had a successful run from October of 1946 to April of 1947 and then the company went on tour throughout the United States. Evans returned to Broadway in October of 1948 to appear with Anne Jeffreys in the musical *My Romance*, which ran through January of 1949.

In December of 1949 Evans opened on Broadway in the original production of the musical *Gentlemen Prefer Blondes* starring Carol Channing at the Ziegfeld Theatre. The play, in which Evans played Sir Francis Beekman, one of Lorelei's suitors, ran for 740 performances, finally closing on September 15, 1951. Returning to Hollywood, Evans alternated between films and television, while working in his spare time as an interior decorator. In 1960 Evans formed a partnership with James Weatherford and took over the second floor of a shop at 748 ½ La Cienega Boulevard in West Hollywood to open the Rex Evans Gallery. The area was rapidly becoming a hub of antique and interior decorator shops and Evans' gallery prospered. The California artist Don Bachardy had his first showing of Hollywood portraits at Evans' gallery in 1962. Evans appeared in his final film *On the Double* (1961) starring Danny Kaye and Dana Wynter and then retired to concentrate on running his gallery. He died at Glendale Community Hospital on April 3, 1969. The Rex Evans Gallery closed in 1972.

JOHN ABBOTT, whose bulging eyes and bobbing Adam's apple helped him to portray a vast array of comic characters and shady individuals, was born on June 5, 1905 in London, England. Abbott, whose real name was John Albert Chamberlain Kefford, was the third son of Edwin Kefford, a dealer in furs, and Annie Kefford. Abbott and his two brothers,

John Abbott (l) as Mr. Childre, with Gerald Hamer in *Pursuit to Algiers*.

Harold and Arthur who were eight and six years older than him and a sister, Ivy, who was younger, received most of their education from private tutors. By 1927 when he was 22, he had officially changed his name to Abbott and was performing in amateur productions at the St. Pancras Theatre in London. He soon turned professional with his appearance at the Westminster Theatre in London's West End in Elizabethan playwright John Dryden's blank verse drama *Aurenz-Zebe*. During the next few years Abbott alternated acting in Shakespearean productions such as *Love's Labor Lost*, *Twelfth Night* and *Hamlet*, with original productions, *The Last Train South* and *Tobias and the Angel*.

John Abbott's British film career began with Alexander Korda's history of man's attempts to fly from ancient times to the present, *Conquest of the Air* (1936), in which he played French balloonist Jean-Francois Pilatre de Rozier. His credits over the next three years would include starring roles in several early BBC television productions and a featured role in an

American film, *The Saint in London* (1939) starring George Sanders and British actress Sally Gray and produced by RKO Pictures as a "quota quickie" in London. As Europe moved inexorably toward war, Abbott worked for a short time at the British Embassy in Moscow, leaving to travel to the United States in 1940 and arriving in New York on the S.S. *Empress of Asia* on September 2, 1940. After a short stay in New York, Abbott left the United States briefly, to re-enter from Tijuana, Mexico on November 26, 1941 at the San Ysidro border crossing in San Diego, California. He auditioned and won a role in former British producer Arnold Pressburger and German director Josef von Sternberg's *The Shanghai Gesture* (1941) which starred Gene Tierney, Victor Mature, Walter Huston and future Roy William Neill repertory player and fellow *Pursuit to Algiers* cast member Rex Evans playing the piano at "Mother" Gin Sling's dinner party.

Abbott's career would ultimately total 150 films and television appearances, with some memorable roles including Jack Rawlings the murderer in *London Blackout Murders* (1943), Webb Fallon the vampire in *The Vampire's Ghost* (1945), the hypochondriac Frederick Fairlie in *The Woman in White* (1948), his humerous performances in the Bob Hope comedy *They Got Me Covered* (1943), and my favorite of my father's films, a wonderful comedy-fantasy called *A Thousand and One Nights* (1945) starring Cornel Wilde, Evelyn Keyes and Phil Silvers, in which my father played the dual roles of the sultan and the sultan's evil twin brother and John Abbott played Ali the tailor, who finds the magic lamp and orders the Genie to grant him all the riches and women he can ask for. His reaction when Cornel Wilde regains possession of the lamp and Ali loses everything is priceless.

Abbott made his Broadway debut in a revival of *He Who Gets Slapped* in 1946, but quickly returned to Hollywood when the play closed after a month and found work in six films that year, including *Anna and the King of Siam*, *Deception* and *Humoresque*. 1947 brought five more films, but by 1948 jobs began to dry up and Abbott returned to Broadway in an original play written and directed by Lillian Hellman called *Montserrat* that managed a run of 65 performances. He had only one film in 1949 and that was Vincente Minnelli's *Madame Bovary* at M-G-M and it was then that he learned that he had been blacklisted as a Communist. In 1950, with the help of a producer who wanted to hire him, he had his name removed from the list when it became clear that he was being mistaken for blacklisted writer Dalton Trumbo who had used the name John Abbott as a *nom de plume*.

In the 1950s, '60s and '70s Abbott worked in hundreds of television series. He would return to Broadway once last time in 1957 to appear as Dr. Bonfant in Jean Anouilh's *Waltz of the Toreadors*. He would even supply the voice of the Wolf in Disney's *The Jungle Book* (1967), but by 1978 he was slowing down and had taken up teaching acting to young actors and actresses. John Abbott would die on May 24, 1996 at Cedars Sinai Medical Center in Los Angeles. His *New York Times* obituary noted that he was survived by his sister Ivy Skeates of Cambridge, England.

ROSALIND IVAN, who gives a slightly overblown, but still amusing performance as Agatha Dunham in *Pursuit to Algiers*, was born in London on November 27, 1880. She had a lengthy career on Broadway, the London stage, films and radio and she even appeared in a number of early live television programs in New York, such as *Lux Video Theatre* and *Philco Playhouse*. Ivan toured the United States in 1901-02 with Henry Irving and Ellen Terry in Shakespeare's *The Merchant of Venice* and later made her

Rosalind Ivan as Agatha Dunham in *Pursuit to Algiers*.

Broadway debut in 1907 in Ibsen's *The Master Builder* with Alla Nazimova and Warner Oland, who would later play Doctor Yogami, the lycanthrope who infects Henry Hull, in *Werewolf of London* (1935) and was of course the first to play Charlie Chan in the Fox series in *The Black Camel* (1931). Ivan continued appearing on the London stage as well as in eleven more Broadway productions, including *Richard III* with John Barrymore in 1920. She would also translate from the Russian language two plays, *Nju* by Ossip Dymow in 1917 and Dostoyevsky's *The Brothers Karamazov* in 1927. In 1934 she appeared with Katharine Hepburn and Colin Clive in *The Lake*.

Ivan made her screen debut in the silent film, *Arms and the Woman* (1916) for director George Fitzmaurice; it was written by Basil Rathbone's wife, Ouida Bergere and featured a little known actor by the name of Edward G, Robinson. Some 30 years later, Ivan and Robinson would reunite in the 1945 *film noir* classic *Scarlet Street*, in which she played Robinson's shrewish wife. Ivan's first sound film was a Philo Vance mystery at M-G-M, *The Garden Murder Case* (1936) starring Edmund Lowe and Virginia Bruce. She would then return to Broadway to appear in three more plays, including a musical biography of Gilbert and Sullivan, *Knights of Song*, with Nigel Bruce as William Gilbert and Ivan as his wife. In 1940, Ivan created the role of Mrs. Watty in the hugely successful production of Emlyn Williams' *The Corn Is Green* that ran for 477 performances starring Ethel Barrymore. When Warner Bros. made the film version starring Bette Davis at the end of 1944, they brought Ivan and her co-star Rhys Williams out to Burbank to recreate their roles in the film.

Ivan's most memorable roles, besides her appearances in *Scarlet Street* and *The Corn Is Green*, are two other nasty characters that earned her the nickname of "Ivan the Terrible." They are Charles Laughton's nagging wife, whom he eventually murders in *The Suspect* (1944) and Morton Lowry's hysterical landlady in *The Verdict* (1946). Her final screen appearance was in Paramount's *Elephant Walk* (1954), the film where Elizabeth Taylor had to replace an ailing Vivien Leigh after the company returned from location filming in Sri Lanka. Rosalind Ivan died of heart failure in New York City on April 8, 1959.

WILSON BENGE, who had previously appeared briefly in *The Pearl of Death* and as Guy Davies, one of the Good Comrades, in *The House of Fear*, was now making his third appearance as a member of the Roy William Neill repertory company as Mr. Norton the minister. (He would return for a fourth time, also as a minister, in *Dressed to Kill*.) Benge, whose real name was George Frederick Benge, was born to Joseph and Mercy Benge on March 1, 1875 in Greenwich, a district of South East London,

Wilson Benge as Mr. Arnold in
Pursuit to Algiers.

England. Joseph Benge worked as a general laborer and the family, which included two more boys and three girls ranging in age from 20 to 4, lived at 14 Old Woolwich Road.

Wilson Benge's education was cursory, for by the time he was 16 he was already working as a rope manufacturer's clerk in London. However, by his 30th birthday he would be married to the former Sarah Lily, and both he and Sarah would be working actors. Six years later they would have a son named George Wilson Benge.

Benge apparently also worked as a theatrical manager in both London and New York and in 1908 traveled with his partner Lester Collingwood to New York, arriving on the S.S. *Mauritania* on June 13, 1908. There is no record of Benge having appeared on Broadway, but in 1922 he arrived in Hollywood and marked his first acting role as a henchman to the villainous Prince John in Douglas Fairbanks' silent *Robin Hood*. For his second film, he appeared for the first of many times as a butler in the modern portion of Cecil B. DeMille's silent version of *The Ten Commandments* (1923). Ultimately, Benge would portray butlers in 97 films between 1923 and his final film, M-G-M's *The Scarlet Coat* (1955). For a few years, during the mid-1940s and the early 1950s, Benge managed to escape his butler's duties and find more diversified roles, such as his work for Roy William Neill; however he still managed to play a half-dozen waiters during that same period. During his 195 film roles, Benge managed to survive Hollywood's type casting and work with virtually every major star in Hollywood, including Laurel and Hardy (*You're Darn Tootin'* [1928] and *Scram!* [1932]) and The Three Stooges (*Pardon My Scotch* [1935] and *A Plumbing We Will Go* [1940]). Wilson Benge died on July 1, 1955 at the age of 80 in Los Angeles, California.

Two more actors who appeared in *Pursuit to Algiers* both coincidentally used three names in their screen credits. The first was WEE WILLIE DAVIS, who played the mute Mr. Gubec. William Davis was born in New York in 1906 and was a wrestler in the 1930s. He parlayed his bulky physique into playing heavies from 1941 to 1978 in some thirty films,

Wee Willie Davis as Mr. Gubec.

Sven Hugo Borg (r) as Johansson the purser, with John Abbott in *Pursuit to Algiers*.

including Basil Rathbone's Nazi thug in M-G-M's *Above Suspicion* (1943), before becoming a wrestling promoter in Louisville, Kentucky and dying there at the age of 74 in 1981. The other actor, SVEN HUGO BORG, who played Johansson the purser, was born in Vinslov, Sweden and in the early 1920s came to the United States as a secretary with the Swedish Consulate in Los Angeles. It was there that he met the newly arrived Greta Garbo, who asked him to interpret for her during her first film at M-G-M, *Torrent* (1926). He stayed with Garbo as her interpreter until he too became an actor when he appeared in the silent version of *Rose-Marie* (1928) starring Joan Crawford. From then until his retirement in 1963, when he played a dead makeup artist in the Paul Newman thriller *The Prize*, he appeared in over seventy films and television series. Borg died in Los Angeles on February 19, 1981 at the age of 84.

The Rialto Theatre, the traditional first-run screening location for Universal's Sherlock Holmes series in New York City, was actually the third theatre to occupy the site at 1481 Broadway. The first was Oscar Hammerstein's Victoria Theatre, which was torn down in 1916 to be replaced by an extravagant movie theatre that was operated under the personal direction of S. L. Rothapfel, better known as "Roxy." The Rialto ran five shows a day that included an orchestra, soloists and "accompaniment contributed by the grand organ." In 1935 this theatre was demolished and rebuilt as a smaller, 594-seat, single-screen house in the Art Deco style of the period. This theatre would be destroyed in 1998 to make way for the 30-story Reuter's building that now occupies the site.

Pursuit to Algiers opened at the Rialto on October 26, 1945, and this time the critics were of no help at all; even the Hollywood trade papers were unhappy. *The Hollywood Reporter* took some heavy swings at Nigel Bruce's performance: "If fault is to be found with this latest issue it is because producer-director Roy William Neill permits Doctor Watson to take center stage so often that the slow-thinking blunderer slows things down for everybody." *PM,* the liberal newspaper that was published daily from 1940 to 1948, devoted a short paragraph to the film declaring: "This Sherlock Holmes episode comes along apparently just to keep the franchise. [It has] no relation to any of the Conan Doyle originals and no apparent connection with present day affairs." The *New York Post* agreed, pronouncing: "*Pursuit to Algiers* does nothing but keep the Sherlock Holmes franchise for Universal and lessen its value."

However, not everyone hated the film entirely, Wanda Hale of the *Daily News* wrote, "*Pursuit to Algiers,* like all Sherlock Holmes mysteries, is good fun and relaxing entertainment…You can just sit back and chuckle over Doctor Watson's blundering and mutterings of protestation at Holmes' subterfuge while Holmes works away, efficiently, doing his job thoroughly and without mishap." Even Bosley Crowther of the *New York Times,* back at his post, had a mild compliment to share in his review: "All that's left is to sit there and chuckle at Doctor Watson's (Nigel Bruce) wretched jokes and sniff at the upstart presumptions of the sleuth's transient enemies." Once again the public figuratively thumbed its collective noses at the critics and bought their tickets, and Universal happily moved on to their next Sherlock Holmes production; this time exchanging the confines of a ship at sea for the more confining compartments of a fast-moving express train—but this time the formula seemed to be working.

TERROR BY NIGHT

UNIVERSAL HIRED FRANK GRUBER, a successful screenwriter and novelist, to create the next Sherlock Holmes film and paid him $5,416 for his efforts. By the time Gruber arrived at Universal Studios he had already written and had published eleven novels, literally hundreds of pulp magazine short stories and had six produced screenplays such as *Northern Pursuit* (1943) starring Errol Flynn and *Johnny Angel* (1945) starring George Raft and Claire Trevor. In 1947, while I was just starting high school, I had read one of Gruber's detective novels called *The Silver Jackass* and decided I would write a screenplay adaptation of the novel. I didn't bother to look into securing the rights and I really had no knowledge of how to con-

struct a screenplay, but that didn't bother me for a moment and I set about writing my first screenplay in longhand, using a pencil and putting it all down in several school notebooks. You can well imagine what a mess this was, but with my youthful impudence, I had the gall to give my workings to a dear friend of my father's, a professional screenwriter named Herb Meadow, and ask for his comments. Herb was gracious enough not only to read my scribbling, but to critique my work. His best advice was "Be sure you own the rights before you start writing a screenplay of somebody else's work." Years later I had the privilege of meeting Frank Gruber when we both had offices at Producers Studio. I would occasionally join Frank and his friend Steve Fisher for lunch at a dingy corner bar across the street next to Paramount Studios. Fisher was another screenwriter who wrote the novel that 20th Century-Fox made into what many consider being the first *film-noir*, *I Wake Up Screaming* (1941). In true *noir* fashion, we would drink our lunch while watching musical shorts on an old Scopitone juke box in the corner. Scopitones were a cross between a jukebox and a 24-inch television that played vintage 16mm short films (Soundies), made in the 1930s and '40s, of bandleaders like Cab Calloway and Woody Herman with their orchestras. One day, after having watched enough of Calloway "Hi-de-hi-de-hoe"-ing and having consumed enough lunch to give me the proper courage, I told Frank about my misguided effort to adapt *The Silver Jackass* and he laughed, saying he was sorry that I didn't succeed as it was one of his favorites and no one had ever made it into a film.

Although *Terror by Night* was basically an original story and screenplay, Gruber did take a couple of elements from Conan Doyle's "The Adventure of the Empty House," specifically the character of Colonel Sebastian Moran and the air gun that was used as the murder weapon. Gruber's "First Revised" screenplay of *Terror by Night* was delivered to the Production Code offices on July 31, 1945, and on the whole the script passed without too much discussion. Oh, there were the usual requests to eliminate overt violence, but the Breen Office seemed far more concerned that Mr. and Mrs. Shallcross would be appropriately punished for pinching the teapot than anything else. As the film moved toward a production date, budgets were drawn up and construction began on the sets. The interiors of the train, the central setting for the film, were constructed on the studio's Stage 20 and included the passenger coach and compartments, the baggage car and the dining car at a cost of $5,400. The budget shows that Roy William Neill received a considerable bump in his salary to $10,000 with no explanation given, but Howard Benedict continued at his regular rate of $3,000. Rathbone and Bruce received their usual salaries of $20,000 and $15,000 respectively and Dennis Hoey was brought back for his final appearance as Inspector Lestrade at his usual rate of $1,000 a week and, because he was featured quite prominently in this film, given a three-week guarantee. Alan Mowbray was hired to play Major Duncan-Bleek at a salary of $1,500 a week for 2 2/3 weeks. *Terror by Night* was budgeted for 16 days of filming, but ended up going 6 days over the schedule. The initial budget was estimated at $224,725, but the final cost would turn out to be $251,954.20, which exceeded the costs for *Pursuit to Algiers* by over $11,000, thereby earning it the dubious honor of becoming the most expensive film in the series.

However, there were extenuating circumstances. *Terror by Night* began filming on October 9, 1945, but two days later production was suspended because of an industry-wide strike. In March of 1945 the Conference of Studio Unions (CSU), an International union belonging to the United Brotherhood of Carpenters and Joiners that had broken away from the International Alliance of Theatrical Stage Employees (IATSE) and represented studio carpenters, painters, cartoonists and several other crafts, went on strike. An estimated 10,500 workers went out and successfully crippled production at most of the Hollywood studios. By October the strike had gone on for six months and both sides were growing frustrated.

The Euston Station set in Universal's Train Shed. From left, Geoffrey Steele, Rene Godfrey and Basil Rathbone.

The studios refused to bargain with the Union and, despite orders from their leaders, many IATSE members refused to cross the picket lines. On October 5, a day that came to be known as "Black Friday," the strike escalated into a violent confrontation between picketers, studio police and strikebreakers in front of Warner's studio in Burbank. Universal, whose rear gate was just down the street on Barham Boulevard, was affected by the strike, when actors and studio personnel refused to cross the picket lines. On March 11, 12 and 13, production ceased on *Terror by Night* and Universal's legal department issued a memo to M-G-M requesting credit on Basil Rathbone's salary for the three lost days. According to the production reports, when work resumed on Monday, October 15 on the Euston Station set in the Train Shed on the studio's back lot, the company was held up for a total of 34 minutes due to planes taking off from nearby Burbank Airport and spoiling the sound—a problem that continues to this day, as I found out while directing a television series at a small studio in North Hollywood that was directly beneath the flight path for what had then become known as Bob Hope Airport. From 7 AM to 9 AM and from 4 PM to 6 PM the planes would fly over at the rate of one every two minutes.

Terror by Night is obviously inspired by Alfred Hitchcock's train-set thrillers, *The 39 Steps* (1935) and *The Lady Vanishes* (1938), but one can still see Roy William Neill's influence in the construction of the screenplay, particularly in the visuals that introduce Euston Station and the night train to Scotland, with provisions being stored in the dining car and baggage being loaded onto the train, imaginatively cross-edited with the arrival and the boarding of the passengers. Many years later an almost identical sequence would be used at the beginning of Sidney Lumet's *Murder on the Orient Express* (1974), but Neill thought of it first. Perhaps this was what he had intended to use in his film version of *The Lost Lady* back in 1937. Once again the film opens with a disembodied voice describing the violent history of the giant diamond, the Star of Rhodesia, over stock footage taken from several old films and appearing remarkably like an old newsreel. The narration goes on to state, "Our story opens in London, within the sound of Bow Bells," a reference to the bells of the church of St. Mary-le-Bow and a tradition that anyone "born with the sound of Bow Bells" was by definition a Cockney. We then arrive at the shop of coffin makers Mock and Son, where a non-grieving Vivian Vedder (Renee Godfrey) is purchasing a coffin to transport her mother's body to Edinburgh from Mr. Mock (Harry Cording) and making sure that it will be delivered to the mortuary in time for the coffin to be loaded onboard the Scotch Express at Euston Station. To be correct, the train should have been referred to as the Scots Express, as Scotch can only refer to the national drink of Scotland. But then again, Ms. Godfrey's high-pitched Cockney accent leaves a great deal to be desired as well.

We now enter the hustle and bustle of activity at Euston Station, in the montage I spoke of earlier, and follow Vivian Vedder and the coffin as it is loaded into the baggage car. Roland Carstairs (Geoffrey Steele) passes her on his way to greet Sherlock Holmes and we learn that Carstairs has hired Holmes to guard his mother and the Star of Rhodesia until they are safely home in Edinburgh. Holmes correctly surmises that an attempt to steal the diamond has already taken place in London. Who should arrive at this point but Inspector Lestrade all decked out for a fishing holiday that Holmes quickly ascertains is merely an excuse for Lestrade to be on board to guard the diamond. The train attendant (Billy Bevan) informs Holmes that the train is about to leave. Just as it starts to pull out of the station, Dr .Watson and his old friend Major Duncan-Bleek (Alan Mowbray) rush down the platform and jump on board. The "Scotch Express" is filled with all sorts of dubious characters besides Vivian Vedder, including Professor Kilbane (Frederick Worlock) and Mr. and Mrs. Shallcross (Gerald Hamer and Janet Murdoch) and they all act suitably suspicious.

Holmes and Watson visit Lady Margaret Carstairs (Mary Forbes) and her son in their compartment and Holmes asks to see the Star of Rhodesia. While the stone and its setting is a remarkable piece of jewelry 423 carats in size, Lady Carstairs informs them that it was originally over 700 carats before her husband had it cut down to make it less ostentatious—a remark that Watson finds ridiculous, muttering, "Ostentatious, it's as big as a duck's egg." Mrs. Shallcross overhears a conversation in the corridor between Holmes, Watson and Lestrade and hurries to inform her husband that police are on the train, adding, "I warned you." Later in the evening, when Holmes joins Watson and Major Duncan-Bleek in the dining car, he discovers a note on his plate warning him to "stop now." Lestrade, who is having dinner in his compartment, hears a crash in the next compartment and goes to investigate, but finds the door locked. When Holmes joins him, they have the attendant unlock the door and find young Carstairs lying dead on the floor and the Star of Rhodesia missing. Watson and Major Duncan-Bleek arrive and Watson examines Carstairs' body, finding no marks of violence, but Holmes insists that it is murder.

As Holmes, Watson and Lestrade confer with the conductor (Leyland Hodgson), Professor Kilbane attempts to leave the carriage, but is stopped by the attendant. The conductor confirms that the train has no stops until it reaches Rugby, and Lestrade declares that they will have a thorough search of the train before that time. Holmes questions Watson about the condition of Carstairs' body and he reveals that there was a small spot of blood on his neck, which Holmes believes was where a poison entered and killed him. Lestrade secures a list of the passengers in the carriage and sets out to question them. Watson decides that he can do as well as Lestrade and goes off to question Professor Kilbane, who turns out to be quite uncooperative, turning the tables on Watson and questioning him instead. Holmes arrives in time to rescue him and suggests that Watson question the couple in the next compartment. When Watson identifies himself as representing the police, Mr. Shallcross confesses and Watson rushes off to get Lestrade. Of course it turns out to be a teapot that Mr. Shallcross has stolen, not the diamond, and Lestrade admonishes Watson to stay out of police business. A chagrined Watson goes off to have a drink with Major Duncan-Bleek while Holmes and Lestrade interrogate Professor Kilbane, who turns out to be a mathematics professor on supposedly legitimate business. Lady Margaret is caught trying to enter her locked compartment (more red herrings) and Holmes and Lestrade retire to Lestrade's compartment to review their case. Holmes is reminded that Colonel Sebastian Moran, Professor Moriarty's most ruthless henchman, specialized in spectacular jewel robberies and was addicted to the study of mathematics. They agree that all of the other passengers on the train are suspects.

Holmes returns to his compartment as Lestrade goes off to have another talk with Lady Margaret. He observes Professor Kilbane sneaking down the corridor and follows him to the end of the carriage, where Holmes finds that the carriage door has been opened. Suddenly, he is pushed out of the train and barely manages to grab hold of a railing to keep from falling to the tracks below. A shadowy figure kicks at him, trying to loosen his grip on the railing and then shuts the carriage door, trapping Holmes outside. Holmes manages to kick in the window and reach inside for the door handle. He climbs back to safety just as the train enters a tunnel. Holmes and Watson return to the baggage car to examine the coffin and discover a secret compartment in the base, large enough for someone to hide in. Watson goes for Lestrade while Holmes questions the rather suspicious-looking guard (Charles Knight). Holmes announces that there are in fact two suspects on board the train. Lestrade, having seen the secret compartment, decides to question Vivian Vedder one more time. Under questioning Vedder admits to Holmes and Lestrade that a man hired her to accompany the coffin to Edinburgh. When Watson and Major Duncan-Bleek join them, Holmes accuses Duncan-Bleek of being that man and of being Colonel Sebastian Moran. Duncan-Bleek insists that he is innocent and Holmes withdraws his accusation, admitting that Watson can supply Duncan-Bleek's alibi and that the Star of Rhodesia wasn't actually stolen. He explains that the real diamond has been in his possession since he first examined it and substituted an imitation. An apoplectic

Lestrade demands that he be given the diamond and then goes off to question Professor Kilbane, only to be shouted down once again.

Holmes and Watson return to the baggage car to discover that the guard has been murdered. As they are examining the body, a figure slips out through the door. Watson removes a tiny dart that appears to have a dissolving substance on it. Holmes is sure that the substance is a poison and that the small scratch on the guard's neck matches the one found earlier on Carstairs' body. A shadowy figure works its way down the passenger car corridor toward the sleeping attendant, then grabbing him and forcing him into the lavatory and locking the door. The figure then moves stealthily to Duncan-Bleek's compartment and enters. The man, whose name is Sands, (Skelton Knaggs) and who is working with Duncan-Bleek, hands him the Star of Rhodesia that he took from Carstairs after he murdered him, but Duncan-Bleek informs him that it is an imitation and that Lestrade now possesses the real diamond. Sands sneaks into Lestrade's compartment and knocks him out, retrieving the real diamond that Lestrade has been examining. Duncan-Bleek then shoots Sands with an air gun that dispenses poison darts, retrieves the diamond. Wiping the gun clean of his fingerprints, he tosses it on the floor and turns off the lights.

Holmes and Watson, returning from the baggage car, realize that the attendant is missing from his post and discover Lestrade and Sands' body. The train makes an unexpected stop so that Scottish police can come on board and Lestrade, still suffering from the hit on his head, asks Holmes to speak with the police. Inspector McDonald of the Edinburgh police (Boyd Davis) informs Holmes that he is taking over the investigation. "This is Scotland," he declares. "You've crossed the border." Lestrade joins the rest in the dining car as McDonald finishes questioning Vivian Vedder. Holmes informs him that Major Duncan-Bleek is in fact Colonel Sebastian Moran. Duncan-Bleek is brought to the dining car and McDonald finds the Star of Rhodesia in a secret pocket of his overcoat. Duncan-Bleek/Moran grabs a gun from one of the officers and pulls the cord to stop the train. Watson manages to knock him down just as the lights go out. In the ensuing scuffle, Holmes throws a coat over Moran, capturing him. McDonald leaves the train, taking Moran with him. As the train pulls out Holmes and Watson pull a shackled Moran from under a table. Holmes explains that McDonald was an accomplice of Moran's with the intent of taking him off the train and helping him to escape. Back at the station, Lestrade (who had substituted himself for Moran) pulls a gun and arrests the false Inspector and his accomplices. Moran informs Holmes that he may have him, but not the diamond. With a smug smile, Holmes brings out the real diamond, explaining that he had several copies made of the original.

By now some members of the Roy William Neill repertory company, such as Leyland Hodgson (Conductor), Gerald Hamer (Mr. Shallcross) and Frederick Worlock (Professor Kilbane), were making their fifth appearances, while Harry Cording (Mock) was returning for the sixth time and would be back again for a seventh time in *Dressed to Kill*. Charles Knight (Guard) and Colin Kenny (Constable) were making their third appearances and Mary Forbes (Lady Margaret Carstairs) and Billy Bevan (Attendant) their second. Dennis Hoey was making his sixth and final appearance as Inspector Lestrade. The new arrivals, though not technically members of the repertory company, were Alan Mowbray (Duncan-Bleek/Sebastian Moran), Renee Godfrey (Vivian Vedder), Skelton Knaggs (Sands), Boyd Davis (Inspector McDonald), Geoffrey Steele (Roland Carstairs) and Janet Murdoch (Mrs. Shallcross).

ALAN MOWBRAY had previously played Colonel Gore-King in Clive Brook's *Sherlock Holmes* (1932) and Lestrade in *A Study in Scarlet* (1933) starring Reginald Owen, and had appeared with Nigel Bruce in the first feature length 3-color Technicolor film, *Becky Sharpe* (1935). He was born Alfred Ernest Allen on August 18, 1896 in London, England, the second of three sons born to London cab driver Edward William Allen and the former Fanny Elizabeth Webb. Mowbray, who was an inveterate storyteller who frequently embellished his own history, could have begun his acting career before entering the service during World War I or he could have started after he was discharged. According to an interview he gave to the *Los Angeles Times* in April of 1932, he supposedly enlisted at the age of 18 in the King's Own Yorkshire Light Infantry and served in France during the entire struggle, with the exception of the last six days. Another biography states that he was awarded the Military Medal and the French Croix De Guerre for bravery. Mowbray took his professional name from a letter he once saw, sent by Robert Louis Stevenson to his cousin Robert Alan Mowbray. According to the *Times* article, Mowbray began his acting career with a speaking role in Edward Childs Carpenter's *The Cinderella Man* that was produced by Oliver Morosco in 1916, which would indicate that he trod the boards before his military service.

Mowbray's colorfully embellished history includes a story quoted in the Gregory William Mank-Charles Heard-Bill Nelson book on the life of John Barrymore, *Hollywood's Hellfire Club*, in which he claims that he got to New York by "stoking a ship… checked into the Webster Hotel and fled the bill two weeks later." He then slept on "a big, black smooth rock" in Central Park and ate leftover rolls at the Automat. The truth of the matter is that he bought passage on the S.S. *President Adams* and arrived in New York on

Alan Mowbray as Duncan-Bleek/Sebastian Moran in *Terror By Night*.

May 22, 1923 and, according to his immigration papers, planned to stay at the Studio Club in Manhattan. Mowbray apparently joined a New York stock company and toured for several years, before making his Broadway debut at the Lyceum Theatre on May 4, 1926 in an original comedy called *Sport of Kings*, which managed to play out the month before closing. In February of 1928 he opened in *These Modern Women* directed by an up-and-coming young Armenian director named Rouben Mamoulian, who had triumphed the previous year with his direction of George Gershwin's *Porgy and Bess*. Unfortunately the magic wasn't there this time and the play closed after 24 performances. For his next outing, Mowbray chose a play that he had written called *Dinner Is Served* that opened at the Cort Theatre with Mowbray in the leading role of Billy Bishop. The reviews were devastating, with the *New York Times* flatly stating, "…Mr. Mowbray, being a glutton for punishment, has given himself a dull part in a dull comedy. Your heart might bleed for Mr. Mowbray, if he were not responsible for his own calamity." *Dinner Is Served* closed after four performances. Mowbray tried one more time to break into Broadway by appearing with Frank Morgan in an original farce called *The Amorous Antic*, but once again the play lasted for only eight performances before permanently turning off the lights. Mowbray wouldn't return to Broadway until 1963, when he appeared with Alan Arkin and Vivian Blaine in Carl Reiner's biographical comedy *Enter Laughing* and this time it was a hit, running for 419 performances.

Mowbray married fellow actor Lorayne Carpenter in 1927 and they eventually had two children, Alan, Jr. and Patricia. They would remain married for 42 years until his death in 1969. In 1960, at the age of 28, Patricia Mowbray married actor Douglass Dumbrille who was 42 years her senior and would remain his wife until his death of a heart attack in 1974.

Alan Mowbray's film career began with the role of a butler in *God's Gift to Women* (1931), but he would earn acclaim later that year with his portrayal of George Washington in George Arliss' *Alexander Hamilton* (1931). In March of 1933 he helped to fund the organization of the Screen Actors Guild and became the Guild's first vice-president. He would continue in films until 1956, when he would turn his efforts to television, even starring in his own series, *Colonel Humphrey Flack* (1959) and co-starring with Howard Duff in *Dante* for two years (1960-1961). Mowbray returned to films one last time in *A Majority of One* (1961) starring Rosalind Russell and Alec Guinness and his last appearance was in an episode of *The Flying Nun* in 1969. On March 22, 1969, Mowbray suffered a severe heart attack and was rushed to Hollywood Presbyterian Hospital in Los Angeles, where he succumbed three days later at the age of 72. He is buried at the Holy Cross Cemetery in Culver City, California.

Mowbray, having been a member of the Lambs Club in New York, had also been an enthusiastic member of the Masquers Club in Hollywood. A haven for actors to drink and socialize, the club had once been the home of silent film star Antonio Moreno and was located just around the corner from Grauman's Chinese Theatre in a classic, English Tudor-style bungalow on North Sycamore. I was never a member, but I visited the Masquers Club on many occasions as a guest and enjoyed the warm atmosphere of the club room and bar in the cellar. The members loved to tell stories of Mowbray's legendary drinking escapades and after his death a brandy glass was placed in his honor on a pedestal behind the bar with a light illuminating it. Legend had it that Mowbray's ghost haunted that bar every evening until the building was finally demolished in 1985 and an apartment house took its place.

RENEE GODFREY's husband, British-born director and sometimes actor Peter God-frey, was a good friend of my father's and I'm sure that I must have seen both of them at some party at our home in Beverly Hills. Renee was a very attractive woman who had begun her career as a model, was a popular World War II pin-up in Coca-Cola ads, and first acted in films play-ing a shopgirl in one scene in *Kitty Foyle* (1940). Renee Vera Haal was born in New York City on September 1, 1919 to German immigrants Emi Haal and Ninny Dering Haal. According to the 1920 census, Emi Haal was working as a bartender in a downtown saloon at the time. Published stories claim that Renee was raised in England, but her life is difficult to track, as she was obviously the product of an over-enthusi-

Rene Godfrey as Vivian Vedder in *Terror By Night*.

astic press agent who gave out numerous press releases over the years, all with different stories to tell. She is shown in newspaper photographs, taken in Atlantic City in September of 1935 when she was barely 16, pos-ing in a bathing suit as a contestant in a Showman's Variety Jubilee beauty contest and later as the winner of the Miss New York State title.

There is a record of a Renee Haal arriving in England aboard the S.S. *Champlain* on September 10, 1938; she was supposedly traveling as part of comedian Danny Kaye's nightclub act. She returned to New York the following year on the S.S. *Normandie*, arriving on May 1, 1939. It was then that the press agent shifted into high gear, announcing her arrival as the "19 year-old songbird, hailed in London as the queen of television, because of her perfect features." Other photographs and stories, which went out all over the country, described her pending marriage to the brother of the Earl of Dudley and that she was on her way to Hollywood for screen tests.

Renee Haal did arrive in Hollywood the following year and was signed to a term contract by RKO Radio Pictures, making her film de-but in *Kitty Foyle*. An article that appeared in newspapers in October of 1940, listing the names of nine young actresses with Renee Haal's name in first position, stated that these actresses had been signed by RKO for Kay Kyser's second film for the studio, *You'll Find Out* (1940). However, the film's screen credits show that Renee was in fact the only one of the nine girls who didn't appear in the film. Instead she played a nurse in Orson Welles' *Citizen Kane* (1941) followed by a small role in a Leon Errol short. Then Renee Haal met her future husband, director Peter Godfrey, who hired her for a featured role in his RKO film *Unexpected Uncle* (1941) starring Anne Shirley and Charles Coburn. Renee and Peter were married later that year and when she appeared in his next film, *Highways by Night* (1942) she took the professional name of Renee Godfrey for her screen appearances. The Godfrey's had three children: a set of twins, Christina and Jill, and another daughter, Roberta. In 1948, shortly after appearing in another of Peter Godfrey's films at Warner Bros., *The Decision of Christopher Blake* (1948), Renee Godfrey retired from films to raise her family and to occasionally appear with her husband, who was an amateur magician, in magic shows. A newspaper photograph that appeared in December of 1949 showed actress Barbara Stanwyck and her then husband actor Robert Taylor holding the Godfreys' twin daughters and becoming their godparents during christening services at the All Saints Church in Beverly Hills.

Peter Godfrey, who directed thirteen feature films for Warner Bros., left the studio in 1950 and, after directing two more low-budget pictures, turned his talents to directing television. Over the next eight years he directed episodes for more than thirty series. In 1954, Renee returned to acting in a number of television series and several films, including *Can-Can* (1960) with Frank Sinatra and Shirley MacLaine and *Inherit the Wind* (1960) with Spencer Tracy and Fredric March. In 1964, even though she was suffering from cancer, she appeared in her final film, Disney Studios', *Those Calloways* (1965). Renee Haal Godfrey died of cancer on May 24, 1964 at the age of 44 and is buried at Forest Lawn Memorial Park in Glendale, California. Peter Godfrey died on March 4, 1970 at the age of 72. The Godfreys' twin daughters have publicly stated that their godmother, Barbara Stanwyck, did nothing to help them after their parents' deaths. Their other daughter, Roberta, now known as Bobbie, would marry and divorce composer Basil Poledouris who wrote the scores for *Conan the Barbarian* (1982), *The Hunt for Red October* (1990) and many other films.

MARY FORBES, who had previously appeared briefly as Mrs. Pettibone in *Sherlock Holmes in Washington,* returned in high style as Lady Margaret Carstairs in *Terror by Night.* Born in the parish of Hornsey, a suburb of London, she began her career on the British stage, and like many actresses of that and later periods, her date of birth tended to fluctuate. The official date appears to be December 30, 1879, but then again it might be January 1, 1880, or even, as she later claimed, 1883. Whatever date the lady prefers we will concede, but what is unquestionably more important is that she was a formidable presence on the British stage. She made her first silent film for Gaumont-British in 1917 (*Ultus and the Secret of the*

Night) and increased the family's acting roots by giving birth to a son, Ralph Forbes, and a daughter Brenda Forbes, both of whom became highly successful stage and screen actors. Mary Forbes was married three times; her first husband, E.J. Taylor, whom she married around 1901, was the father of both Ralph Taylor, born September 30, 1902, and Brenda Taylor, born January 14, 1908. Both son and daughter would eventually take on their mother's maiden name when they joined her in the acting profession.

Mary Forbes as Lady Margaret Carstairs in *Terror By Night.*

In November of 1912, Mary Forbes made her first journey to the United States, arriving in New York on November 11 of that year on board the S.S. *Caronia.* She would open the following February at the Maxine Elliott's [sic] Theatre in an original drama called *Romance.* After a respectable run of 160 performances, Forbes returned to London, her family and several more roles in silent films and theatre. Her next trip to New York was in 1913 to appear with British comedienne Marie Tempest in one half of a comedy double bill, *The Duke of Killcranki* at the Lyceum Theatre, and then go on tour, appearing throughout the Midwest. By 1929, Mary Forbes had apparently divorced E.J. Taylor and moved permanently to the United States and Hollywood, making her stateside film debut in Alexander Korda's *Her Private Life* (1929) starring Walter Pidgeon, Billy Dove and Thelma Todd. In her next film, *The Thirteenth Chair* (1929) she met her future husband, British actor Charles Quatermaine, to whom she remained married until his death in 1958.

As she moved into the character acting phase of her career, Forbes played roles in such blockbusters as *A Farewell to Arms* (1932), *Cavalcade* (1933), *Captain Blood* (1935), *The Awful Truth* (1937) and *Stage Door* (1937), in which she appeared for the first time on screen with her son Ralph Forbes, playing his mother-in-law. In *You Can't Take It With You* (1938), she reprised a role similar to that she had played in *The Awful Truth,* playing Jimmy Stewart's snobbish mother, who disapproves of his girlfriend Jean Arthur's family, and she was Lady Conyngham in *The*

Adventures of Sherlock Holmes (1939) with Rathbone and Bruce. Forbes remained busy throughout the 1940s in such films as *Back Street* (1941), *Jane Eyre* (1944), *I'll Remember April* (1945) and *The Secret Life of Walter Mitty* (1947), but by 1950 the roles became fewer and were mostly in television. She made her final screen appearance in a small role in *Houseboat* (1958) with Cary Grant and Sophia Loren, the same year that her husband Charles Quatermaine died. Her son, Ralph Forbes, had died prematurely at the age of 49 in New York in 1951, shortly after starring in a revival of Shaw's *Caesar and Cleopatra*. Some time in the early '70s, Mary Forbes married Wesley Hall and moved to his home in Beaumont, California, where she would reside until her death on July 22, 1974.

SKELTON KNAGGS, who had made a career of playing bizarre characters in horror films such as *Isle of the Dead* (1945), *House of Dracula* (1945) and *Bedlam* (1946), was a tragic figure in life as well. Born Skelton Barnaby Knaggs on June 27, 1911 in Sheffield, England, he was the son of a grocer's assistant named Harry Knaggs and the former Beatrice Ellen Skelton—hence the rather unusual first name. When Skelton was 12–years- old, the Knaggs family traveled to Canada and a month later, on August 23, 1923, settled in Syracuse, New York. A photo that appeared in the *Syracuse Herald* on September 3, 1924 under the heading "Kids in Our Block," shows a group of children smiling at the camera, with a young, unsmiling Skelton Knaggs seated somewhat apart from the others, outside of their intimate circle. Judging from the facial scars he exhibited as an adult, as well as his stunted growth, it was likely that at some point in his youth he was exposed to small pox. Knaggs showed an interest in acting at an early age and was very active in his high school's drama department, continuing to act with a local drama group after his graduation. Knaggs lived with his family, which had grown with the birth of two more sons, Cecil and Melvin, through the mid-1930s and continued to act in local productions. Judging from another newspaper article in the September 11, 1935 issue of the *Syracuse Herald*, Knaggs' drinking problem, which would ultimately kill him, had already begun. The article reported that Knaggs attempted to commit suicide by drinking a small bottle of poison after discovering that he had spent all of the $1,000 that he

Skelton Knaggs as he appeared as X-Ray in *Dick Tracy Meets Gruesome* (1947).

had withdrawn from the bank a few days earlier, even though he couldn't remember doing it. Knaggs survived because he had driven to a friend's home and told him what he had done and the friend had taken him to a hospital.

Later in 1935, Knaggs traveled to England and enrolled as a student in the Royal Academy of Dramatic Art. While appearing in a production of Shakespeare's *Cymbeline*, he caught the eye of casting director Harold Huth, who offered him a role in Gaumont-British's production *Everything Is Thunder* (1936) starring Constance Bennett. This led to his appearance in small roles in a number of "quota films," as well as two notable films, *Rembrandt* (1936), starring Charles Laughton, Gertrude Lawrence and Elsa Lanchester, and *The Spy in Black* (1939), starring Conrad Veidt and Valerie Hobson. As war broke out in Europe, Knaggs returned to the United States and found work in his first Hollywood film, a low-budget potboiler called *Torture Ship* (1939) that starred Irving Pichel, who played Sandor in *Dracula's Daughter* (1936) and would later direct *Destination Moon* (1950) . In this film Knaggs first wore the Coke-bottle glasses that he would use again in several other films, including his portrayal of Sands in *Terror by Night*.

The 1940s were busy years for Skelton Knaggs: He appeared in twenty films and two Broadway plays, the first being *Heart of a City* (1942) which starred my father and Margot Grahame, who was considered the Jean Harlow of British films. The play was a fictitious dramatization of the true story of the Windmill Theatre in London that stayed open during the Blitz to entertain British servicemen. The same story was later dramatized twice in films, the first being *Tonight and Every Night* (1945) starring Rita Hayworth and the second, *Mrs. Henderson Presents* (2005) with Judi Dench and Bob Hoskins. Knaggs briefly returned to England and in the summer of 1949 married Thelma Crawshaw in Croydon, returning with her to the United States and his home on North Highland Avenue in Hollywood, where his brother Melvin would also live with them. Skelton Knaggs would appear in thirteen more films and television episodes before dying of cirrhosis of the liver on May 1, 1955, a month before his 44th birthday. He is buried in the Hollywood Forever Cemetery, next door to Paramount Studios on Santa Monica Boulevard in Hollywood.

GEOFFREY STEELE, whose full name was Geoffrey Herbert Steele, was born on June 27, 1914 in Potchefstroom, South Africa, the son of George Frederick Steele, a regimental commander in the Royal Dragoons, known as The Royals. His mother, Muriel, had come to South Africa to visit her husband and Geoffrey was born while she was there. Soon after Steele and his mother had returned to England, his father was killed in a battle in Northern France in the early days of World War I. Steele was educated at Eton and Sandhurst, where he became a medalist in the high-hurdles and was selected to participate in the Berlin Olympics of 1936. Unfortunately his army career got in the way and he was ordered to join his father's old regiment in Egypt for a tour of duty instead of joining the British Olympic team.

Steele's interest in acting was first realized when he appeared in a minor role in the British "quota quickie" *Marigold* (1938). Eventually he and his mother traveled to Hollywood and it was there in 1941 that he first met actress-heiress Mildred Shay at a cocktail party. She was the daughter of a wealthy lawyer who represented several Hollywood studios and through his connections she had appeared in a few films. Mildred was better known for her eccentric

Geoffrey Steele as Roland Carstairs in *Terror By Night*.

social life and her previous stormy marriages and when she and Geoffrey Steele ran off to be married, the gossip columnists gave it at most three to six months, although in fact the marriage lasted until his death in 1987. Steele managed to secure some minor, uncredited roles in several films, including *Casablanca* (1942) and *The Constant Nymph* (1943), before returning to England with Mildred to rejoin his regiment. Shay's cavalry regiment was still being mobilized as a mechanized regiment so Steele, because of his show-business background, was assigned to make training films for the army. After the war Mildred gave birth to a daughter, Georgiana, and the couple returned to Hollywood where Steele again tried to pursue a career in acting. After appearing in a small role in Warner's *Confidential Agent* (1945), he was signed by Universal to play Roland Carstairs in *Terror by Night*. He would work sporadically in half a dozen other small parts in films and television before leaving the business entirely in 1967. Geoffrey Steele would die in Los Angeles, California at the age of 72 on February 7, 1987.

The two remaining members of the cast, Boyd Davis (Inspector McDonald) and Janet Murdoch (Mrs. Shallcross), had dissimilar careers. BOYD DAVIS, who was born in Santa Rosa, California on June 19, 1885, was 40–years-old before he made his first film *The Spider* (1931), in which

| Boyd Davis as Inspector McDonald. | Janet Murdoch as Mrs. Shallcross with Gerald Hamer in *Terror By Night*. |

he appeared as a member of the audience watching Lois Moran perform on stage. From then on he divided his time between Broadway plays and the movies, until 1938 when he devoted himself exclusively to films. All in all he appeared in fifteen Broadway productions and seventy one films until his retirement in 1953, ten years before his death on January 25, 1963 in Los Angles at the age of 77. JANET MURDOCH, on the other hand although British born, had a much briefer career in films appearing in only seven films from 1934 to 1948. The roles were occasionally important enough for her to receive screen credit including, *Smash Up: The Story of a Woman* (1947), in which she played Miss Kirk, the Nanny for Susan Hayward's baby, Angelica. Her final film appearance would be in a low-budget version of Robert Louis Stevenson's *Kidnapped* (1948) that Roddy McDowall produced and starred in for Monogram Pictures.

Terror by Night opened in New York at (where else?) the Rialto Theatre on February 8, 1946, but for the first time Bosley Crowther actually had some nice things to say in his *New York Times* review the following day—although he still couldn't resist an opening jab: "There is not a great deal of difference between one Sherlock Holmes film and the next," he began. "But the little there is weighs in favor of *Terror by Night*. That is because this episode in the famous detective's career is told in tight continuity and with flavorsome atmosphere." Crowther closed with another compliment, "Obviously, Hitchcock's *The Lady Vanishes* inspired the author of the script, but that's not a bad inspiration. And the action has been handled well. Mr. Rathbone is silky smooth, as usual; Nigel Bruce plays Doctor Watson blimpishly, and a good cast of Universal actors are passengers aboard the train."

Terror by Night retains a special place in my heart because of the first time that I viewed it. It was in 1946, my parents had divorced and I had been shipped off to a rather bleak, British-style boarding school in Ottawa, Canada called Ashbury College. I arrived on a dreary Saturday afternoon at the end of April, feeling rather glum and friendless, just as the students were returning from their Spring break. Imagine my surprise when I learned that each Saturday the school ran 16mm copies of current films and that night's film was to be *Terror by Night*. For 60 minutes I escaped my unhappy surroundings and lost myself in the film's action, enjoying seeing my father's important role in the story. As it turned out, I became somewhat of a junior celebrity when the boys saw my father's name in the credits. I was asked all sorts of questions about Hollywood and moviemaking, which I happily answered whether I knew what I was talking about or not. Of course my time as a celebrity was brief, as my classmates quickly tired of Hollywood and went back to more important matters such as sports. *Terror by Night* became my favorite Sherlock Holmes film that night, not just because it helped to break the ice with my classmates, but because of its excellent pacing and style. It was, in my opinion, arguably the best of the series.

With a tight 60-minute running time, *Terror by Night* was the shortest of all the Sherlock Holmes films. For some reason it began with an entirely new fanfare, replacing the theme that traditionally played over the Universal letters circling the globe, but then the film reverted to the standard Sherlock Holmes main title music. It is interesting to note that *Sherlock Holmes Faces Death* was the first film in the series not to have an original musical score written. Universal's attitude regarding the music used in its films seemed to be based largely on economics. Composers were hired to write the music for the studio's larger budgeted films and the scores would then be kept in a music library to be used over and over in less important films. Frank Skinner wrote the original music for *Sherlock Holmes and the Voice of Terror, Sherlock Holmes and the Secret Weapon* and *Sherlock Holmes in Washington*. He had been under contract to Universal since 1936 and had written the scores for such films as *Son of Frankenstein* (1939), *Destry Rides Again* (1939) and *Tower of London* (1939). In later years he would also compose the music for *Francis* (1950), *All*

That Heaven Allows (1955) and *The Ugly American* (1963). All of the nine remaining Sherlock Holmes films reused Skinner's compositions, as well as library music selected from various other composers' works, that was rearranged and rerecorded with an orchestra to fit the timings for the new films. Skinner's theme for the Sherlock Holmes main title would be repeated in every one of the subsequent films. A musical director would be assigned to select the appropriate music and conduct the orchestra on the scoring session. In later years studios could use "canned music" to score their TV shows, but in the 1940s the American Federation of Musicians and its leader James C. Petrillo demanded that each score be recorded by an orchestra, and so as a result every studio maintained their own orchestras. At first these musical directors, most of whom were under contract to Universal and composers in their own right, included Hans J. Salter, who was the music director on *Sherlock Holmes Faces Death* and *The Spider Woman*. Salter had been with the studio for almost 30 years and wrote scores for such films as *The Invisible Man Returns* (1940), *Black Friday* (1940), *The Wolf Man* (1941) and *The Ghost of Frankenstein* (1942). Another was Paul Sawtell, who was the music director on *The Scarlet Claw*, *The Pearl of Death* and *The House of Fear* and wrote the music for *Calling Dr. Death* (1943), *The Mummy's Curse* (1944) and *The Cat Creeps* (1946).

Toward the end of the series however, the studio began using musical directors who were not predominantly composers, such as Mark Levant (*The Woman in Green*), who had been the concert master for Metro, Edgar Fairchild (*Pursuit to Algiers*) who had been at the studio for many years and had been Deanna Durbin's musical director, and Milton Rosen (*Terror by Night* and *Dressed to Kill*), who had contributed to the scores of many Universal films and serials. By 1946 the studio was in the midst of a transition and would soon be controlled by the former president of RKO Pictures, Leo Spitz, and former 20th Century-Fox executive William Goetz. Perhaps that was the reason that Milton Rosen chose to have both *Terror by Night* and *Dressed to Kill* begin with a dramatic new fanfare, replacing the old theme that traditionally played over the Universal logo. By the end of the year the logo itself would be gone and an entirely new image would introduce Universal-International Pictures, the studio's new name, on all of its forthcoming films. An edict would announce, "[h]enceforth no feature that bore the Universal-International imprimatur would run under 70 minutes." The day of the studio's "B" pictures was coming to an end, but there was still time for one last Sherlock Holmes film that would begin life as *Prelude to Murder*.

DRESSED TO KILL

HAPPY WITH THE WAY that he had developed the *Terror by Night* screenplay, Universal retained Frank Gruber to write the next Sherlock Holmes film. Although his draft was ostensibly an original, it did take some inspiration from Sir Arthur Conan Doyle's " A Scandal in Bohemia," the first chapter of *Adventures of Sherlock Holmes*, and a few elements from several previous Holmes films, including the music boxes vs. the busts of Napoleon in *The Pearl of Death* and an indecipherable code as in *Sherlock Holmes and the Secret Weapon*. Apparently Gruber's first draft wasn't totally satisfactory and Leonard Lee, who had written the screenplay for *Pursuit to Algiers*, was brought in for one week to do a quick revision for $750; the job eventually stretched out into nine weeks and $6,750. Lee's revised draft dated (January 16, 1946) was submitted to the Breen Office the following day and their reaction was primarily concerned with the showing of drinks, which in their view "does not seem particularly essential for a proper telling of the story." And of course they were also concerned about the female lead's evening dress not being too revealing, "Specifically, Hilda's breasts should be adequately covered," stated the Breen office's letter. And finally they questioned the manner in which the heavies tried to dispose of Holmes saying it was "unacceptable as now written for the reason that it presents a detailed method of committing murder." Now admittedly it was a cumbersome way to attempt to kill Holmes, but how could seeing him suspended from a hook while a car spewed a deadly chemical smoke into a garage be any more detailed than seeing someone being shot by a gun, a most popular means of murder in films both then and now? It amazes me how anyone in those days could concentrate on creating a successful film with the Breen Office constantly giving such "helpful" advice. And they were still making comments like that, right up to the very end of the Production Code Administration's reign in the late 1960s. Howard Hughes was the first to challenge the Breen Office with his production of *The Outlaw* (1943) starring Jane Russell and won, proving that a film could make a sizable profit without code approval. Otto Preminger sank the knife in deeper with his films *The Moon Is Blue* (1953), *The Man with the Golden Arm* (1955) and *Anatomy of a Murder* (1959). The Code was eventually replaced by the Motion Picture Association of America's system, with its alphabet soup collection of film ratings.

Art directors Jack Otterson and Martin Obzina requested that Universal's London offices arrange to have a photographer take stills of the interior of Doctor Samuel Johnson's home at 17 Gough Square. The home, built in the 1700s, was where Doctor Johnson compiled his first comprehensive English dictionary; it would become the setting for the finale of *Dressed to Kill*. Meanwhile the studio's publicity department was busy sending out releases announcing that Mr. and Mrs. Nigel Bruce would be celebrating their silver wedding anniversary on May 15 of that year, adding, "Mrs. Bruce, formerly Violet Shelton, was prominent on the English stage as Violet Campbell. They have two daughters, Pauline and Jennifer (Mrs. Jay Gould III), and they have a brand-new grandson, Bruce Jay Gould." Patricia Morison, who had previously been at the studio to star in the first of the Inner Sanctum series *Calling Dr. Death* (1943) with Lon Chaney and had last played David Bruce's girlfriend in the Deanna Durbin starrer *Lady on a Train* (1945), was hired to play Mrs. Hilda Courtney at a salary of $1,500 a week, with a three-week guarantee. According to the studio's production report, director Roy William Neill began filming *Prelude to Murder*, which would eventually have its title changed to *Dressed to Kill*, on Tuesday, January 22, 1946 on Stage 11 in Sherlock Holmes' Baker Street flat. When the first shot for scene 66 was printed at 9:45 AM the final Sherlock Holmes film was officially underway. The title *Dressed to Kill* had been used twice before, once in 1928 for a silent film starring Mary Astor and Edmund Lowe and again in 1941 at 20th Century-Fox for a Michael Shayne mystery starring Lloyd Nolan. It would be used again in 1980 in Brian De Palma's film starring Michael Caine as a transvestite killer.

Dressed to Kill opens with another disembodied voice describing Dartmoor Prison over what appears to be an aerial still photograph of the prison. A quick scene between prisoner John Davidson (Cyril Delevanti) and another prisoner, who is actually an undercover officer from Scotland Yard (Guy Kingsford), establishes the music boxes that Davidson makes. From there it's a quick jump to the Gaylord Art Gallery where the owner Ebenezer Crabtree (Holmes Herbert, with a lovely Cockney dialect and no hairpiece) is offering three identical music boxes at auction to his audience. Julian Emery (Edmond Breon) bids on the first, only to be outbid by an attractive young lady, Evelyn Clifford (Patricia Cameron), who we will later learn owns a toy shop. Emery bids successfully on the second music box and we then meet the young Miss Kilgour (Topsy Glyn) who will soon become the proud owner of the third music box. (What a wonderfully Hollywood name, it's too bad that this child appeared in only two films, the other being *Enter Arsene Lupin* (1944).) A short time later Colonel Cavanaugh (Frederick Worlock) arrives at the Gaylord Art Gallery and questions Ebenezer Crabtree and his bookkeeper Alfred (Olaf Hytten). Having secured the names and addresses of two of the purchasers and a description of the third, Cavanaugh joins his accomplice Hamid (Harry Cording), who is waiting outside in a taxi. Growing impatient when Hamid continues to read his book, Cavanaugh pulls it away from him and we see the inscription, "With affection from Hilda Courtney." Hamid is angry, but Cavanaugh dismisses him with a warning that Hilda Courtney is above his station.

The scene then transitions to 221-B Baker Street and its two occupants. Holmes is playing his violin while Watson reads a copy of the *Strand*. Watson proudly quotes from an article that he has written entitled "A Scandal in Bohemia," about a woman named Irene Adler who once bested Holmes on a case. Holmes replies, "If you must record my exploits, I do hope you've given 'The Woman' a soul. She had one, you know." This discussion is interrupted by the arrival of Julian Emery, Watson's old school friend, who greets Watson as "Fatso" and is called "Stinky" in reply. (Rather disagreeable names for old friends to call one another, don't you think?) Emery has been robbed and has come to Holmes for help. The three return to Emery's flat, where he proudly displays his collection of music boxes. The Universal prop department did an excellent job of gathering a number of intriguing items, including one where a small bird jumps out and whistles happily and another where a rabbit pops up and wiggles its ears, much to Watson's displeasure. Holmes is fascinated to learn that the stolen box resembles one that Emery bought at the Gaylord Art Gallery. He advises Emery to be more cautious in the future—advice that both Emery and Watson dismiss as over-reacting. A short time later, after a preliminary phone call, Hilda Courtney (Patricia Morison) visits Emery's flat and flirts with him, while attempting to gain possession of the music box. Hamid has followed her into the flat and, when he sees Emery put his arms around Hilda, hurls a knife into his back, killing him. What follows is that much discussed moment by film fans where Hilda's white stole is slowly extricated from beneath Emery's body—a nice touch by Roy William Neill.

Hilda returns to the taxi, where Cavanaugh is waiting, and displays the purloined music box in answer to his gruff question, "Did you get it?" The relationship between Hilda and Cavanaugh is somewhat ill-defined, causing confusion as to who is actually in command of the gang of thieves. Although Cavanaugh's concern in the earlier scene in the taxi that he hadn't successfully carried out Hilda's orders indicated that he answers to her, in this and several other scenes his autocratic behavior would imply the opposite.

Holmes and Watson arrive at Emery's flat in answer to a call from Inspector Hopkins (Carl Harbord) and are informed of the time of Emery's death from Sergeant Thompson (Tom P. Dillon). Upon learning that the music box is gone, Holmes and Watson visit the Gaylord Art Gallery to speak with Ebenezer Crabtree, who tells them about Cavanaugh's visit and that he will possibly return the next day for the auction. Having also learned the name and address of Mr. Kilgore, the man who bought the third box, they pay him a visit. The door to Kilgore's home is opened by a charwoman (Patricia Morison in an excellent character makeup and exhibiting a wonderfully accurate Cockney dialect) who lets them enter as she is leaving. A thumping sound leads Holmes to discover Kilgore's daughter (Topsy Glyn) trussed up in a closet. Realizing that the charwoman was actually Hilda Courtney and that she now possesses two of the music boxes, Holmes leaves Watson with Kilgore's daughter while he goes off to find the young woman who bought the third music box. Watson tries unsuccessfully to amuse the frightened child by doing duck impressions, but all he gets for his labors are more tears.

Evelyn Clifford, the young woman for whom Holmes is searching, is again at the auction at the Gaylord Art Gallery and purchases a small antique doll. When she leaves the gallery she is followed by the three conspirators to her toy shop, where Hilda and Cavanaugh learn that the last music box has been sold to Sherlock Holmes. They return to the taxi and are followed by Sergeant Thompson, who has been standing outside the shop. Hilda spots Thompson's cab following them and orders Hamid to take evasive action. Holmes and Watson are in the Scotland Yard Commissioner's office (Ian Wolfe), along with Inspector Hopkins, where Holmes is unsuccessful in finding Hilda amongst the photographs of known criminals. A technician (Boyd Irwin) brings in X-rays taken of the third music box, but they show nothing out of the ordinary. They learn that Dartmoor prisoner John Davidson made all three of the music boxes and that he had been apprehended two years before for stealing a set of plates used in printing £5 notes from the Bank of England. Unfortunately the plates were not on Davidson when he was arrested and Scotland Yard has been unable to find where he hid them. Holmes is certain that a message revealing the location of the plates is contained in the three music boxes and he will try to deduce the message from the one box in his possession. He listens again to the tune and reflects that somehow it is different than the tune played by Emery's music box. A phone call informs them that Sergeant Thompson has been killed, run over by a taxi. Holmes is certain that it is not an accident, but murder.

At a Limehouse pub (a redressed version of the set used in *Sherlock Holmes and the Voice of Terror*), a rendezvous for street performers known as "Buskers," an entertainer (Delos Jewkes) is singing a Cockney ditty called "Ya Never Know Just 'Oo You're Gonna Meet" as Holmes and Watson come down the stairs. Holmes approaches the little man playing the piano, Joe Cisto (Wallace Scott), and asks him to identify the music box tune for him. Cisto quickly recognizes the tune as an Australian song called "The Swagman," but points out that Holmes played several wrong notes. Holmes is now certain that the different notes are part of a code. When Holmes and Watson return to their flat, they find the rooms in turmoil; someone has been searching for the music box, but Holmes reveals that it is safely hidden in a biscuit jar. When Mrs. Hudson (Mary Gordon) informs them that a young lady and an older gentleman called while they were out, Holmes is certain that their visitors were Hilda and the colonel, particularly after he discovers a fancy cigarette lying on the desk.

The following morning Watson finds Holmes at his desk, having been up all night trying unsuccessfully to break the code. A passing comment from Watson, about his old music teacher numbering the keys on a piano for him, gives Holmes the clue he has been looking for and he deciphers the notes of the tune into a message. He brings the partial message to the commissioner and Inspector Hopkins, telling them that what he has is the first and third parts of the message and that Hilda and the colonel have the first and second parts. He assures the commissioner that the third music box is being guarded by Doctor Watson and that the key words in the message are, "It's behind books, third shelf secretary, Dr. S." He asks that Scotland Yard search for doctors with all variations of the initial S.

Holmes goes off to a tobacconist (Sally Shepherd) to inquire about the cigarette he found on his desk and learns that one of only three customers for these particular cigarettes is Mrs. Hilda Courtney of Park Mansions, Briarstone Square. Holmes arrives at Hilda's flat and ends up being captured by Hamid and Colonel Cavanaugh. What follows is the scene that so upset the Breen Office, with Holmes being strung from a hook over the idling taxi as toxic monosulfite fumes escape from an attachment to its engine. What does bother me is, if the fumes were as deadly as Cavanaugh describes them (reference to the German's use of this gas and their "undesirables") then why, once Hamid starts the motor and the fumes are seen to be filling the garage, do they take their sweet time taping Holmes' mouth and hanging him from the hook before driving away? Monosulfite must be a very slow acting poison gas. Holmes of course is quickly able to free himself with the help of keys he picked from Cavanaugh's pocket in the taxi and an energetic double (stunt man Robert Tafur) who swings his legs onto the rafter, releasing his hands from the hook, then dropping to the floor. Holmes still has to pull the tape from his mouth and unlock the handcuffs while deadly smoke swirls about him, but after one cough for effect the scene quickly dissolves.

Hilda pays a visit to Holmes's flat; misleading Doctor Watson with a trumped-up story about a missing sister, she maneuvers him momentarily out of the room while she plants a smoke bomb in one of the cabinets. Watson, thinking the room is on fire, instinctively goes to protect the cookie jar, allowing Hilda to learn where the music box is hidden. In the smoke and confusion, Hilda removes the music box from the jar and exits, leaving a chagrined Watson to realize that he has been duped. Hilda returns with the music box to her flat to join Cavanaugh and Hamid in deciphering the final message. When Holmes returns to his rooms, Watson confesses to him that Hilda has tricked him and stolen the music box. Holmes is amused to hear that she used a smoke bomb, saying she undoubtedly got the idea from reading Watson's story, "A Scandal in Bohemia" in the *Strand* magazine. When Watson quotes one of Doctor Samuel Johnson's sayings, he inadvertently gives Holmes the missing clue.

A museum guide (Leyland Hodgson) is conducting a group of visitors through Doctor Samuel Johnson's home as Hilda, Cavanaugh and Hamid arrive. They join the group just as the guide is interrupted by a minister's wife (Lillian Bronson), who whispers an old rumor to her husband (Wilson Benge). The group continues up the stairs to Doctor Johnson's library where, the guide explains, Johnson wrote his famous dictionary. As the group moves on, the guide points out Johnson's secretary containing many of his valued books. Hilda and the others remain behind and quickly force the lock on the secretary, pulling out books until they find a hidden package that contains the Bank of England plates. Their moment of victory is quickly dashed by the appearance of Holmes and soon after by Watson, Inspector Hopkins and several policemen. The group is arrested and Holmes gives the credit for his success to Watson, who receives Inspector Hopkins' congratulations by replying, "I don't think I could've done it entirely, without Mr. Holmes' help, you know."

Hilda Courtney and her gang are apprehended by Sherlock Holmes and Dr. Watson in the finale of *Dressed to Kill.*

The Roy William Neill repertory company was out in full force once again in *Dressed to Kill,* with Frederick Worlock (Colonel Cavanaugh), Holmes Herbert (Ebenezer Crabtree), Harry Cording (Hamid), Mary Gordon (Mrs. Hudson), Ian Wolfe (Commissioner), Olaf Hytten (Bookkeeper), Sally Shepherd (Tobacconist), Leyland Hodgson (Museum Guide), Wilson Benge (Minister), Lillian Benson (Minister's Wife), Cyril Delevanti (John Davidson), Guy Kingsford (Undercover Convict), Boyd Irwin (Technician) and Ted Billings (Pub Patron). The non-members were Patricia Morison (Hilda Courtney), Edmond Breon (Julian Emery) and Carl Harbord (Inspector Hopkins).

PATRICIA MORISON, although not technically a member of the Universal Films Repertory Company, is one of only two surviving principal cast members from any of the Sherlock Holmes films and on March 19, 2011 she celebrated her 97th birthday. (The other survivor is Marjorie Lord from *Sherlock Holmes in Washington*, whose 93rd birthday was on July 26, 2011.) Born in 1914 in New York City, Eileen Patricia Augusta Fraser Morison is the daughter of English parents then living in the United States. Her father William R. Morison was a playwright and sometime actor (stage name Norman Rainey) and her mother, the former Selena

Patricia Morison as Hilda Courtney and Basil Rathbone as Sherlock Holmes
examine her exotic cigarettes in *Dressed to Kill.*

Fraser, worked for British Intelligence during World War I. According to her comments on the DVD audio commentary for *Dressed to Kill*, at some point when Patricia was quite young the family returned briefly to England, for Morison speaks of years later visiting the church in London where she was christened. She was part of the first group from Hollywood to go overseas to entertain the troops. She flew in a seaplane with Merle Oberon, Al Jolson, Frank McHugh and Alan Jenkins. War correspondent Quentin Reynolds took her to see the church where she was christened, but it had been destroyed by German bombs.

Morison began her education at New York's P.S. #9 and then graduated from Washington Irving High School with a scholarship to study art in Paris. However, her interest in performing led her to study acting with Sanford Meisner at the Neighborhood Playhouse School of the Theatre and dance under the tutelage of Martha Graham. To make her living expenses, Morison was working at the same time as a dress shop designer at Russeks Department Store.

Her first appearance on the Broadway stage was on November 23, 1933, when she opened at the Ambassador Theatre in the comedy *Growing Pains*, produced and directed by Arthur Lubin, the future director of *Hold*

That Ghost (1941), *Phantom of the Opera* (1943) and *The Spider Woman Strikes Back* (1946). Unfortunately the play closed after 28 performances and Morison was back at Russeks working as a designer. As mentioned earlier, in December of 1935 Morison was hired to understudy Helen Hayes in *Victoria Regina* and for the next year and a half she stood in the wings and watched Hayes and Vincent Price performing as the Queen and her Prince Consort. When Hayes took her vacation in June of 1936 the producers temporarily closed down the play, rather than continue with Morison in the role. So it wasn't until May of 1938 that Morison had her first big break when she co-starred with Alfred Drake in the musical operetta, *The Two Bouquets* at the Windsor Theatre. The play ran just long enough for Morison to receive some nice reviews from critics such as Brooks Atkinson, who wrote that she sang "with uncommon skill" and acted "with willowy elegance," and a term contract with Paramount Pictures.

Patricia Morison's film career was a series of frustrations for her, never realizing the potential she knew she was capable of attaining. She made her debut at Paramount in *Persons in Hiding* (1939), based on a book by J. Edgar Hoover. She played an ambitious woman who goads a small-time crook, played by J. Carrol Naish, into becoming a cold-blooded killer. As she told William Peper in a *New York World-Telegram* interview in 1965, "I was typed as a gun moll or a spy after that." Paramount's publicity department came up with the catchphrase "The fire and ice girl." When asked what she thought that meant, Morison replied, "I haven't the foggiest." Morison made eleven films in three years for Paramount, including a Cisco Kid western *Romance of the Rio Grande* on loanout to 20th Century-Fox, and never sang a note. It wasn't until she left Paramount in 1942 and took a role in a low-budget Monogram musical, *Silver Skates* (1943) co-starring Kenny Baker and the British skater Belita, that she supposedly sang the duet "A Girl Like You, A Boy Like Me" with Baker and the Ted Fio Rito Orchestra, but according to Morison it wasn't her voice that you heard. Monogram had already recorded the song with another singer before Morison was hired and the budget wouldn't allow them to re-record the song with Morison singing. It wasn't until she played a Romanian spy posing as a cabaret singer in an independent film shot in Mexico called *Sophia* (1948), which co-starred Gene Raymond and Sigrid Gurie, that Morison finally got to sing on the screen, even though the song was in Romanian.

In 1948, after appearing in 27 films, Patricia Morison made the decision to leave Hollywood and return to New York. It was a propitious move on her part as she soon auditioned for Cole Porter, who promised her the lead in his new musical *Kiss Me Kate*. The musical had not yet received its financial backing and Morison signed for a role in an early television series called *Cases of Eddy Drake* while she waited for Porter to call. The series was cancelled after nine episodes, just as *Kiss Me Kate* went into rehearsals. When the play opened in Philadelphia, everybody thought they were in trouble, but the show was a huge success. Morison's performance as Lilli Vanessi, once again opposite Alfred Drake, earned her the following comments from the *New York Times:* "As a greasepaint hussy, Miss Morison is an agile and humorous actress who is not afraid of slapstick and who can sing enchantingly." After appearing on Broadway for two and a half years in *Kiss Me Kate*, Morison went on to play the role in the London production for another year and a half. The play was such a success that King George VI, who was ill and unable to attend a performance, requested a special closed circuit TV presentation at Buckingham Palace. Morison then returned to the United States and eventually replaced Gertrude Lawrence on Broadway in *The King and I*. Although neither Morison or Drake was in the cast of the M-G-M film version of *Kiss Me Kate* in 1953 that starred Howard Keel and Kathryn Grayson, they did recreate their roles in 1958 for a live television special directed by George Schaefer. Morison continued working in television in New York and later in Hollywood, her last film appearance was in *Won Ton Ton: The Dog That Saved Hollywood* (1976) and her most recent appearance to date was in an episode of the popular television series *Cheers* in 1989. As of this writing she continues to live in Hollywood near CBS Television City and the Farmers Market.

EDMOND BREON gives a wonderfully droll performance as Julian Emory in *Dressed to Kill*. Breon, whose full name was Iver Edmond de Breon MacLaferty, was born on December 12, 1888 in the village of Hamilton in Lanark, Scotland. He matriculated from the United Services College in Westward Ho, Devon when he was 18 and in 1908 he married his wife, Margaret and returned to Scotland to begin his career as an actor. One of his first performances was in a one-act play called *Lonesome-Like* at the Royalty Theatre in Glasgow on February 6, 1911. The next year he starred as Fedor Protasov in the English translation of Leo Tolstoy's play *The Living Dead*, now called *The Man Who Was Dead*, produced by the Literary Theatre Society in London. The following year, 1913, he starred in another play with a Russian background, George Bernard Shaw's little known *Great Catherine (Whom Glory Still Adores)* and shortly after, he left the stage to begin appearing in silent films and moved to France. He played Inspector Juve, the tenacious nemeses of Fantomas the thief, in Louis Feuillade's eponymous series of films based on the novels by Marcel Allain, *Fantomas—A l'ombre de la guillotine* (1913) and *Juve Against*

Fantomas (1913), and then remained in France to appear in four more films before the outbreak of World War I. It was during this period that he began the habit of changing the spelling of his first name to "Edmund" when appearing in films, a habit that would continue sporadically throughout his career in Hollywood. When the War broke out, Breon joined the 1st Battalion of the Hampshire Regiment and served in France until the end of hostilities.

Edmond Breon as Julian Emery in *Dressed to Kill*.

In December of 1922 Breon appeared briefly in a drama called *The Rumor* starring Claude Rains at The Globe Theatre and then began a highly successful run in John Galsworthy's *Loyalties*. It was Galsworthy's biggest success and ran for 407 performances. In 1928 Breon made his first British film, *Skirts*, a silent comedy starring Charlie Chaplin's older half-brother Sydney Chaplin. Following a quick trip to New York to appear in a comedy written and starring Elliott Nugent and an even quicker sojourn in Hollywood where he appeared as Lt. Phipps in Howard Hawks' 1930 production of *The Dawn Patrol* with Douglas Fairbanks, Jr., he returned to England and began a series of "quota films," several of which starred Douglas Fairbanks, Jr. After appearing in M-G-M's *Goodbye Mr. Chips* (1939), Breon and his wife left for America and on November 26, 1940 he opened at the National Theatre in Emlyn Williams' *The Corn Is Green,* supporting Ethel Barrymore and Richard Waring. The play was an enormous success, playing for 477 performances before closing on January 17, 1942.

Edmond and Margaret Breon moved to Beverly Hills and took an apartment at 216 South Rodeo Drive. His Hollywood film career began in earnest with his appearance in 20th Century-Fox's *The Lodger* (1944) and continued throughout that year with films such as *Gaslight* (1944) and *The White Cliffs of Dover* (1944), followed by *The Woman in the Window* (1944). As luck would have it, when Warner Bros. made the film version of *The Corn Is Green* (1945), several of Breon's fellow stage actors were signed to recreate their roles, but Breon's character of the Squire was played by Nigel Bruce. He would continue making films, including his final appearance, working again for director Howard Hawks in his very popular science-fiction film *The Thing from Another World* (1951). Shortly after completing this film, Edmond Breon sailed for London on

July 25, 1951 and returned to his native Scotland, where he died at the age of 68 later that year.

CARL HARBORD, whose real name was John Kerslake Harbord, was born on January 26, 1908 in Salcombe, a onetime fishing and ship-building center and today a popular seaside resort in Devon in Southern England. Harbord, his brother Joseph Thwaites Harbord (two years his senior) and their parents, George Thwaites Harbord and the former Agnes Louise Payne Ovenden, continued living in Salcombe until Harbord's father died and his mother moved the family to London. Carl Harbord began acting in his early twenties and one of the first plays that he appeared in was an American comedy by actor James Gleason called *Iz Zat So*, which opened at the Apollo Theatre in London in 1926 and ran for 234 performances. Shortly after, Harbord appeared in *Paul I* at the Royal Court Theatre with a young Charles Laughton. By 1928 Harbord was appearing in his first film, playing Lt. Gunther in a World War I silent drama starring Elissa Landi called *The Betrayal* (1928). This was followed by another military officer role in *The American Prisoner* (1929) with Carl Brisson and Madeleine Carroll. Harbord's next film was a forgotten early (1929) silent version of Liam O'Flaherty's play *The Informer* that director John Ford would immortalize in 1935. Harbord starred in his next few films and then was signed for Anthony Asquith's *Tell England* (1931) to play the leading role of Edgar Doe, the sensitive young Australian who

goes off to war filled with enthusiastic patriotism only to become disillusioned by the horrors of the battlefield and ultimately die in the battle of the Gallipoli Peninsula. It was in this film, later retitled *The Battle of Gallipoli* and in which my father appeared as The Padre who tries to calm the fears of Edgar Doe and his best friend Rupert Ray, that Carl Harbord and my father first met and began a friendship that lasted until Harbord's death many years later.

On October 16, 1934 Harbord arrived in the United States onboard the S.S. *Aquitania* with the rest of the cast of Noel Coward's musical comedy *Conversation Piece*. Coward had

Carl Harbord as Inspector Hopkins in *Dressed to Kill.*

From left, C.M. Hallard, unidentified, Dennis Hoey, Tony Bruce and Carl Harbord in *The Battle of Gallipoli*.

starred in a very successful run of his play in London and it was now opening on Broadway at the 44th Street Theatre with Pierre Fresnay replacing Coward and Harbord replacing Louis Hayward. Another member of the cast was George Sanders, making his one and only appearance on Broadway. While in the United States, Harbord made a brief appearance in M-G-M's *The Mystery of Mr. X* (1934) before returning to England and several more films. In 1937 he revisited Broadway in a revival of Gustave Flaubert's *Madame Bovary* with Constance Cummings and Eric Portman. By 1942 Harbord was in Hollywood appearing in two films, *Captains of the Clouds* with James Cagney at Warner Bros. and *Eagle Squadron* at Universal with a large contingent of future Roy William Neill repertory company members including Nigel Bruce, Evelyn Ankers, Edgar Barrier, Frederick Worlock, Paul Cavanaugh, Gavin Muir, Ian Wolfe, Harold De Becker, Olaf Hytten, Rudolph Anders, Alec Harford, Guy Kingsford and his future wife Isobel Elsom. Harbord and Elsom, otherwise known as Isabella Jeanette Reed, were married later that year. Soon after, Harbord played one of his best remembered roles as Marty Williams, the British soldier who dies quoting poetry in *Sahara* (1943) starring Humphrey Bogart. Elsom and Harbord were frequent dinner guests at our home; she and my father had been friends in England and had appeared together in an early NBC television production of Noel Coward's play *Hay Fever* in New York in 1939. By the time of the Harbord-Elsom marriage, Harbord's career had slipped from starring roles to playing sometimes uncredited supporting roles and Isobel Elsom was a highly sought-after character actress in films. Perhaps as a means of escaping this unpleasant reality, on April 10, 1943, at the age of 35, Harbord voluntarily joined the Army Air Corps and after basic training was stationed at a military hospital in Palm Springs, California. He would often come and stay with us at our home at 167 North Crescent Drive in Beverly Hills, when he was on leave and Isobel was in New York appearing in a play.

Carl was a charming man and I always enjoyed the times he would arrive in his khaki uniform, toting his B4 bag and move into our guest room, but he had one big problem; he drank and when he did he became unpleasant. Eventually my father had to ask him to find other accommodations when he came up from Palm Springs, although we continued to visit with him and Isobel at their apartment in Santa Monica. In 1951 both Carl and Isobel appeared with Olivia de Havilland and Jack Hawkins in a revival of *Romeo and Juliet* at the Broadhurst Theatre in New York. Harbord would follow that with another revival of a Shakespeare play, *Much Ado About Nothing*, while Elsom was appearing down the street in *The Climate of Eden*. Apart from a few television roles, Harbord's career in films was over and his last professional appearance was to join his wife and Basil Rathbone in an unsuccessful production of an original mystery called *Hide and Seek*, which closed after seven performances. Carl Harbord died in Santa Monica, California on October 18, 1958 at the age of 50. Isobel Elsom remained close friends with my mother for many years, until my mother's death in 1974. Elsom died on January 12, 1981 at the Motion Picture & Television Country House and Hospital in Woodland Hills, California at the age of 85. I always thought it was quite ironic that Carl Harbord would be the actor chosen to replace my father in *Dressed to Kill*.

GUY KINGSFORD represented the Roy William Neill repertory company's book ends, having appeared in both Neill's first and last of the Holmes series. He was however a frequent performer in Universal films during the 1930s and 1940s. His father, the popular character actor Walter Kingsford, appeared in only two Universal films during that same period, *The Invisible Ray* (1936) and *Ghost Catchers* (1944), and was best remembered as Doctor Walter Carew in M-G-M's series of *Dr. Kildare* films. Guy Duncan

Guy Kingsford as he appeared as the foot patrolman, with Basil Rathbone
in *Sherlock Holmes and the Secret Weapon*.

Kingsford Pearce was born to Walter Kingsford Pearce and his wife, the actress Winifred Hanley, on September 30, 1911 in the town of Redhill, Surrey, England. In a curious coincidence, Kingsford, born of an acting family, came from a town known as one of the few places in England where Fuller's Earth could be extracted. Among its other applications, Fuller's Earth is used in motion pictures to create dust effects and to conceal protective pads used by stunt men in falls. At the age of three, Guy Kingsford traveled with his parents to the United States, where both were appearing on Broadway with a repertory company performing children's plays. He would return once again in 1922, when his parents decided to move permanently to New York to pursue their acting careers. Walter and Winifred eventually divorced and Guy continued to live with his mother at 215 West 79th Street in Manhattan until his 18th birthday, when he traveled to Cuba as a student.

In 1935, Kingsford appeared as a taxi driver in his first Hollywood film *The Headline Woman*, starring Heather Angel. His next film was *Dracula's Daughter* (1936) and from that point on Kingsford worked steadily in films and occasional television series until his retirement in 1960. 1936 was a banner year for Kingsford, as he appeared in seven films, became a U.S. citizen and on March 14, 1936 married his wife, Adelaide. Kingsford appeared only once in a film with his father, Walter, and that was in 20th Century-Fox's *Bomber's Moon* (1943). In a newspaper interview with Jimmie Fidler that Kingsford gave while he was appearing in the Humphrey Bogart film *Sahara* (1943), he recounted an incident that took place while he was appearing with a touring stock company in Berlin in 1938. "One day he received a phone call from Doctor Goebbels, propaganda minister of the Third Reich," Fidler wrote. "Would Kingsford be interested in playing a leading role in a picture produced by the German Reichs' Filmkammer? The pay, Goebbels said, would be excellent—10,000 reichsmarks on signing the contract, and 50,000 more on completing the picture. Kingsford coveted that kind of pay, but nixed the role when he read the script and the billing. He was to be publicized as a leading American star—and the picture, laid in America, called for him to play a 'patriotic' bundsman who turned American military secrets over to the German High Command!" Kingsford returned directly to Hollywood and a Republic picture called *Sabotage* (1939), but two years later he did return briefly to London to portray Captain Troubridge in the Laurence Oliver-Vivian Leigh starrer *That Hamilton Woman* (1941). Guy Kingsford appeared in a total of 102 films and television episodes, with his final performance in the early supernatural TV series *One Step Beyond* in 1960. He would die at the Encino Hospital in Encino, California on November 9, 1986 at the age of 75.

In December of 1945 my father appeared in his final film for Universal Pictures, a lesser entry in their horror catalogue called *She-Wolf of London* (1946) starring June Lockhart and Don Porter. From there he went immediately over to 20th Century-Fox to join the cast of *Anna and the King of Siam* (1946), which filmed through all of January and February, thereby making him unavailable for the final Sherlock Holmes film, *Dressed to Kill* that began filming on January 22, 1946. Whether the Lestrade character was rewritten into a purely functional detective named Inspector Hopkins because of my father's unavailability, or because the screenwriters and Roy William Neill felt that the presence of the Lestrade character would fail to add anything to the proceedings, is a matter of pure conjecture and unfortunately no one is alive to provide the answer. But whatever the reason, it denied my father his chance to take a final bow along with his fellow cast mates Basil Rathbone and Nigel Bruce. The friendly atmosphere on the Holmes set was described by Howard C. Keyn in an *AP* Newsfeatures titled *Elementary Doctor Watson* that appeared in Sunday papers on February 2, 1946: "The Holmes sets have become rather famous in Hollywood," he wrote. "The players are nearly all of British or Scottish extraction and are frequently referred to jocularly as 'The London Art Players.' Tea is served each afternoon on the Holmes set. The kidding is abundant, deadpan and very British. Bruce is apt to say to Rathbone, 'Do you know, Basil, I think Dennis Hoey is the very WORST Lestrade we've ever had! Oh—frightfully sorry, Dennis old man—didn't see you there.'"

When *Dressed to Kill* was released on June 7, 1946, the Hollywood trade papers, perhaps knowing by then that it was to be the final film in the series, gave it generally good reviews. *The Hollywood Reporter* said, "Story-wise, *Dressed to Kill* heads the list of the modern Sherlock Holmes pictures ... It poses a puzzle worthy of the Doyle tradition and gives Doctor Watson a large, if unwitting share in pointing to the solution." *Daily Variety* singled out the principals for recognition, saying, "Film moves at speedy tempo which early attracts attention and cleverly-contrived plot holds this interest. Basil Rathbone and Nigel Bruce are up to usual form ... and Roy William Neill, in dual capacity of producer-director, has accorded picture showmanship treatment." Even the *Weekly Variety* had kind words to say: "Like most of the Universal series it is expertly put together and excellently played by a cast familiar with technique necessary to keep the Holmes fans satisfied. Film gets good production and direction from Roy William Neill and plot is neatly contrived to hold interest."

But time had finally run out for the series. Despite the fact that the studio had renewed its option with the Conan Doyle estate in December of 1944, as soon as *Dressed to Kill* completed filming in mid-February of 1946, Nigel Bruce was notified by the studio that the series was to be discontinued and his term contact ended. Basil Rathbone, feeling stifled by the role, had informed the studio that he no longer wished to play Holmes. Whether Bruce felt unhappy with his co-star's decision, as has been suggested, I don't know, but in his unpublished memoir Bruce speaks fondly of his relationship with Rathbone: "My association with Basil had been a very long one. We had acted together in fourteen Sherlock Holmes pictures, in the film of *Frenchman's Creek* [1944] and on the radio in countless programs since October 2nd, 1939. Ours had been a very happy association and one which had brought me much publicity and a lot of money. During our long time together Basil and I never had a row or any unpleasantness of any sort." Bruce continued to play Dr. Watson on the radio programs, this time with Tom Conway as Holmes, and co-starred in eight more films, including *The Two Mrs. Carrolls* (1947) with Humphrey Bogart, *Limelight* (1952) with Charles Chaplin and the very first 3-D feature, Arch Oboler's *Bwana Devil* (1952), which caused quite a commotion when it first opened. I was invited to a preview screening and found that I could never get the red and blue paper framed glasses to fit properly and consequently missed half of the 3-D effects and came away with a splitting headache. William Nigel Ernle Bruce, who was born in Ensenada, Mexico on February 4, 1895, would die in Santa Monica, California of a coronary thrombosis on October 8, 1953 at the age of 58, after having already suffered a serious heart attack the previous year. According to newspaper articles at the time, over 300 friends and colleagues attended his funeral. He is buried at the Chapel of the Pines in Los Angeles, California.

Basil Rathbone would live for another 14 years, continuing to claim in numerous interviews that Sherlock Holmes had ruined his career, even though he received a Tony nomination as Best Actor for his performance in the original Broadway production of *The Heiress* in 1948 and still attempted to star in a production of *Sherlock Holmes*, written by his wife Ouida Bergere, that opened and closed in three performances in 1953. In the *Hollywood Reporter*'s 25th Anniversary issue that came out on November 14, 1955, Rathbone authored an article entitled "Spillane Killed Sherlock," in which he bemoaned the public's taste for violence as the reason his stage production of *Sherlock Holmes* had failed, ignoring the fact that the play had received mediocre reviews. It's ironic to note that only in these films that he professed to hate so much would his name appear above the title. I would see Rathbone once again in 1965 when I was working at Producers Studios in Hollywood and I heard that he was working that day on the adjoining stage to ours in an AIP production with the dreadful title, *The Ghost in the Invisible Bikini,* which was no improvement over its original title *Beach Party in a Haunted House.* Wanting to pay my respects, during a break in filming I went next door and found him seated in a director's chair away from all of the activity. It had been 21 years since I had last seen him at Universal and, although I had watched him perform in numerous films over the years, I was nonetheless shocked to see the frail old man seated in the shadows, drinking a cup of tea. I introduced myself, reminding Mr. Rathbone of my father, and of our meeting in 1944 on the set of the Sherlock Holmes film. He seemed vaguely to remember my father and politely asked about his health. When I informed him that my father had died several years earlier, he nodded silently, as if to acknowledge his own mortality. I couldn't help feeling that I was intruding, as he seemed to drift off into his own thoughts, so I made some self-conscious comment about the continuing popularity of the old Sherlock Holmes films, to which he smiled graciously and I then excused myself. As I walked back to my stage I grew angry that this once great actor was now reduced to playing a supporting role to a cast of callow teenagers in a low-budget exploitation film. Philip St. John Basil Rathbone, born in Johannesburg, South Africa on June 13, 1892, would die of a heart attack in his New York apartment on July 21, 1967 at the age of 75. Ouida Bergere Rathbone would die on November 29, 1974 at the age of 88 and be buried alongside her husband at the Ferndale Mausoleum in Hartsdale, New York.

EPILOGUE

When all is said and done, the Sherlock Holmes series was arguably the most successful franchise in Universal Pictures history, with its twelve films far outnumbering even the highly influential *Frankenstein* series of seven sequels, or *The Mummy* and its four sequels. As part of the research for this book I viewed each of the twelve Sherlock Holmes films that starred Basil Rathbone and Nigel Bruce several times. Even on a small monitor screen I was amazed at the quality of the films and their ability to hold your interest. These films have survived over 60 years and, in spite of other film and television versions and the ongoing argument regarding Universal's arbitrary alterations to the original setting, they are still considered by many to be the quintessential motion picture representation of the Sir Arthur Conan Doyle stories. Much credit must indeed be given to its two stars and to its brilliant director, but I would like to think that the support given by the many talented and unsung performers that made up the repertory company also had a great deal to do with the continuing praise for the series. These character actors and actresses would grace hundreds of other films with their diversified performances and more often than not these films, be they star-studded spectacles or poverty row quickies, would be that much the better for their presence. United Press Hollywood correspondent Frederick C. Othman, who has been quoted several times previously in this book, wrote an article in 1940 about George Zucco in which he praised all character actors. "They're not bothered much by studio press agents," he wrote. "They don't have to appear in night clubs unless they feel like it. They're all comfortably middle-aged and they all earn around $1,000 a week—and don't care if they never earn any more. They're getting a little bald, some of them. But that's okay. Some are getting extra inches around their middle. They're not

257

glamour boys. They're the character actors, the gentlemen who are mentioned in the small type under the names of the stars—and the gentlemen who, more often than not, turn a bad picture into a good one." It would have been nice if Othman had included the distaff side of the profession in his praise, but if we merely change the male references to female, his comments apply to our actresses as well. They were all exceptional, and perhaps now we will remember their names. I hope so.

ACKNOWLEDGMENTS

I must first thank my good friend Scott P. Gallinghouse, whose amazing research was an incalculable contribution to this book.

Also film historian Tom Weaver, whose friendship and support have helped me through the writing of all three of my books, but most particularly for his invaluable aid in the development of this book.

Kris Marentette, a true Sherlockian film fan who was tremendously helpful with gathering many of the photographs and lobby cards for this book.

Author Scott Allen Nollen, who helped to find some of the additional lobby cards that introduce each chapter.

Dan Scapperotti, for several additional photographs from his fabulous collection.

John Antosiewicz for providing the photographs of Edgar Barrier and Skelton Knaggs.

James Clatterbaugh of *Monsters From the Vault* magazine for the photographs that illustrate the chapter on Roy William Neill.

Frederick Rappaport for the photographs of Charles Knight, Boyd Irwin and Arthur Stenning.

Ned Comstock, Archivist, at the University of Southern California Cinematic Arts Library, for his invaluable help in locating the old Universal Pictures production files.

And Jenny Romero, Department Coordinator of the Special Collections section of the Margaret Herrick Library at the Academy of Motion Picture Arts and Sciences and Academy Foundation, for allowing me access to the Universal Pictures Sherlock Holmes correspondence and publicity files.

THE UNIVERSAL FILMS OF THE ROY WILLIAM NEILL REPERTORY COMPANY (1920–1947)

John Abbott *(1905-1996)*
Nightmare (1942)
Pursuit to Algiers (1946)
Time Out of Mind (1947)
The Web (1947)

Rudolph Anders *(1895-1987)*
A Dangerous Game (1941)
Eagle Squadron (1942)
Sherlock Holmes and the Voice of Terror (1942)
Sherlock Holmes and the Secret Weapon (1943)
The Strange Death of Adolf Hitler (1943)

Evelyn Ankers *(1918-1985)*
Hold that Ghost (1941)
The Wolf Man (1941)
Ghost of Frankenstein (1942)
Eagle Squadron (1942)
Sherlock Holmes and the Voice of Terror (1942)
The Great Impersonation (1942)
Keep 'Em Slugging (1943)
Captive Wild Woman (1943)
All by Myself (1943)
Hers to Hold (1943)
You're a Lucky Fellow Mr. Smith (1943)

Son of Dracula (1943)
The Mad Ghoul (1943)
His Butler's Sister (1943)
Ladies Courageous (1944)
Weird Woman (1944)
Pardon My Rhythm (1944)
Jungle Woman (1944)
The Invisible Man's Revenge (1944)
The Pearl of Death (1944)
Bowery to Broadway (1944)
The Frozen Ghost (1945)

Lionel Atwill (*1885-1946*)
Man Made Monster (1941)
The Mad Doctor of Market Street (1942)
The Ghost of Frankenstein (1942)
The Strange Case of Doctor Rx (1942)
Night Monster (1942)
Sherlock Holmes and the Secret Weapon (1943)
Frankenstein Meets the Wolf Man (1943)
House of Frankenstein (1944)
House of Dracula (1945)
Lost City of the Jungle (1946)

Edgar Barrier (*1907-1964*)
Eagle Squadron (1942)
Sherlock Holmes and the Voice of Terror (1942)
Arabian Nights (1942)
The Adventures of Smilin' Jack (1943)
We've Never Been Licked (1943)
Phantom of the Opera (1943)
Crazy House (1943)
Flesh and Fantasy (1943)
Cobra Woman (1944)

Wilson Benge (*1875-1955*)
The Man Who Cried Wolf (1937)
One Hundred Men and a Girl (1937)
The Witness Vanishes (1939)
Call a Messenger (1939)
Green Hell (1940)

The Green Hornet (1939)
Half a Sinner (1940)
The Man Who Lost Himself (1941)
It Started with Eve (1941)
You're Telling Me (1942)
Jungle Woman (1944)
The Pearl of Death (1944)
The House of Fear (1945)
Pursuit to Algiers (1945)
Dressed to Kill (1946)

Billy Bevan (*1887-1957*)
Dracula's Daughter (1936)
The Invisible Man Returns (1940)
The Invisible Man's Revenge (1944)
The Pearl of Death (1944)
Terror by Night (1946)

Ted Billings (*1880-1947*)
Frankenstein (1931)
Murders in the Rue Morgue (1932)
The Impatient Maiden (1932)
The Invisible Man (1933)
The Man Who Reclaimed His Head (1934)
Bride of Frankenstein (1935)
The Invisible Ray (1936)
Tower of London (1939)
Seven Sinners (1940)
The Flame of New Orleans (1941)
Sherlock Holmes and the Voice of Terror (1942)
Pittsburgh (1942)
Flesh and Fantasy (1943)
The Scarlet Claw (1944)
The Invisible Man's Revenge (1944)
Dressed to Kill (1946)

Mathew Boulton (*1893-1962*)
The Invisible Man Returns (1940)
Two Tickets to London (1943)
The Woman in Green (1945)

Edmond Breon (*1882-1951*)
The Woman in the Window (1944)
Dressed to Kill (1946)

Lillian Bronson (*1902-1995*)
Ladies Courageous (1944)
The Invisible Man's Revenge (1944)
The Pearl of Death (1944)
The Suspect (1944)
Dressed to Kill (1946)

Hillary Brooke (*1914-1999*)
Unfinished Business (1941)
Sherlock Holmes and the Voice of Terror (1942)
Sherlock Holmes Faces Death (1943)
The Woman in Green (1945)

John Burton (*1904-1987*)
The Sun Never Sets (1939)
Dark Streets of Cairo (1940)
Horror Island (1941)
Eagle Squadron (1942)
Invisible Agent (1942)
Sherlock Holmes and the Secret Weapon (1943)
Sherlock Holmes in Washington (1943)
Two Tickets to London (1943)
The Spider Woman (1944)
Enter Arsine Lupin (1944)
The Woman in Green (1945)

Paul Cavanagh (*1888-1964*)
Uncertain Lady (1934)
The Under-Pup (1939)
The Strange Case of Doctor Rx (1942)
Eagle Squadron (1942)
The Scarlet Claw (1944)
The House of Fear (1945)
The Woman in Green (1945)
Night in Paradise (1946)
Ivy (1947)
Secret Beyond the Door (1947)

David Clyde (*1885-1945*)
Eagle Squadron (1942)
Nightmare (1942)
Frankenstein Meets the Wolf Man (1943)
Two Tickets to London (1943)
The Scarlet Claw (1944)
Enter Arsine Lupin (1944)
The House of Fear (1945)

Harry Cording (*1891-1954*)
Captain of the Guard (1930)
My Pal, the King (1932)
The Black Cat (1934)
Strange Wives (1934)
The Man Who Reclaimed His Head (1934)
The Mystery of Edwin Drood (1935)
Lady Tubbs (1935)
Sutter's Gold (1936)
The Road Back (1937)
Son of Frankenstein (1939)
The Sun Never Sets (1939)
Tower of London (1939)
Destry Rides Again (1939)
The Invisible Man Returns (1940)
The House of Seven Gables (1940)
When the Daltons Rode (1940)
Law and Order (1940)
Trail of the Vigilantes (1940)
The Green Hornet Strikes Again (1940)
San Francisco Docks (1940)
Bury Me Not on the Lone Prairie (1941)
The Lady from Cheyenne (1941)
Mutiny in the Arctic (1941)
Raiders of the Desert (1941)
Rawhide Rangers (1941)
Badlands of Dakota (1941)
The Wolf Man (1941)
Ride 'Em Cowboy (1942)
The Ghost of Frankenstein (1942)
The Spoilers (1942)
Sherlock Holmes and the Voice of Terror (1942)

Overland Mail (1942)
The Mummy's Tomb (1942)
Pittsburgh (1942)
Arabian Nights (1942)
Sherlock Holmes and the Secret Weapon (1943)
Two Tickets to London (1943)
Ali Baba and the Forty Thieves (1944)
The Spider Woman (1944)
Phantom Lady (1944)
The Great Alaskan Mystery (1944)
The Pearl of Death (1944)
Gypsy Wildcat (1944)
Lost in a Harem (1944)
Strange Confession (1945)
Jungle Queen (1945)
The House of Fear (1945)
Sudan (1945)
Terror by Night (1945)
Night in Paradise (1946)
Dressed to Kill (1946)
Inside Job (1946)

Alec Craig (*1884-1945*)

Charlie McCarthy, Detective (1939)
Zanzibar (1940)
Meet the Chump (1941)
Calling Dr. Death (1943)
The Spider Woman (1944)
Ghost Catchers (1944)
Jungle Woman (1944)
The Mystery of the Riverboat (1944)
The Woman in the Window (1944)
The House of Fear (1945)
Girl on the Spot (1946)

Henry Daniell (*1894-1963*)

Sherlock Holmes and the Voice of Terror (1942)
Nightmare (1942)
The Great Impersonation (1942)
Sherlock Holmes in Washington (1943)
The Suspect (1944)
The Woman in Green (1945)

Harold De Becker (*1889-1947*)

Winners of the West (1940)
Eagle Squadron (1942)
Nightmare (1942)
Sherlock Holmes and the Secret Weapon (1943)
Two Tickets to London (1943)
Sherlock Holmes Faces Death (1943)
Flesh and Fantasy (1943)
The Pearl of Death (1944)
The Woman in Green (1945)

Cyril Delevanti *(1887-1975)*

Red Barry (1938)
Night Monster (1942)
When Johnny Comes Marching Home (1942)
The Adventures of Smilin' Jack (1943)
Frankenstein Meets the Wolf Man (1943)
All by Myself (1943)
Two Tickets to London (1943)
Phantom of the Opera (1943)
Son of Dracula (1943)
Phantom Lady (1944)
Her Primitive Man (1944)
The Invisible Man's Revenge (1944)
Strange Confession (1945)
Jungle Queen (1945)
The House of Fear (1945)
The Daltons Ride Again (1945)
Lost City of the Jungle (1946)
The Mysterious Mr. M (1946)

Leslie Denison (*1905-1992*)

Paris Calling (1941)
Danger in the Pacific (1942)
Eagle Squadron (1942)
Invisible Agent (1942)
Sherlock Holmes and the Voice of Terror (1942)
Sherlock Holmes and the Secret Weapon (1943)
The Amazing Mrs. Holliday (1943)
Sherlock Holmes in Washington (1943)
Corvette K-225 (1943)

Follow the Boys (1944)
The Pearl of Death (1944)
Enter Arsene Lupin (1944)
She Gets Her Man (1945)
The House of Fear (1945)
Her Lucky Night (1945)
The Woman in Green (1945)

Reginald Denny (*1891-1967*)
18 silent short films (1922-1923)
24 silent feature films (1922-1929)
One Hysterical Night (1929)
Embarrassing Moments (1930)
One More River (1934)
Two in a Crowd (1936)
Spring Parade (1940)
Seven Sinners (1940)
Appointment for Love (1941)
Sherlock Holmes and the Voice of terror (1942)
Tangier (1946)

Vernon Downing (*1913-1973*)
East of Java (1935)
Sherlock Holmes Faces Death (1943)
Corvette K-225 (1943)
The Spider Woman (1944)
The Time of Their Lives (1946)

Rex Evans (*1903-1969*)
First Love (1939)
The Invisible Man Returns (1940)
I'm Nobody's Sweetheart Now (1940)
The Flame of New Orleans (1941)
The Great Impersonation (1942)
Frankenstein Meets the Wolf Man (1943)
Ali Baba and the Forty Thieves (1944)
Swing Out, Sister (1945)
Pursuit to Algiers (1945)
Night in Paradise (1946)

Mary Forbes (*1879-1974*)

East is West (1930)
One Hundred Men and a Girl (1937)
The Rage of Paris (1938)
Risky Business (1939)
You Can't Cheat an Honest Man (1939)
Three Smart Girls Grow Up (1939)
The Sun Never Sets (1939)
I Stole a Million (1939)
Private Affair (1940)
Back Street (1941)
Paris Calling (1941)
Almost Married (1942)
The Great Impersonation (1942)
Sherlock Holmes in Washington (1943)
Two Tickets to London (1943)
Flesh and Fantasy (1943)
Ladies Courageous (1944)
I'll Remember April (1945)
That's the Spirit (1945)
Lady on a Train (1945)
That Night with You (1945)
Terror by Night (1946)
Ivy (1947)

Charles Francis (*1885-1968*)

The Jury's Secret (1938)
Strange Faces (1938)
The Scarlet Claw (1944)
The Pearl of Death (1944)

Thomas Gomez (*1905-1971*)

Sherlock Holmes and the Voice of Terror (1942)
Who Done It? (1942)
Pittsburgh (1942)
Arabian Nights (1942)
White Savage (1943)
Frontier Badmen (1943)
Corvette K-225 (1943)
Crazy House (1943)

Phantom Lady (1943)
In Society (1944)
The Climax (1944)
Bowery to Broadway (1944)
Dead Man's Eyes (1944)
Can't Help Singing (1944)
Frisco Sal (1945)
Patrick the Great (1945)
I'll Tell the World (1945)
The Daltons Ride Again (1945)
Night in Paradise (1946)
Swell Guy (1946)

Mary Gordon (*1882-1963*)

The Home Maker (1925)
The Claw (1927)
Hell's Heroes (1929)
Roaring Ranch (1930)
Frankenstein (1931)
A House Divided (1931)
Scandal for Sale (1932)
Radio Patrol (1932)
The Kiss Before the Mirror (1933)
The Invisible Man (1933)
Beloved (1934)
I Give My Love (1934)
Bride of Frankenstein (1935)
Yellowstone (1936)
The Man in Blue (1937)
Code of the Streets (1939)
The Invisible Man Returns (1940)
When the Daltons Rode (1940)
The Invisible Woman (1940)
Sealed Lips (1942)
Bombay Clipper (1942)
The Strange Case of Doctor Rx (1942)
Half Way to Shanghai (1942)
Sherlock Holmes and the Voice of Terror (1942)
The Mummy's Tomb (1942)
Sherlock Holmes and the Secret Weapon (1943)

Keep 'Em Slugging (1943)
Sherlock Holmes in Washington (1943)
Two Tickets to London (1943)
Sherlock Holmes Faces Death (1943)
You're a Lucky Fellow, Mr. Smith (1943)
The Spider Woman (1944)
Ladies Courageous (1944)
Hat Check Honey (1944)
The Pearl of Death (1944)
The Woman in Green (1945)
Strange Confession (1945)
Little Giant (1946)
Dressed to Kill (1946)
The Dark Horse (1946)

Gerald Hamer (*1886-1972*)

Sherlock Holmes in Washington (1943)
Sherlock Holmes Faces Death (1943)
The Scarlet Claw (1944)
Enter Arsine Lupin (1944)
Hi, Beautiful (1944)
The Suspect (1944)
Pursuit to Algiers (1945)
Terror by Night (1946)
Ivy (1947)

Kay Harding (*1924-1984*)

Weird Woman (1944)
Hi, Good Lookin' (1944)
Follow the Boys (1944)
The Scarlet Claw (1944)
Ghost Catchers (1944)
The Mummy's Curse (1944)
The Woman in Green (1945)

Alec Harford (*1888-1955*)

Eagle Squadron (1942)
Sherlock Holmes and the Voice of Terror (1942)
Hi, Beautiful (1944)
The Woman in Green (1945)

Rondo Hatton (*1894-1946*)

The Big Guy (1939)
Sin Town (1942)
The Pearl of Death (1944)
The Jungle Captive (1945)
The Royal Mounted Rides Again (1945)
The Spider Woman Strikes Back (1946)
House of Horrors (1946)
The Brute Man (1946)

Holmes Herbert (*1882-1956*)

Up the Ladder (1925)
The Charlatan (1929)
The Invisible Man (1933)
Beloved (1934)
The Black Doll (1938)
Mystery of the White Room (1939)
The Sun Never Sets (1939)
The House of Fear (1939)
Tower of London (1939)
The Ghost of Frankenstein (1942)
Danger in the Pacific (1942)
Lady in a Jam (1942)
Invisible Agent (1942)
Strictly in the Groove (1942)
Sherlock Holmes and the Secret Weapon (1943)
Sherlock Holmes in Washington (1943)
Two Tickets to London (1943)
Corvette K-225 (1943)
Calling Dr. Death (1943)
The Pearl of Death (1944)
Enter Arsine Lupin (1944)
The Mummy's Curse (1944)
The House of Fear (1945)
The Strange Affair of Uncle Harry (1945)
Dressed to Kill (1946)
Ivy (1947)

Halliwell Hobbes (*1877-1962*)

Dracula's Daughter (1936)
Love Letters of a Star (1936)

The Jury's Secret (1938)
Service de Luxe (1938)
Sherlock Holmes Faces Death (1943)
His Butler's Sister (1943)
The Invisible Man's Revenge (1944)
Canyon Passage (1946)

Leyland Hodgson (*1892-1949*)

Once in a Lifetime (1932)
The Mummy (1932)
The Human Side (1934)
The Girl on the Front Page (1936)
One Hundred Men and a Girl (1937)
The Kid From Kansas (1941)
The Wolf Man (1941)
Road Agent (1941)
The Ghost of Frankenstein (1942)
The Strange Case of doctor Rx (1942)
Escape from Hong Kong (1942)
Danger in the Pacific (1942)
Sherlock Holmes and the Voice of Terror (1942)
Sherlock Holmes and the Secret Weapon (1943)
Sherlock Holmes in Washington (1943)
Two Tickets to London (1943)
Adventures of the Flying Cadets (1943)
Flesh and Fantasy (1943)
Follow the Boys (1944)
The Invisible Man's Revenge (1944)
The Pearl of Death (1944)
Enter Arsine Lupin (1944)
The Frozen Ghost (1945)
Strange Confession (1945)
Terror by Night (1946)
Dressed to Kill (1946)

Dennis Hoey (*1893-1960*)

Sherlock Holmes and the Secret Weapon (1943)
Sherlock Holmes Faces Death (1943)
Frankenstein Meets the Wolf Man (1943)
The Spider Woman (1944)
The Pearl of Death (1944)

The House of Fear (1945)
Terror by Night (1946)
She-Wolf of London (1946)

Arthur Hohl (*1889-1964*)

Show Boat (1936)
The Road Back (1937)
You Can't Cheat an Honest Man (1939)
The Spider Woman (1944)
The Scarlet Claw (1944)
Salome Where She Danced, (1945)
The Frozen Ghost (1945)
The Vigilantes Return (1947)

Olaf Hytten (*1888-1955*)

The Impatient Maiden (1932)
Glamour (1934)
Let's Talk it Over (1934)
Secret of the Chateau (1934)
Strange Wives (1934)
Mister Dynamite (1935)
His Night Out (1935)
Sutter's Gold (1936)
Love Letters of a Star (1936)
We Have Our Moments (1937)
California Straight Ahead! (1937)
I Cover the War (1937)
Youth Takes a Fling (1938)
The Sun Never Sets (1939)
Rio (1939)
Little Accident (1939)
The Wolf Man (1941)
The Ghost of Frankenstein (1942)
You're Telling Me (1942)
Eagle Squadron (1942)
Sherlock Holmes and the Voice of Terror (1942)
Destination Unknown (1942)
The Great Impersonation (1942)
The Amazing Mrs. Holliday (1943)
Sherlock Holmes Faces Death (1943)
Flesh and Fantasy (1943)

The Scarlet Claw (1944)
The Invisible Man's Revenge (1944)
Babes on Swing Street (1944)
House of Frankenstein (1944)
The Suspect (1944)
The Woman in Green (1945)
Pursuit to Algiers (1945)
She-Wolf of London (1946)
Dressed to Kill (1946)

Boyd Irwin (*1880-1957*)

The Marriage Pit (1920)
The Gilded Dream (1920)
The Long Chance (1922)
Around the World in Eighteen Days (1923)
The Man Who Reclaimed his Head (1934)
Werewolf of London (1935)
His Night Out (1935)
Risky Business (1939)
The Witness Vanishes (1939)
The Invisible Man Returns (1940)
Jungle Queen (1945)
The Woman in Green (1945)
Scarlet Street (1945)
Girl on the Spot (1946)
Dressed to Kill (1946)
The Time of Their Lives (1946)
Ivy (1947)

Rosalind Ivan (*1880-1959*)

It Started with Eve (1941)
Paris Calling (1941)
The Suspect (1944)
Pursuit to Algiers (1945)
Pillow of Death (1945)
Scarlet Street (1945)
Ivy (1947)

Colin Kenny (*1888-1968*)

The Triflers (1920)
The Fighting Lover (1921)

Merry-Go-Round (1932)
The Kiss Before the Mirror (1933)
The Man Who Reclaimed His head (1934)
The Oregon Trail (1939)
Tower of London (1939)
The Invisible Man Returns (1940)
The House of Seven Gables (1940)
Eagle Squadron (1942)
Sherlock Holmes in Washington (1943)
Two Tickets to London (1943)
The Pearl of Death (1944)
Jungle Queen (1945)
Terror by Night (1946)

Guy Kingsford (*1911-1986*)

Dracula's Daughter (1935)
Yellowstone (1936)
Lucky Devils (1941)
Sea Raiders (1941)
Don Winslow of the Navy (1942)
Eagle Squadron (1942)
Junior G-Men of the Air (1942)
When Jonny Comes Marching Home (1942)
Sherlock Holmes and the Secret Weapon (1943)
Corvette K-225 (1943)
Strange Confession (1945)
The Invisible Man's Revenge (1944)
Dressed to Kill (1946)

George Kirby (*1879-1953*)

Glamour (1934)
The Human Side (1934)
Mystery of Edwin D rood (1935)
Werewolf of London (1935)
Dracula's Daughter (1936)
The Invisible Man Returns (1940)
His Butler's Sister (1943)
The Spider Woman (1944)
The Scarlet Claw (1944)

Skelton Knaggs (*1911-1955*)
Diamond Frontier (1940)
The Invisible Man's Revenge (1944)
House of Dracula (1945)
Terror by Night (1946)

Charles Knight (*1885-1979*)
The Scarlet Claw (1944)
The Pearl of Death (1944)
The Suspect (1944)
Jungle Queen (1945)
Terror by Night (1946)
Ivy (1947)

Martin Kosleck (*1904-1994*)
The Great Alaskan Mystery (1944)
The Mummy's Curse (1944)
The Frozen Ghost (1945)
Pursuit to Algiers (1945)
House of Horrors (1946)
She-Wolf of London (1946)

Doris Lloyd (*1896-1968*)
The Drake Case (1929)
Back Street (1932)
Glamour (1934)
One Exciting Adventure (1934)
The Man Who Reclaimed His Head (1934)
A Shot in the Dark (1935)
Straight from the Heart (1935)
Don't Get Personal (1936)
The Luckiest Girl in the World (1936)
The Black Doll (1938)
Letter of Introduction (1938)
Three Smart Girls Grow Up (1939)
The Under-Pup (1939)
First Love (1939)
The Boys from Syracuse (1940)
Appointment for Love (1941)
Keep 'Em Flying (1941)

The Wolf Man (1941)
The Ghost of Frankenstein (1942)
Frankenstein Meets the Wolfman (1943)
Two Tickets to London (1943)
Flesh and Fantasy (1943)
Phantom Lady (1944)
Follow the Boys (1944)
The Invisible Man's Revenge (1944)
The House of Fear (1945)

Marjorie Lord (*1918-*)
Escape from Hong Kong (1942)
Timber! (1942)
Moonlight in Havana (1942)
The Adventures of Smilin' Jack (1943)
Hi, Buddy (1943)
Sherlock Holmes in Washington (1943)
Flesh and Fantasy (1943)

Montagu Love (*1880-1943*)
The Last Warning (1929)
Silks and Saddles (1929)
The Cat Creeps (1930)
Stowaway (1932)
Sutter's Gold (1936)
Adventure's End (1937)
Private Affairs (1940)
Sherlock Holmes and the Voice of Terror (1942)

Morton Lowry (*1914-1987*)
Corvette K-225 (1943)
Pursuit to Algiers (1945)

Edmund MacDonald (*1908-1951*)
Prison Break (1938)
I Stole a Million (1939)
Destry Rides Again (1939)
The Invisible Man Returns (1940)
Black Friday (1940)
Trail of the Vigilantes (1940)
Nice Girl? (1941)

The Strange Case of Doctor Rx (1942)
Timber (1942)
Who Done It? (1942)
Madame Spy (1942)
Hi'ya, Chum (1943)
Sherlock Holmes in Washington (1943)
Corvette K-225 (1943)
The Mysterious Mr. M (1946)

Aubrey Mather (*1885-1958*)
The Great Impersonation (1942)
The House of Fear (1945)

Miles Mander (*1888-1946*)
Tower of London (1939)
The House of Seven Gables (1940)
Phantom of the Opera (1943)
The Scarlet Claw (1944)
The Pearl of Death (1944)
Enter Arsine Lupin (1944)

Patricia Morison (*1914-*)
Calling Dr. Death (1943)
Lady on a Train (1945)
Dressed to Kill (1946)
Danger Woman (1946)

Alan Mowbray (*1896-1969*)
Nice Women (1931)
Little Man, What Now? (1934)
One More River (1934)
Embarrassing Moments (1934)
Night Life of the Gods (1935)
Four Days' Wonder (1936)
As Good as Married (1937)
The Boys from Syracuse (1940)
His Butler's Sister (1943)
My Gal Loves Music (1944)
Men in Her Diary (1945)
Terror by Night (1946)
Idea Girl (1946)

Gavin Muir (*1900-1972*)
Eagle Squadron (1942)
Sherlock Holmes and the Voice of Terror (1942)
Nightmare (1942)
Sherlock Holmes in Washington (1943)
Sherlock Holmes Faces Death (1943)
The Merry Monahans (1944)
The House of Fear (1945)
Patrick the Great (1945)
Salome Where She Danced (1945)
Ivy (1947)

Clarence Muse (*1889-1979*)
Outside the Law (1930)
Night World (1932)
Laughter in Hell (1933)
Alias Mary Dow (1935)
East of Java (1935)
Show Boat (1936)
Mysterious Crossing (1936)
Secrets of a Nurse (1938)
Zanzibar (1940)
The Flame of New Orleans (1941)
Tough as They Come (1942)
Sin Town (1942)
Shadow of a Doubt (1943)
Sherlock Holmes in Washington (1943)
Honeymoon Lodge (1943)
Flesh and Fantasy (1943)
San Diego I Love You (1944)
Jungle Queen (1945)
Scarlet Street (1945)

Minna Phillips (*1885-1963*)
Gals, Incorporated (1943)
Hers to Hold (1943)
Sherlock Holmes Faces Death (1943)
Hat Check Honey (1944)

Sally Shepherd (*1896-1982*)

Enter Arsine Lupin (1944)
The Suspect (1944)
The House of Fear (1945)
The Woman in Green (1945)
Dressed to Kill (1946)

Gale Sondergaard (*1899-1985*)

The Black Cat (1941)
Paris Calling (1941)
The Strange Death of Adolf Hitler (1943)
Crazy House (1943)
The Spider Woman (1944)
The Invisible Man's Revenge (1944)
Christmas Holiday (1944)
Gypsy Wildcat (1944)
The Climax (1944)
Enter Arsine Lupin (1944)
The Spider Woman Strikes Back (1946)
Night in Paradise (1946)
The Time of Their Lives (1946)

Arthur Stenning (*1883-1972*)

Tower of London (1939)
Sherlock Holmes and the Voice of Terror (1942)
Two Tickets to London (1943)
Flesh and Fantasy (1943)
The Spider Woman (1944)
The Pearl of Death (1944)
Enter Arsine Lupin (1944)
Strange Confession (1945)
The Woman in Green (1945)

Milburn Stone (*1904-1980*)

His Night Out (1935)
Nobody's Fool (1936)
Two in a Crowd (1936)
The Man I Marry (1936)
Wings Over Honolulu (1937)
The Man in Blue (1937)

The Wildcatter (1937)
Reported Missing (1937)
Sinners in Paradise (1938)
Wives Under Suspicion (1938)
The Storm (1938)
Society Smugglers (1939)
The Spirit of Culver (1939)
When Tomorrow Comes (1939)
Tropic Fury (1939)
Charlie McCarthy, Detective (1939)
The Big Guy (1939)
Framed (1940)
Enemy Agent (1940)
Give Us Wings (1940)
Frisco Lil (1942)
Invisible Agent (1942)
Keep 'Em Slugging (1943)
Captive Wild Woman (1943)
Get Going (1943)
Sherlock Holmes Faces Death (1943)
Corvette K-225 (1943)
The Mad Ghoul (1943)
'Gung Ho!' (1943)
Phantom Lady (voice only) (1944)
Strange Confession (The Imposter) (1944)
Hat Check Honey (1944)
Hi, Good Lookin'! (1944)
Moon Over Las Vegas (1944)
The Great Alaskan Mystery (1944)
Twilight on the Prairie (1944)
Jungle Woman (1944)
She Gets Her Man (1945)
I'll Remember April (1945)
The Master Key (1945)
Swing Out, Sister (1945)
The Frozen Ghost (1945)
On Stage Everybody (1945)
The Beautiful Cheat (1945)
Strange Confession (1945)
The Royal Mounted Rides Again (1945)
The Daltons Ride gain (1945)

Smooth as Silk (1946)
The Spider Woman Strikes Back (1946)
Strange Conquest (1946)
Her Adventurous Night (1946)
Inside Job (1946)
Danger Woman (1946)
Little Miss Big (1946)

Harry Stubbs (*1874-1950*)
Night Ride (1930)
The Invisible Man (1933)
Werewolf of London (1935)
Sutter's Gold (1936)
The Man I Marry (1936)
The Invisible Man Returns (1940)
The House of Seven Gables (1940)
Zanzibar (1940)
The Mummy's Hand (1940)
Margie (1940)
Burma Convoy (1941)
The Wolf Man (1941)
Eagle Squadron (1942)
Sherlock Holmes and the Voice of Terror (1942)
Frankenstein Meets the Wolf Man (1943)
Flesh and Fantasy (1943)

Don Terry (*1902-1988*)
Her First Mate (1933)
You Can't Cheat an Honest Man (1939)
Mutiny in the Arctic (1941)
In the Navy (1941)
Tight Shoes (1941)
Hold that Ghost (1941)
Don Winslow of the Navy (1942)
Unseen Enemy (1942)
Escape from Hong Kong (1942)
Danger in the Pacific (1942)
Top Sergeant (1942)
Drums of the Congo (1942)
Overland Mail (1942)
Moonlight in Havana (1942)

Don Winslow of the Coast Guard (1943)
Sherlock Holmes in Washington (1943)
White Savage (1943)

David Thursby (*1899-1977*)

Princess O'Hara (1935)
Werewolf of London (1935)
Nobody's Fool (1936)
Tower of London (1939)
The Invisible Man Returns (1940)
The Bank Dick (1940)
Burma Convoy (1941)
The Pearl of Death (1944)
The House of Fear (1945)
She-Wolf of London (1946)
Ivy (1947)

Ian Wolfe (*1896-1992*)

The Raven (1935)
Paris Calling (1941)
Saboteur (1942)
Eagle Squadron (1942)
Nightmare (1942)
Sherlock Holmes in Washington (1943)
Corvette K-225 (1943)
Flesh and Fantasy (1943)
Her Primitive Man (1944)
The Scarlet Claw (1944)
The Invisible Man's Revenge (1944)
The Pearl of Death (1944)
In Society (1944)
Reckless Age (1944)
The Merry Monahans (1944)
Babes on Swing Street (1944)
The Mystery of the Riverboat (1944)
Murder in the Blue Room (1944)
Blonde Ransom (1945)
Strange Confession (1945)
Dressed to Kill (1946)

Frederick Worlock (*1886-1973*)

Eagle Squadron (1942)
Sherlock Holmes in Washington (1943)
Sherlock Holmes Faces Death (1943)
The Woman in Green (1945)
Pursuit to Algiers (1945)
Terror by Night (1946)
She-Wolf of London (1946)
Dressed to Kill (1946)

George Zucco (*1886-1960*)

The Mummy's Hand (1940)
Dark Streets of Cairo (1940)
Half Way to Shanghai (1942)
The Mummy's Tomb (1943)
Sherlock Holmes in Washington (1943)
The Mad Ghoul (1943)
The Mummy's Ghost (1944)
House of Frankenstein (1944)
Sudan (1945)

INDEX

Numbers in **_bold italics_** indicate pages with illustrations.
Names of people in _italics_ indicate principal characters.